Missio Dei:
Joining God on the Adventure of a Lifetime

missio Dei

joining God on the adventure of a lifetime

Elizabeth Renicks and JuLee Davis

Teacher Edition

purposeful design®
p u b l i c a t i o n s

Colorado Springs, Colorado

Purposeful Design Publications is the publishing division of the Association of Christian Schools International (ACSI) and is committed to the ministry of Christian school education, to enable Christian educators and schools worldwide to effectively prepare students for life. As the publisher of textbooks, trade books, and other educational resources within ACSI, Purposeful Design Publications strives to produce biblically sound materials that reflect Christian scholarship and stewardship and that address the identified needs of Christian schools around the world.

References to books, computer software, and other ancillary resources in this series are not endorsements by ACSI. These materials were selected to provide teachers with additional resources appropriate to the concepts being taught and to promote student understanding and enjoyment.

Printed in the United States of America
17 16 15 14 13 12 11 10 09   1 2 3 4 5 6 7

Renicks, Elizabeth, and JuLee Davis
   Missio Dei: Joining God on the adventure of a lifetime
   ISBN 978-1-58331-250-6   Teacher edition   Catalog # 7077S

Design team: Bethany Kerstetter, Daron Short
Managing editor: JuLee Davis
Editorial team: Karen Friesen, Cheryl Chiapperino

Purposeful Design Publications
A Division of ACSI
PO Box 65130 • Colorado Springs, CO 80962-5130
Customer Service: 800-367-0798 • www.acsi.org

Table of Contents

Preface...ix

Acknowledgments xi

Course Introduction

Introduction to the Teacher Edition xiv

Lesson 1 The Beginning of the Journey xxviii

Bible Unit

Bible Unit Introduction 2

Lesson 2 What I Know About the Bible 4

Lesson 3 The Bible as One Story 8

Lesson 4 Bearers of God's Purpose 14

Lesson 5 A Heart for All Nations 19

Lesson 6 Relationships, Redemption, and Reconciliation: Part 1 24

Lesson 7 Relationships, Redemption, and Reconciliation: Part 2 29

Lesson 8 What a Blessing Is 32

Lesson 9 The Faith of Abraham 36

Lesson 10 Cats, Dogs, and Footraces 41

Lesson 11 The Kingdom: Now and Not Yet 44

Lesson 12 Our Need for Eyes to See 48

Lesson 13 Who the Enemy Is 52

Lesson 14 Abiding in Christ 57

Lesson 15 The Weapons of War 61

Lesson 16 Review: God's Purpose and Mission 65

Culture Unit

Culture Unit Introduction 68

Optional Enrichment Extension Projects for the Culture Unit 70

Lesson 17 Culture and God's View of It 71

Lesson 18 Misunderstandings, Ethnocentrism, and Premature Judgments 75

Lesson 19 The Nacirema and Ethnocentrism 79

Lesson 20 The Incarnation 82

Lesson 21 Going to the Margins in Love 86

Lesson 22 A Big, Big World 90

Lesson 23 Identifying Cultural Distance 94

Lesson 24 Incarnational Living 98

Lesson 25 Evaluating Case Studies 102

Lesson 26 Review: The Lens of Culture 106

History Unit

History Unit Introduction 110

Lesson 27 God's Purpose Advancing Throughout History 112

Lesson 28 Introduction to the Era Chapters 117

Lesson 29 Era One 123

Lesson 30 Era Two 128

Lesson 31 Era Three 132

Lesson 32 Era Four 136

Lesson 33 Era Five: Part 1 141

Lesson 34 Era Five: Part 2 146

Lesson 35 Review: The Ultimate Completion of God's Purpose 151

Practices Unit

Practices Unit Introduction 156

Lesson 36 Intimacy with God 158

Lesson 37 Practicing Intimacy with God 164

Lesson 38 More Practicing Intimacy with God 168

Lesson 39 Passion: Part 1 172

Lesson 40 Passion: Part 2 176

Lesson 41 Loving God, Loving People 179

Lesson 42 Taking the Opportunity 183

Lesson 43 Community 186

Lesson 44 The Purpose of Community 190

Lesson 45 Christian Community as Witness 194

Lesson 46 The Rest of the Story 198

Lesson 47 A Celebration! 202

Lesson 48 Reflecting and Looking Forward 206

References 209

Credits 213

We can be overjoyed every time someone creates a window into the basic theme of the Bible and transforms it from a book about our personal salvation into a divine revelation of God's concern to reach out to all peoples and to restore all creation.
—*Ralph D. Winter, PhD, U.S. Center for World Mission, Pasadena, CA*

Preface

Divine interruptions. They are all around us. If only we have eyes to see what God is doing and ears to hear what He is saying to us.

Sometimes a particular event, a set of circumstances, or a person comes into our lives—a "divine" interruption—at just the right time to move us in a different direction. I had recently joined ACSI and was developing a curricular product on unreached people groups of the 10/40 Window. We were partnering with another organization on the project, and someone there recommended that I take the Perspectives on the World Christian Movement course. I knew that adding *one more thing to my plate* would make life more difficult—after all, I was starting a new job in a new city—but I decided to go ahead and enroll in the course. Little did I know that God would use the first speaker on the first night to turn my world upside down.

That speaker, Dr. Don McCurry, talked about the Bible as being "one story," and he (and of course, the Holy Spirit!) throughout his talk proceeded to unravel every underlying assumption I had held about the Bible and its message. Pieces that hadn't made sense in the past fell away, and new insight started to form. I had been maneuvering through life with a skewed view—like trying to drive a car that has wheels out of alignment. God was beginning to bring my focus back into alignment. I started seeing the world differently. A new passion formed.

A missional hermeneutic for interpreting the Bible provides much more than a lens through which to understand the Bible. It provides meaning and purpose for our lives. And when Jesus said, "Come, follow me," He wasn't inviting His followers to have an intellectual discussion; He was showing them *a way of life*. God wants us to fully experience life with Him, and our participation in missio Dei provides a window into the kingdom of God here on earth and the opportunity we have to influence the world around us.

Near the end of the fifteen-week Perspectives course, the speaker asked the "what" question: "What are you going to do with what you have learned from this course?" The answer came quickly, for the Lord had been preparing me for what would come next. His answer was to introduce concepts I had learned in the Perspectives on the World Christian Movement course to a new generation, and that is our purpose for writing this book. The *Missio Dei* materials were developed from the framework and some of the overarching concepts of the original course. They are designed to set you on a path of discovery, a journey worth exploring and investigating. Life is not always easy, and there are no easy answers. In this book we encourage you to ask the hard questions, such as, Why am I here? Is there a purpose for my existence? Ultimately our goal is to help you recognize that you have been placed on this earth for a purpose, for something much larger than yourself.

God formed a fabulous team of people to carry this project forward. While there were bumps in the road along this journey, God continued to reveal and reconfirm His call in the midst of challenges and setbacks. I'll never forget one of our first meetings as a writing team. At the time the task seemed enormous and impossible, but the Lord impressed Zechariah 4:10 upon my heart, and He reminded us *to not despise the day of small things*. Here we are, eight years later, with a finished book! My encouragement to you is to remember that there are no "small things" in God's economy. God takes our lives and connects us to something significant. We are a part of an epic story that has been going on from the beginning of time until this very day. I am reminded each day that we are just vessels, jars of clay. The power comes from Him (2 Corinthians 4:7).

On earth we are living "between two trees"—a tree at the beginning of God's story (the tree of the knowledge of good and evil described in Genesis 2) and a tree for the healing of the nations (found in Revelation 22:2).* May you fully experience God's presence and power as you set your feet on this path of discovery and join Him on the adventure of a lifetime!

JuLee Davis

*Concept from Rob Bell's *Nooma: Trees 003* (2005).

Acknowledgments

We are grateful to our families for their support and encouragement throughout the development of this book:

- To my husband, Marshall: Your support, understanding, prayers, and love are reflected throughout this book. The words *thank you* are not enough. To my sons, Will and Jackson: May God bless you through this work when you get old enough to read what Mommy was writing when you were little boys. You both brought much to bear on what is here. (ER)

- To my children and grandchildren—Gabrielle, Brenton, Jamie, Kiara, and Brooke: You are my inspiration! Your presence and encouragement were a "cup of cold water" during many stages of this journey. To my parents, LeRoy and Joyce: Your love and support are a precious gift, something I will always be thankful for. (JD)

It is impossible for a project of this scale to be completed without the diligent and faithful prayers of God's people. We are thankful for the quiet "warriors" behind the scenes who lifted our hands in the midst of battle (similar to what Aaron and Hur did for Moses in Exodus 17:10–12): Thank you for faithfully praying during each step of the process.

We are indebted to Jim Sawyer at Jim Elliot Christian School in Colorado for his involvement in the project during the early days of research for the book: Jim, your passion for inspiring high school students to live missionally is contagious, and we appreciate your insight and expertise.

We are extremely thankful that the Newbigin family and Regent Publishers allowed us to reprint Lesslie Newbigin's amazing book *A Walk Through the Bible*. May a new generation of people be exposed to the *story* of the Bible.

We are blessed to work with Pete Gannon in producing the music video *Carrier*: Pete, thank you for your passion in revealing God's heart through visual tools. We are also grateful for the ministry of Jared Anderson and for the permission we received from the team at Integrity Music to use Jared's song "Carrier."

We want to thank the church bodies at Grace Church in Alabama and at New Life Church in Colorado: Thank you for your prayers, support, and encouragement during the development of this book. Your provision of opportunities to discuss, pray through, and teach the contents of this book was a tool God used to shape and refine much of what is here. What wonderful environments to be immersed in during the writing process!

We are privileged to work with like-minded organizations that share the same vision and desire to see God's kingdom reign here on earth:

- We are deeply grateful to Dr. Ralph Winter, Greg Parsons, and others at the U.S. Center for World Mission: Thank you for your encouragement through the years of "testing the idea" to actually developing the book. Thank you for allowing us to adapt the original material for a new generation. We appreciate the work you do to inspire people to join God in His mission.

- We want to thank the staff from Caleb Resources (formerly Caleb Project): We are thankful for your partnership and encouragement while the book was being developed. We are also thankful for your beautiful images of people around the world, which we used in the music video *Carrier*.

- We are thankful for Bryan Nicholson and others at Global Mapping International: Thank you for your work in developing the maps for the History Unit. We also want to thank Patrick Johnstone at WEC International: Thank you for allowing us to use, in the creation of our maps, concepts and statistics from your upcoming publication, *The Future of the Worldwide Church: Possibilities for 21st Century Ministry*.

We are so grateful for the "collective voices" (and their publishers) that contributed to the content of *Missio Dei*. One of the exciting things we discovered while writing the book was how other authors shared a similar message. Isn't that just like God to drop a pebble and let us see the ripples!

We are blessed to have such a dedicated team of editors, designers, and support personnel who worked together to make this book a reality. It was truly a joy to see the hands, feet, eyes, and ears working together in unity for the glory of God (1 Corinthians 12:12–27).

We dedicate this work to our Lord and Savior, Jesus Christ: Thank You for inviting us to participate in Your mission here on earth. We are humbled to be a part of the work You are doing. "We have this treasure in jars of clay to show that this all-surpassing power is from God and not from us" (2 Corinthians 4:7).

Introduction
to the teacher edition

Introduction to the Teacher Edition

Course Overview

Missio Dei: Joining God on the Adventure of a Lifetime is a semester Bible textbook for upper–high school students. The term *missio Dei* means literally "the mission of God." This course provides opportunities for students to explore and engage in God's mission as the foundation for the story of the Bible, as the lens through which we all relate to others cross-culturally, as the centerpiece of history, and as the driving force for living "missionally" in whatever context we find ourselves.

The Missio Dei course invites students to enter into a deeper understanding of God through joining Him on the adventure of a lifetime. Throughout the book we introduce the concept of a journey. Students are challenged to reconsider how they live their day-to-day experience with God and others. This is not an experience that begins and ends with salvation, but it is a journey that lasts a lifetime.

The course uses a missional hermeneutic to study the Bible and see the world (worldview), connecting our individual stories with God's story. This interdisciplinary course includes biblical studies, history, and cultural studies. Through the study of missio Dei, students are introduced to concepts and ideas they may also be learning in other classes, thus creating an opportunity for you to collaborate with other colleagues to build upon and enhance what your students are learning elsewhere.

The following is a portion of the student edition introduction:

> *Missio Dei: Joining God on the Adventure of a Lifetime* is a collection of things to think about and practices to embrace as you move down the path of your life. The contents of this book are like the items you might put together in preparation for a hiking trip or some other sort of cross-country sojourn. So, what can you expect?
>
> Well, don't expect this book to be a guide to life with one-size-fits-all answers for you. Only God can give you the answers you need to navigate the terrain of your own life. And only in close relationship with Him can you discover what He has in store for your particular journey with Him. What you will find in this book are some tools to help you along your journey. These tools fall into four categories—Bible, culture, history, and practice—so there are four units within this book. They can be thought of as four different lenses through which to view the mission of God.
>
> The first unit focuses specifically on the Bible, the compass part of your travel kit. It is the tool that points you in the right direction for meeting God and joining Him in His mission. You cannot participate with Him without knowing what the Bible says. So, naturally, that is our starting point. And if you think you already know what the Bible has to say about your life with God, you might be in for a surprise!
>
> The second unit looks through the lens of culture. You can think of this section as the binoculars in your travel kit—the lenses that give you an opportunity to see beyond your immediate surroundings to the bigger, wondrous world around you. Doing this is important because we tend to be consumed by our own surroundings and our own culture. But God is not limited to one culture or one context to work through. He is at work all around the world, in ways that might amaze you. In the chapters on culture, we are going to pick up the binoculars and take a wide-angle look around to see what God's thoughts are on these matters.

The third section of the course focuses on the narrative of history. You can think of this section of the course as a travelogue, a collection of stories from those who have come before you on this journey. Many, many people have participated with God on His mission throughout history. Checking out their perspectives, successes, and failures is instructive to us as we consider our world today. If you were planning a trip to a city that is new to you, you might consult someone who had been there before to find out the best places to stay and eat, and to learn about the best activities there. The History Unit lets you read about the varied experiences of those in the past as you prepare to journey with God in the future. Henri J. M. Nouwen says, "I have to keep my eyes fixed on Jesus and on those who followed him and trust that I will know how to live out my mission to be a sign of hope in this world" (1994). We focus on mission in the past as a way of affirming that God has always been at work and that He continues to invite us to join Him in that work to the present moment.

Finally, *Missio Dei* concludes with a unit called "Practices." Think of this section as a backpack full of essentials. On a hiking trip, you would want to make sure you have some food and water in your pack as well other items to make your hike more manageable. In the same way, the final chapters of this book will help you explore some basic and essential practices that will nourish and assist you on your journey with God. From intimacy with God, to spiritual passion, to embracing community, we will explore some things you'll want to have as you move through life. Just as you wouldn't leave town without a few basic necessities, you won't want to go too far down the road with God without understanding some of the things you need to make that journey the best it can be.

Throughout the coming chapters, you can expect to be challenged not only in your thinking but in how you live your day-to-day experience with God and others. You will be asked to consider new ideas and to take steps into new experiences in your relationship with Jesus. Perhaps some of this thinking and action will take you outside your comfort zone. But stretching our muscles is the only way we can hike farther and longer than we have before. You are invited to stretch yourself, to participate, and to enter into a deeper understanding of the adventure of a lifetime that God invites you to join Him on.

We close with another quote from [Leonard I.] Sweet: "Imagine how different the Christian life would be if it was understood not as something to ponder or to observe in others—but as the one thing in life that has to be fully experienced" (2007, 29). Furthermore, imagine how different life would be if we as believers in Christ understood that the experience of life with God isn't simply to make our own lives richer—in other words, to fulfill *our* individual needs—but it is to fulfill a much-larger purpose. What if we recognized that God is calling us to something grand, larger than ourselves, and best lived not individually but in community, in a *kingdom*? These are some of the terrains we will be covering during the course of this book.

Course Components

The course is made up of four components: a student edition, a teacher edition, a student journal (*Missio Dei: The Journey*), and a website. The student edition contains the core of the material for the course, and it is divided into four units—Bible, Culture, History, and Practices—twenty-six chapters in all. Big Ideas, which provide the overarching framework for concepts introduced throughout the course, are clearly stated for the student. Printed in both the student edition and the teacher edition are reflective questions (titled "What Difference Does It Make?" in the student edition and "Reflective Questions" in the teacher edition) that challenge students to deeply and personally reflect on what they are learning. These questions are distributed throughout the student edition and are used in the teacher edition as writing prompts, as checks for reading comprehension, or as discussion starters.

The student journal was developed after the concept of *vade mecum* (Latin for "go with me") as a companion piece and an integral part of the student's experience with missio Dei. The journal, which contains the majority of the course work, is filled with article excerpts, Bible verses, quotations, places for reflection, and activities directly related to the material from the TE lessons. Since the journal is a reflection of what the student is learning throughout the course, it can also be used as an assessment piece. Pages not tied to any specific assignment are sprinkled throughout the journal, and they provide places for students to refine their thinking, maybe through drawing or just reflecting. Be aware of these places and remind your students to make use of these pages as they move through the journal. You may also want to have your own copy of the journal for personal reflection so that you can follow along with your students.

The forty-eight lessons in this teacher edition will guide you step-by-step through the teaching of the material and through the leading of various activities and assignments. The course is designed to culminate in the activities and lessons found in the final unit, and especially those accompanying the last chapter of the student book. These final activities and information in very practical ways set the stage for a life-long journey of participating with God in His mission. Therefore, your planning and pacing should reflect a commitment to completing the entire course.

The Missio Dei course is specifically designed so that each unit builds on the other units, all leading up to the final unit (Practices). This unit is what you could call the "So what?" unit—the unit that asks, Now that you know these things, what are you going to do with what you have learned? While the lessons throughout the course emphasize personal application alongside new concepts, the final unit is focused exclusively on challenging and inspiring students to understand and adopt deeper levels of living out their faith.

At the beginning of each unit are several Bible memory verses to reinforce concepts from the material in the unit and to incorporate memory work into the lesson plans. Though not an exhaustive list of all the biblical passages that your students are exposed to throughout the course, these verses correspond to some of the key concepts and Big Ideas of the course. You may want to incorporate additional verses (including other Bible versions) to fit your particular needs.

At the end of this teacher edition is a CD with the following items: blackline masters (BLMs), a music video (several computer versions), unit exams, and rubrics. The CD has a menu feature that allows you to easily access each item. Many of the BLMs, which correspond to material in the teacher edition, will have answer keys, though not all because answers will vary among students, depending on level of content and type of questions in the BLMs.

As already mentioned, a music video called *Carrier* is provided for use with the celebration in TE lesson 47. This visual tool will help students reflect on the message of this course and prepare for a time of celebration. The CD contains several versions of the video that can be played on a computer, and a separate DVD, included for your convenience, contains a version that plays in a DVD player.

Unit exams are provided as formal assessment options at the end of the first three units (Bible, Culture, and History). While there are plenty of assessment-type activities and assignments provided in the course, you may wish to utilize a more-traditional approach by using these exams. Rubrics are provided to assist you in evaluating alternative assessments found throughout this course.

Finally, in addition to the materials listed above, a website has been developed specifically for this course. The website, www.missiodei-thejourney.com, is an online resource you may want to use as part of your planning and teaching of this course. It includes an ongoing blog discussion (which you or your students may want to participate in at various times throughout the course) as well as discussion forums and additional resources that enhance and expand the content of this course.

Teaching Schedule

The course is designed as a semester course, but there is ample material to use for a yearlong Bible course format or a block schedule. Each individual lesson is designed to accommodate a 45-to-50-minute time frame, but in many cases there are "If Time Activity," "Extra Mile," and "Further Study" sections provided to give you more material for longer class periods. These options could also be used to expand the TE lessons over several days.

Some TE lessons are designed to take more than one class period to complete. The following Course Instructional Plan Overview will guide you through the process of identifying what pieces go together (SE chapters, TE lessons, journal entries, BLMs) and will help you decide how to pace the course to meet the needs of your school schedule.

Big Ideas

Course

CR1   Participating in missio Dei is the adventure of a lifetime.

Bible Unit

B1   The Bible, from Genesis to Revelation, tells the story of God's purpose.

B2   God's purpose is relationship, redemption, and reconciliation.

B3   God invites us to participate in His purpose; He blesses us so that we can bless others.

B4   God's story is unfolding as we see and participate in God's kingdom throughout the earth.

B5   The spread of God's kingdom takes place in the context of warfare with Satan.

Culture Unit

C1   Effectively communicating God's story requires an intimate understanding of culture and God's view of it.

C2   The incarnation of Jesus is the model for reaching out to all people, whether within one's own culture or across cultural boundaries. Jesus tells us not only what to communicate but how to communicate it.

C3   The process of reaching out across cultures can be enhanced by a study of people.

C4   God's people must learn to connect incarnationally with others in significant cross-cultural relationships.

History Unit

H1   God initiates and advances His purpose throughout human history.

H2   History reveals the challenges, successes, and shortcomings that people throughout history have experienced as they have participated with God in completing His purpose.

H3   God's redemptive purpose will come to an ultimate completion in human history.

Practices Unit

P1   Participating in missio Dei requires a personal intimacy with God.

P2   Participating in missio Dei requires spiritual passion.

P3   Participating in missio Dei is lived out in the context of community.

P4   Missio Dei culminates in the gathering of every tribe, tongue, language, and nation around the throne of God.

Course Instructional Plan Overview

Student Edition	Teacher Edition	Journal Entries	Blackline Masters	Big Ideas
Course Introduction: Welcome to the Journey	**Course Introduction**			All
	Lesson 1 The Beginning of the Journey	JE 1 Reflection on Missio Dei		CR1
Chapter 1 The Bible, God's Story	**Lesson 2** What I Know About the Bible	JE 2 Viewpoints About the Bible JE 3 Reflective Writing: My View of the Bible		B1
	Lesson 3 The Bible as One Story		BLM 1.1 Plot Components	B1
	Lesson 4 Bearers of God's Purpose	JE 4 Bearing God's Purpose		B1
	Lesson 5 A Heart for All Nations	JE 5 My Worship of God	BLM 1.2 Attractive and Expansive Forces	B1
Chapter 2 The Mission of God	**Lesson 6** Relationships, Redemption, and Reconciliation: Part 1			B2
	Lesson 7 Relationships, Redemption, and Reconciliation: Part 2	JE 6 Broken or Restored? JE 7 Redemption Coupons		B2
Chapter 3 The Invitation: Blessed to Be a Blessing	**Lesson 8** What a Blessing Is	JE 8 Abraham's Diary Entry JE 9 Top Lines, Bottom Lines		B3
	Lesson 9 The Faith of Abraham	JE 10 Reflection on the Lesson JE 11 "The Parable of the Race"		B3
	Lesson 10 Cats, Dogs, and Footraces	JE 12 Cat and Dog Theology JE 13 Inflow/Outflow Inventory	BLM 3.1 Unpacking "The Parable of the Race" BLM 3.1K Answer Key	B3
Chapter 4 The Kingdom of God	**Lesson 11** The Kingdom: Now and Not Yet	JE 14 Blinders JE 15 Assess Yourself		B4
	Lesson 12 Our Need for Eyes to See	JE 16 Consider This About the Kingdom		B4
Chapter 5 Behind Enemy Lines	**Lesson 13** Who the Enemy Is	JE 17 Christ and the Counterfeiter JE 18 A Believer's True Identity	BLM 5.1K Christ and the Counterfeiter (Answer Key) BLM 5.2K A Believer's True Identity (Answer Key)	B5
	Lesson 14 Abiding in Christ	JE 19 Be Still JE 20 Garbage In, Garbage Out JE 21 What Fruit?	BLM 5.3 Abide in Him BLM 5.3K Answer Key	B5

Student Edition	Teacher Edition	Journal Entries	Blackline Masters	Big Ideas
	Lesson 15 The Weapons of War			B5
Chapter 6 Review: God's Purpose and Mission	Lesson 16 Review: God's Purpose and Mission			B1–B5
Chapter 7 God's View of Culture	Lesson 17 Culture and God's View of It	JE 22 A Sketch of My Culture	BLM 7.1 Five Views of God and Culture BLM 7.1K Answer Key	C1
Chapter 8 Cultural Pitfalls	Lesson 18 Misunderstandings, Ethnocentrism, and Premature Judgments	JE 23 Cultural Pitfalls JE 24 Empathy	BLM 8.1 Excerpts from "Body Ritual Among the Nacirema"	C1
	Lesson 19 The Nacirema and Ethnocentrism	JE 25 Discoveries		C1
Chapter 9 The Incarnation	Lesson 20 The Incarnation	JE 26 Responding to the Incarnation		C2
	Lesson 21 Going to the Margins in Love	JE 27 Reaching Out		C2
Chapter 10 God's View of People	Lesson 22 A Big, Big World	JE 28 A Global Village	BLM 10.1 Looking Outside: A Cross-Cultural Research Project BLM 10.2 Culture Analysis Template	C3
	Lesson 23 Identifying Cultural Distance	JE 29 Uncovering My Cultural Context JE 30 E-Scale Thoughts		C3
Chapter 11 Between a Rock and a Hard Place	Lesson 24 Incarnational Living	JE 31 Kingdom Culture JE 32 "Between a Rock and a Hard Place" Response		C4
Chapter 12 Cross-Cultural Case Studies	Lesson 25 Evaluating Case Studies	JE 33 Think About These Things JE 34 Imagine This	BLM 12.1 Case Study Talking Points	C4
Chapter 13 Review: The Lens of Culture	Lesson 26 Review: The Lens of Culture			C1–C4
Chapter 14 How God Works Through History	Lesson 27 God's Purpose Advancing Throughout History	JE 35 Proverbs 19:21	BLM 14.1 Abraham: A Man of Faith and Doubt BLM 14.1K Answer Key	H1
	Lesson 28 Introduction to the Era Chapters	JE 36 Coping with Cultural Limitations	BLM 14.2 K-W-L Reading Organizer	H2

Student Edition	Teacher Edition	Journal Entries	Blackline Masters	Big Ideas
Chapter 15 Era One: The Beginnings of the Church	**Lesson 29** Era One	JE 37 James, Son of Zebedee JE 38 Phoebe, Dorcas, and Lydia JE 39 Paul JE 40 Reflection on Era One	BLM 15.1 Era One Time Line BLM 15.1K Answer Key BLM 15.2 Who, What, When, Where, How BLM 15.2K Answer Key BLM 15.3 All Shook Up BLM 15.3K Answer Key BLM 15.4 Challenges, Successes, and Shortcomings	H2
Chapter 16 Era Two: AD 100 to 600	**Lesson 30** Era Two	JE 41 Antony JE 42 Perpetua and Felicitas JE 43 Ulfilas JE 44 Patrick JE 45 Reflection on Era Two	BLM 16.1 Era Two Time Line BLM 16.1K Answer Key BLM 16.2 Who, What, When, Where, How BLM 16.2K Answer Key BLM 16.3 All Shook Up BLM 16.3K Answer Key BLM 16.4 Challenges, Successes, and Shortcomings	H2
Chapter 17 Era Three: AD 600 to 1500	**Lesson 31** Era Three	JE 46 Cyril and Methodius JE 47 Peter Waldo JE 48 Raymond Lull JE 49 Monastic Prayers JE 50 Reflection on Era Three	BLM 17.1 Era Three Time Line BLM 17.1K Answer Key BLM 17.2 Who, What, When, Where, How BLM 17.2K Answer Key BLM 17.3 All Shook Up BLM 17.3K Answer Key BLM 17.4 Challenges, Successes, and Shortcomings	H2
Chapter 18 Era Four: AD 1500 to 1800	**Lesson 32** Era Four	JE 51 Matthew Ricci JE 52 Count Zinzendorf and the Moravians JE 53 David Brainerd JE 54 Reflection on Era Four	BLM 18.1 Era Four Time Line BLM 18.1K Answer Key BLM 18.2 Who, What, When, Where, How BLM 18.2K Answer Key BLM 18.3 All Shook Up BLM 18.3K Answer Key BLM 18.4 Challenges, Successes, and Shortcomings	H2

Student Edition	Teacher Edition	Journal Entries	Blackline Masters	Big Ideas
Chapter 19 Era Five: Nineteenth and Twentieth Centuries	**Lesson 33** Era Five: Part 1	JE 55 Ann and Adoniram Judson JE 56 Lott Carey JE 57 Mary Slessor JE 58 Semisi Nau JE 59 Cameron Townsend JE 60 William Wade Harris JE 61 Mother Teresa JE 62 Reflection on Era Five	BLM 19.1 Era Five Time Line BLM 19.1K Answer Key BLM 19.2 Who, What, When, Where, How BLM 19.2K Answer Key BLM 19.3 All Shook Up BLM 19.3K Answer Key BLM 19.4 Challenges, Successes, and Shortcomings	H2
	Lesson 34 Era Five: Part 2	JE 63 Looking Back—Going Forward JE 64 Present Era Mission Snapshot JE 65 Back to Jerusalem	BLM 19.5 People in History Profile Template	H2
Chapter 20 Review: The Ultimate Completion of God's Purpose	**Lesson 35** Review: The Ultimate Completion of God's Purpose	JE 66 God's Purpose Will Stand JE 67 Thoughts on the Nature of Mission	BLM 20.1 Stephen Neill on God's Work Going Forward BLM 20.2 Getting to Know a People Group: An Ethnographic Study BLM 20.3 People Group Profile Template	H3
Chapter 21 Intimacy with God	**Lesson 36** Intimacy with God	JE 68 Assessing My Assumptions JE 69 Intimacy Versus No Intimacy JE 70 A Second Look		P1
	Lesson 37 Practicing Intimacy with God	JE 71 Listening Is Key JE 72 Conversation with God JE 73 Hearing from God JE 74 Intentionally Pursuing God		P1
	Lesson 38 More Practicing Intimacy with God	JE 75 A Beautiful Mind and Life JE 76 Foundational Truths JE 77 I Am Thankful		P1
Chapter 22 Spiritual Passion	**Lesson 39** Passion: Part 1		BLM 22.1 A Tree Shall Be Known by Its Fruit	P2
	Lesson 40 Passion: Part 2	JE 78 Check Your Focus JE 79 Isn't He Good? JE 80 Transformed Desires JE 81 The Passion of William Wilberforce JE 82 Be the Change		P2

Student Edition	Teacher Edition	Journal Entries	Blackline Masters	Big Ideas
Chapter 23 The Spiritual Passion of Jesus	**Lesson 41** Loving God, Loving People	JE 83 The One Thing Challenge	BLM 23.1 Are You Walking like Jesus?	P2
	Lesson 42 Taking the Opportunity	JE 84 Ryan and the Empty Bowls JE 85 Serving God by Saving the Planet JE 86 Incarnational Living		P2
Chapter 24 Community Life	**Lesson 43** Community	JE 87 Where Do I Belong? JE 88 Getting In JE 89 Your Misery, Your Ministry		P3
Chapter 25 The Purpose of Community	**Lesson 44** The Purpose of Community	JE 90 BELLS JE 91 Crowd or Community? JE 92 Your Community JE 93 Four Souls JE 94 Breaking Ground JE 95 Waterskiing Community		P3
	Lesson 45 Christian Community as Witness	JE 96 God and Basketball JE 97 Every Part Matters JE 98 Missional Community		P3
Chapter 26 Celebration: The End of the Story	**Lesson 46** The Rest of the Story	JE 99 What Are You Waiting For? JE 100 What Is Worship? JE 101 Sacrifice—the Soil of True Life JE 102 Being Missional		P4
	Lesson 47 A Celebration!	JE 103 Celebrate God!		P4
	Lesson 48 Reflecting and Looking Forward	JE 104 A Time of Reflection JE 1 Reflection on Missio Dei JE 11 "The Parable of the Race" JE 105 Created in Christ Jesus to Do Good Works JE 106 Next Steps JE 107 My Journey with God … a Year Later		P4

Lesson Components

Each lesson contains the following components:

 Big Idea: a sentence or two explaining the big-picture idea of a chapter or group of chapters

 Key Concepts: a short list of key concepts from the chapter, designed to quickly focus your thinking as lesson preparation begins

 Reflective Questions: outcome-based questions (titled "What Difference Does it Make?" in the student edition) that reflect the Big Ideas and key concepts of the chapter and that promote higher-level thinking skills

 Teacher's Heart: a devotional section written to stimulate your thinking as you begin preparation for teaching the lesson

 Teacher's Preparation: a background and preparation section designed to prepare you to effectively present and communicate the content for each lesson and to provide an overview of the content; also designed to provide hard-to-obtain reference material and other resources for further preparatory study (such as, in some lessons, a section called "Word Play," which is a listing of words and definitions that might be unfamiliar to students and that could be the basis of preteaching vocabulary or assigning in-class work or that could simply serve as reference material)

 Objectives: student learning objectives for the lesson

 Unpacking: a bullet-point presentation of the lesson plan (the heart of the chapter-concepts presentation), outlining one or more activities designed to "unpack" the text with the students—activities that may introduce new information, make connections to previously taught information, informally provide for assessing student understanding, prepare students for or challenge them with further study, or apply key concepts

Most lessons include one or more of the following components:

 If Time Activity (or Activities): one or more extra activities/assignments that in some lessons are provided for use if the schedule allows

 Extra Mile: an activity or a short list of activities to challenge students who express an interest in learning more about a particular lesson or who are interested in a personal experience related to the lesson topic; material that might also be offered for extra credit or for the enrichment of interested students

 Formal Assessment: both traditional and alternative assessments provided at the end of each unit as formal assessment options

What's Next: any homework assignments required for the next class

Looking Ahead: a reminder of upcoming lessons, assignments, or projects that you will need to begin planning and preparing for

Further Study: additional material provided as a starting place for further research on a particular topic related to the lesson

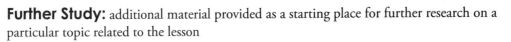

Assessment

Provided throughout the course is a variety of assessment options, including journal entries, BLMs, quizzes, class discussions, activities, and major projects and assignments, and provided at the end of each unit is a formal assessment. Most lessons contain specific suggestions for how to assess the activities in the lesson. Some lessons begin with scripted reading checks, whereas others make specific homework assignments.

You could keep anecdotal records of student participation in class discussions, periodically check progress in the student journal, or collect any of the other assignments you make as you go along. You could evaluate open-ended discussions, essays, or journal entries with a simple plus/minus system, or you could use a rubric (sample included in the CD). Also included is an assortment of rubrics for evaluating major assignments such as portfolios, written reports, and oral presentations as well as a comprehension self-assessment rubric that can be used following the reading of a chapter. On the self-assessment rubric, the students rate their understanding of concepts in the SE chapter on a scale of 0 to 3. Students then write out two concepts they understand well from the chapter. The results of this self-assessment may point you to specific items to reinforce in another class period. And as already mentioned, a formal unit test is provided for each of the first three units as one of several options for formal assessment following each unit.

The final project for the course (see the Major Assignments/Projects chart) is to have students turn in their journal as part of a portfolio project. There is no specific lesson in which this is introduced to the student (thus giving you the opportunity to introduce it when you believe it is appropriate), but it is important to inform the students early on in the course that you will be looking at their journal. You may want to do periodic evaluations throughout the course (many lessons involve discussions regarding what they have written the night before in their journal), in which case you could evaluate their work on the basis of participation in the discussion and evidence of thoughtful reflection. The other option is to wait until the completion of the course to evaluate the journals and any other assignments you have given students as part of a culminating portfolio. Encourage your students to embrace their experience and to journey with God throughout the course. Ask that they honestly reflect this experience in what they write.

Because of the intensely personal nature of the journal, students may be reluctant to answer questions openly and honestly if they know that this material will be evaluated by the teacher. Remember that one of the underlying goals of this course is to ask the hard questions and give students the opportunity to wrestle with these questions. In many cases there are no right or wrong answers because each student's experience and journey with God will be different. It is important that you provide an environment in which students are free to openly and fully embrace their experience with God. Keeping that underlying assumption in mind, reassure your students regarding how you intend to evaluate their work.

Major Assignments/Projects

The following assignments/projects give students an opportunity to use higher-level thinking skills to build upon the concepts and ideas introduced throughout the course. In many cases, these alternative assessments serve as a culminating unit project or a formal assessment (although traditional types of assessment are also provided). You will find rubrics in the CD of this teacher edition to assist you in the evaluation of these assignments.

Project	Unit/Course	Type of Assignment	TE Lesson Assigned	TE Lesson Completed	Blackline Masters or Journal Entries
The Story of the Bible: Version 1 Students will write a brief one-page narrative of the Bible in their own words.	Bible	Essay	**Lesson 1** The Beginning of the Journey	**Lesson 1** The Beginning of the Journey	None
The Story of the Bible: Version 2 Students will repeat the assignment, writing a brief one-page narrative of the Bible in their own words. Versions 1 and 2 will be compared to each other.	Bible	Essay	**Lesson 16** Review: God's Purpose and Mission	**Lesson 16** Review: God's Purpose and Mission	None
Looking Outside: A Cross-Cultural Research Project Students will research an international current events news story and examine the cultural context behind the story.	Culture	Research project (may include an in-class presentation; written report to include essays and research activities)	**Lesson 22** A Big, Big World	Time frame determined by teacher but completed by the end of the Culture Unit	BLM 10.1 Looking Outside: A Cross-Cultural Research Project BLM 10.2 Culture Analysis Template
Looking Back: A Review of History Students will review over 2,000 years of history through the lens of missio Dei. This culminating assignment provides a synthesis of the learning experience that students had throughout the unit.	History	Portfolio project (to include reflective writing assignments, research activities, BLMs, and notes from lectures or class discussions)	**Lesson 28** Introduction to the Era Chapters	**Lesson 35** Review: The Ultimate Completion of God's Purpose	BLM 15.1 Era One Time Line BLM 15.2 Who, What, When, Where, How BLM 15.3 All Shook Up BLM 15.4 Challenges, Successes, and Shortcomings BLM 16.1 Era Two Time Line BLM 16.2 Who, What When, Where, How BLM 16.3 All Shook Up BLM 16.4 Challenges, Successes, and Shortcomings BLM 17.1 Era Three Time Line BLM 17.2 Who, What When, Where, How BLM 17.3 All Shook Up BLM 17.4 Challenges, Successes, and Shortcomings

Project	Unit/ Course	Type of Assignment	TE Lesson		Blackline Masters or Journal Entries
			Assigned	Completed	
Looking Back: A Review of History (continued)					BLM 18.1 Era Four Time Line
					BLM 18.2 Who, What When, Where, How
					BLM 18.3 All Shook Up
					BLM 18.4 Challenges, Successes, and Shortcomings
					BLM 19.1 Era Five Time Line
					BLM 19.2 Who, What When, Where, How
					BLM 19.3 All Shook Up
					BLM 19.4 Challenges, Successes, and Shortcomings
People in History Profile Students will research and write one (or more, if assigned) contemporary people profile.	History	Written report and presentation	Lesson 34 Era Five: Part 2	Lesson 35 Review: The Ultimate Completion of God's Purpose	BLM 19.5 People in History Profile Template
Getting to Know a People Group: An Ethnographic Study Students will complete a basic ethnographic study of a people group.	Practices	Portfolio project and presentation (written report, research activities, and assignments)	Lesson 35 Review: The Ultimate Completion of God's Purpose	Lesson 46 The Rest of the Story	BLM 20.2 Getting to Know a People Group: An Ethnographic Study BLM 20.3 People Group Profile Template
Missio Dei: The Journey Students will put together a culminating course portfolio.	Entire Course	Portfolio project (student journal and any other assignments, as determined by the teacher)	To be determined by the teacher	Lesson 48 Reflecting and Looking Forward (or following course completion)	Student journal (*Missio Dei: The Journey*) and any BLMs or other assignments the teacher determines should be included

Lesson 1 — The Beginning of the Journey

Big Idea

Participating in missio Dei is the adventure of a lifetime.

Key Concepts

- God invites each of us to participate in a very specific journey with Him during our lives.

- Each of us has a unique reaction to the idea of a new beginning, an adventure, or a journey—particularly those that are spiritual in nature.

Reflective Questions

- How do you feel about journeys or adventures? Does the idea of a new adventure thrill you or make you nervous? Why is that? (SE p. xiii)

- What expectations or desires do you have in relation to this course? Are you dreading it? looking forward to it? Why do you think you have those feelings? (SE p. xvii)

Teacher's Heart

If you are teaching this course, then you are old enough to have discovered that life is full of beginnings, passages, and adventures of all kinds. There are three general reactions to those sorts of events—excited expectation, unmitigated dread, or sheer boredom and disinterest. You are likely to experience a variety of those reactions right now as you begin a new semester. My prayer for you, as you familiarize yourself with the contents of this course and as God directs your steps, is that you will be filled with anticipation about what God will bring into your life and into the lives of your students. Perhaps the beginning of this course includes new students and many other unknown elements for you. Spend a few minutes in prayer before reading the rest of this lesson plan. Ask God to help you prepare for this time of new beginnings. Talk to Him about your hopes, fears, expectations, and desires. Then rest in the assurance that He is present with you both in the current moment and on the road ahead. Blessings to you on your journey this semester!

Teacher's Preparation

Today's lesson is a time to begin introducing the course. It is a time to take note of your present surroundings as you prepare to journey to the places God will take you in the coming semester. It is also a time to capture some thoughts about your expectations as you begin. At the end of the course, your students will have the opportunity to look back and see how far they have come. To that end, there are basically two components to today's lesson: read and react. Along with reading and discussing the student edition introduction in class today, you'll spend some time looking through the student book and the student journal and discussing some of their elements. The second component of the lesson is to let students capture their reactions in the first entry of the journal that goes along with the text. Designed to be an integral part of your students' participation in the course, the journal is styled after the concept of *vade mecum*, Latin for "go with me." According to *Merriam-Webster Online Dictionary*, *vade mecum* is "1 : a book for ready reference : manual 2 : something regularly carried about by a person."[1] Not only will the journal be an important part of completing assignments throughout the course, but it also contains supplemental material to stimulate and reinforce ideas from the student book, and it is designed as a place for students to capture their ideas and impressions as they go along the journey of *missio Dei*—the mission of God. You and your students can read a little more about the concept of *vade mecum* in the introduction to the journal.

There are several concepts in the student edition introduction that you may wish to emphasize during your class discussion. The goal is not to instruct on or resolve any of the possible topics of conversation, but to simply call attention to those ideas that stand out to you and your students as you read the introductory material. Your students are likely to have their own observations to make, but here are some suggestions to get the conversation going:

• Talk about the concept of different paths that is discussed in the introduction (SE p. xiii). Many students are probably feeling overwhelmed with "life decisions" at this point in their high school careers. Discuss how they're feeling, how they make decisions, and what they believe about an "intended path." You might want to also talk about the idea of cookie-cutter answers mentioned on that same page.

• Discuss the concept of missio Dei. Do the students conceive that God has a mission on earth at the present time? Do they think of themselves as having a role to play?

• Talk about the idea that experience is at the heart of a relationship with God (SE p. xv). Leonard I. Sweet says, "Christians have much to learn about faith as a lived experience, not a thought experiment" (2007, 5; SE p. xiv). Have students compare and contrast these two ideas of relating to God.

• Draw attention to each of the four units and the corresponding metaphorical "tools for the journey" that students will encounter in the course (see SE pp. xv–xvi). Let them react to the idea of the Bible as a compass, the study of culture as a type of binoculars, the study of history as a travelogue, and some key practices of Christ-followers as a backpack of essential items. Discuss what items your students must have when they travel. Ask them to project what essentials they need (and have used) on their journey with God. Discuss why each view (each unit) is important in studying the mission of God.

• Point out and discuss the quotation from Sweet in the final paragraph of the introduction (2007, 29; SE p. xvii).

Remember, the goal of today's lesson is to give students a small taste of the course through the introduction. After your discussion about the contents of the book, draw attention to the book's cover. Then point out and discuss the elements mentioned in the introduction to this course, asking students to watch for how each of these ideas is revealed during the course. You might also want to look together through the table of contents or the unit introductions (SE pp. 3, 103, 169, and 247) as a way of heightening anticipation for the material in the course. Remind students to write down any impressions or thoughts they have during the class discussion. These notes can form the basis of their response to the final assignment of today's lesson, in which students respond to **JE 1 Reflection on Missio Dei**.

Perhaps you have already noticed by looking through the course materials that there are some different voices, perhaps even new ideas, presented in various ways throughout the text. In some ways, your students may be more attuned than you are to some of these elements, since they are immersed in a world that communicates, interacts, and thinks in ways that may be very different from the world of even fifteen or twenty years ago. If this is your first time to teach this course, you may find yourself encountering new ideas, teaching methods, and voices that reflect the realities of the world we live in. Some of these elements may initially be challenging or new to you. God knows exactly where you are, where your students are, and how He will connect all of you with the big things He is doing all around this world. That is the adventure that awaits you and your students!

By permission. From *Merriam-Webster Online Dictionary* ©2009 by Merriam-Webster, Incorporated (www.merriam-webster.com).

Objectives

- Students will read and discuss the introduction of this course.

- Students will react to the overarching ideas of the course and think through what the course might teach them.

Unpacking

Reading and Discussing (20–30 minutes)

Give students an opportunity to individually and silently read the student edition introduction at the beginning of class. Then, using the suggestions in the "Teacher's Preparation" section, discuss the introduction, the student book itself, and the student journal.

Reacting (5–10 minutes)

Direct students to the first journal entry, **JE 1 Reflection on Missio Dei**. Give students time to answer the questions in class. You may want to collect the student journals to use **JE 1** as a means of assessment. Listening carefully during class discussion to determine your students' attitudes and expectations is another way of assessing the starting point of your students. If they don't have time to finish, ask them to complete the assignment as homework.

You could also have your students write and turn in an essay in response to this lesson's Reflective Questions.

The Story of the Bible: Version 1 (10–15 minutes and out-of-class assignment)

For this project, The Story of the Bible: Version 1, have your students write a brief narrative of the Bible. They should write the story of the Bible in their own words, and the length should be no longer than a page. Don't give your students a lot of parameters or structure. Regard this task for your students as a starting point—even an informal personal assessment—for identifying beliefs and understandings about the Bible. You will be asking your students to re-create this assignment in lesson 16.

❧

Note

1. *Merriam-Webster Online Dictionary*, s.v. "vade mecum," http://www.m-w.com/dictionary/ (accessed June 30, 2009).

Bible Unit

unit one

Bible Unit Introduction

Student Edition Introduction

In this unit, we will take a look at the story of the Bible. Be prepared for it not to sound as familiar as you might expect. You see, most of us come at reading the Bible in ways that may not give us the true picture. Maybe you think you know the story of the Bible. But this may be your chance to hear it from a new perspective, as though for the first time. As we unpack it, we'll take a look at the dynamic adventure of a lifetime that God invites you to be a part of. So, let's pick up the compass and see what it reveals to us about where we are.

Big Ideas

- The Bible, from Genesis to Revelation, tells the story of God's purpose.

- God's purpose is relationship, redemption, and reconciliation.

- God invites us to participate in His purpose; He blesses us so that we can bless others.

- God's story is unfolding as we see and participate in God's kingdom throughout the earth.

- The spread of God's kingdom takes place in the context of warfare with Satan.

Memory Verses

2 Corinthians 5:17–19

Therefore, if anyone is in Christ, he is a new creation; the old has gone, the new has come! All this is from God, who reconciled us to himself through Christ and gave us the ministry of reconciliation: that God was reconciling the world to himself in Christ, not counting men's sins against them. And he has committed to us the message of reconciliation.

Isaiah 26:8

Yes, Lord, walking in the way of your laws, we wait for you; your name and renown are the desire of our hearts.

Genesis 12:1–3

The Lord had said to Abram, "Leave your country, your people and your father's household and go to the land I will show you. I will make you into a great nation and I will bless you; I will make your name great, and you will be a blessing. I will bless those who bless you, and whoever curses you I will curse; and all peoples on earth will be blessed through you."

Ephesians 6:10–18

Finally, be strong in the Lord and in his mighty power. Put on the full armor of God so that you can take your stand against the devil's schemes. For our struggle is not against flesh and blood, but against the rulers, against the authorities, against the powers of this dark world and against the spiritual forces of evil in the heavenly realms. Therefore put on the full armor of God, so that when the day of evil comes, you may be able to stand your ground, and after you have done everything, to stand. Stand firm then, with the belt of truth buckled around your waist, with the breastplate of righteousness in place, and with your feet fitted with the readiness that comes from the gospel of peace. In addition to all this, take up the shield of faith, with which you can extinguish all the flaming arrows of the evil one. Take the helmet of salvation and the sword of the Spirit, which is the word of God. And pray in the Spirit on all occasions with all kinds of prayers and requests. With this in mind, be alert and always keep on praying for all the saints.

Web Resources

Link to more resources in our community at www.missiodei-thejourney.com.

What I Know About the Bible

Big Idea

The Bible, from Genesis to Revelation, tells the story of God's purpose.

Key Concepts

- Story is a powerful means of communicating truth.
- A person's perspective influences the way that person reacts to and responds to a story.
- The Bible is God's story.
- The Bible is an interpretation of the whole of history from beginning to end, and of the human story within that entirety.
- Though told in terms of one nation and one man within that nation, the story of the Bible reveals that God has a purpose regarding all nations.
- The story of the Bible reveals that we are invited to participate with God as bearers of His purpose.

Reflective Questions

- What have you learned about God by understanding the Bible as His story and understanding that He is the main character? Now that you know those things, what effect will they have on your life? (SE p. 90)
- Do you read the Bible differently after having studied this unit? If so, what difference does that make in the way you perceive the Bible? What about in the way you live your day-to-day life? (SE p. 90)
- Most of the time we don't think about the fact that our lives are telling a story to other people. What sorts of truths is the story of your life revealing to those around you? How can you be more intentional about the story your life is telling? (SE p. 90)

Teacher's Heart

I was reminded today of the idiom about looking at the world through rose-colored glasses. Rain was pouring down, traffic was creeping along on the interstate, and I couldn't have been happier. After several months of severe drought conditions—weeks since the last rain—my locality's annual rainfall totals were twenty inches below average. Obviously, my perspective on driving in a downpour was heavily influenced by the realities of the drought.

We are not often challenged to think about our perspective, our preconceived notions, and our biases—the lenses through which we view everything around us. But these lenses can play a huge role in how we interact with our world, what we spend our time thinking about, even how we read the Bible and interact with God. When we have a skewed perspective, the Bible, instead of being the epic story of God's purpose and plans for all of history, can become merely a book of rules or a tome of comforting snippets of advice—pieces and parts we construct together to fit our needs or desires at the time. Just as driving in the rain can be a nuisance unless you have the perspective of coming through a drought, the story of the Bible can be greatly influenced by your own perspective.

Jesus knew all about perspective. He often took the Pharisees to task for failing to have the proper perspective. In the Sermon on the Mount, Jesus gave this beautiful illustration of the power of perspective: "Why do you look at the speck of sawdust in your brother's eye and pay no attention to the plank in your own eye? How can you say to your brother, 'Let me take the speck out of your eye,' when all the time there is a plank in your own eye? You hypocrite, first take the plank out of your own eye, and then you will see clearly to remove the speck from your brother's eye" (Matthew 7:3–5). Notice how Jesus taught that our own perspective must be aligned with truth before we have even a chance of helping another person see truth.

Thankfully, the Holy Spirit is our guide in reading the Bible and understanding the truth of its story. We are reminded in John 16:13–14 of the sure guidance and true perspective of the Counselor: "But when he, the Spirit of truth, comes, he will guide you into all truth. He will not speak on his own; he will speak only what he hears, and he will tell you what is yet to come. He will bring glory to me by taking from what is mine and making it known to you."

My prayer for you as you prepare this lesson, and all the other lessons in this course, is that the Holy Spirit will guide you into all truth. I pray that you will be empowered to journey with your students to a deeper love relationship with God, that He will teach you and challenge you in unexpected ways, and that you will see and feel His hand leading you to join Him as He carries out His purpose all around you.

Teacher's Preparation

This first chapter of the Bible Unit is the longest chapter in the entire course. Included in this student chapter is the full text of Lesslie Newbigin's book *A Walk Through the Bible* (2005), which is literally a retelling of the entire story of the Bible in an engaging narrative form. This piece offers students the opportunity to hear the narrative of the Bible as one story, a concept that is foundational for this entire course. Though this chapter is long, in it are depths of truth and wisdom we will be unpacking throughout the remainder of this course. While teaching this chapter, you will perhaps be tempted to veer off into the many fascinating themes brought out by the reading. Rest assured that many of the themes presented by Newbigin are ones we will revisit throughout this unit and the remainder of the course. When you work with the entire story of the Bible, you will be unavoidably tempted to explore many things. But these first lessons have very specific purposes that lay foundations for the remainder of the course.

The heart of chapter 1 is to bring students to understand the Bible as one big story that reveals the purpose of God. This may be a somewhat different perspective than many of your students will have regarding the Bible, since some may view the Bible as a lot of little stories or may fall prey to the idea that only the New Testament has bearing on our lives today. Some of your students may have had little exposure to the Bible, and thus they have a less-specific perspective about what it contains. Mature adults and young people alike often are tempted to have a self-centered approach when relating to the Bible—looking for how God is going to bless them, sustain them, or save them. But the Bible is primarily a story about God, not man. The implications of that perspective of the Bible are enormous, especially in terms of our individual purposes and our relationships with God. So, we begin today's lesson with an exploration of preconceived notions that students have about the Bible and, by extension, about God. Keep in mind that you are likely to be dealing with a range of assumptions and perceptions on the part of your students. The objective is to get your students to consider what their assumptions about the Bible mean in terms of their daily lives and relationships with God.

Another benefit of shifting our perception to understanding that the Bible is God's story is the sense of purpose that new understanding can bring to our lives. Individuals can be responsible actors and participants with God in history. Newbigin's text clearly has this focus in mind. Newbigin writes about the ultimate vision of the Bible, as described in Revelation, as "a vision that enables us to see the whole human story and each of our lives within that story as meaningful, and which therefore invites us through Jesus Christ to become responsible actors in history" (2005, 84–85; SE p. 35). In other words, when we understand the story of the Bible as that of God at work to accomplish His purpose and also as a story of God inviting us to participate in His purpose, we find a whole new level of understanding our place in this world. Chapter 1 sets a foundation that will allow us to explore throughout this unit the purpose of God revealed in the Bible.

Today, students will be examining their own perspectives about the Bible and the story it tells. The previous assignment to write the story of the Bible in their own words has challenged them to identify the story of the Bible. Be sensitive regarding the struggle some students may have experienced in completing the assignment. Even as mature adults, many of us are still wrestling with the larger questions that are embodied in that writing assignment. As stated earlier, this assignment should be seen as a starting point—even an informal personal assessment—for identifying beliefs and understandings. Another activity (**JE 2 Viewpoints About the Bible**) introduced today extends that thinking by helping your students identify their own perceptions of what the Bible is and their attitudes toward it. As you begin to understand their perceptions about the Bible, you will start to see some of their ideas about who God is. And knowing what they believe about God and about the Bible is foundational to helping them develop a desire to be on mission with God. As you work through the remaining lessons in this unit, you will be helping the students see a bit at a time that the Bible, from Genesis to Revelation, tells the story of God's purpose.

Objectives

- Students will tell the story of the Bible in their own words.
- Students will examine and describe their own views of the Bible.
- Students will discuss their individual views of the Bible.
- Students will explain the relationship between their own perceptions of the Bible and their understanding of God.

Unpacking

Story-Writing Discussion (15–20 minutes)

To discuss The Story of the Bible: Version 1, the assignment of writing the story of the Bible in the students' own words, divide the class into several small groups of four to six students. Instruct each small group to briefly share their completed writing and to listen for common themes and ideas. After discussion time, ask each group to summarize its stories for the class. On the board, list common themes and repeated ideas. After students have discussed this assignment, help them draw conclusions regarding what this assignment revealed about their understanding of the Bible. Perhaps there is a great diversity of ideas about the story of the Bible. Perhaps many struggled to summarize the Bible in a short writing. Perhaps a specific theme or set of ideas emerged as a central story.

As students work in small groups, you may wish to assess whether they completed the story-writing assignment. Or you may want to observe your students' engagement with the material, to "take the pulse" of your students and their views of the Bible and God, and to establish a helpful benchmark as you move forward through the course. You may also wish to collect this reflective writing at the end of class.

Viewpoints Discussion (10–15 minutes)

Direct students to **JE 2 Viewpoints About the Bible**, and give them time to independently complete the survey. When they are finished, discuss the various views of the Bible that are represented on the survey. Ask students to consider how these various viewpoints might affect a person's view of God or the way in which a person makes daily choices.

Reflection (5–10 minutes)

Give students the time to complete **JE 3 Reflective Writing: My View of the Bible**, which asks them to respond to the following:

• Summarize your perspective of what the Bible is about.

• How do your views regarding the Bible affect the way you interact with God or with others?

• How do they influence your view of yourself?

Preparation for Reading (5 minutes)

Emphasize to students that understanding the Bible as one story of God's purpose can be a very eye-opening perspective. Encourage them to try to read chapter 1 in one sitting so that they can experience the idea of the one big story of the Bible.

What's Next

Have students complete the reading of chapter 1 before the next lesson.

The Bible as One Story

Big Idea

The Bible, from Genesis to Revelation, tells the story of God's purpose.

Key Concepts

- Story is a powerful means of communicating truth.
- A person's perspective influences the way that person reacts to and responds to a story.
- The Bible is God's story.
- The Bible is an interpretation of the whole of history from beginning to end, and of the human story within that entirety.
- Though told in terms of one nation and one man within that nation, the story of the Bible reveals that God has a purpose regarding all nations.
- The story of the Bible reveals that we are invited to participate with God as bearers of His purpose.

Reflective Questions

- What have you learned about God by understanding the Bible as His story and understanding that He is the main character? Now that you know those things, what effect will they have on your life? (SE p. 90)
- Do you read the Bible differently after having studied this unit? If so, what difference does that make in the way you perceive the Bible? What about in the way you live your day-to-day life? (SE p. 90)
- Most of the time we don't think about the fact that our lives are telling a story to other people. What sorts of truths is the story of your life revealing to those around you? How can you be more intentional about the story your life is telling? (SE p. 90)

Teacher's Heart

I was really struck by what Newbigin had to say about the beauty of the prohibitions found in the Ten Commandments: "But you see the great point about a negative command is that it leaves you free. Positive commandments telling you exactly what to do in every situation don't leave you any freedom. A negative commandment leaves you freedom within limits" (2005, 20; see SE p. 13). He goes on to compare a negative commandment to a fence around a playground: the fence offers protection yet leaves plenty of room for play. What love is expressed by the one who offers us such boundaries!

A most powerful effect of understanding the Bible as one big story of God's purpose is that it removes from our hearts the idea of the Bible as a judgmental, static book of rules and regulations that must be followed to please God. That notion can put the most submissive and loving of hearts in a straitjacket. Surely God does desire our obedience, but He is dynamic—a living, relational being. He gives us fences that provide for our protection *and* our freedom. Over and over again the Bible shows us that relationship with God is not a cookie-cutter, one-size-fits-all experience. What joy and freedom our loving Father desires to bestow on us! How great is His grace! How much bigger He is than we sometimes allow.

As a teenager, I was constantly questioning and pushing against boundaries set for me by those in authority. I had no understanding of the insight Newbigin so wonderfully offers. Some of your students may be in the same place. Perhaps you are as well. As you prepare this lesson, ask God to reveal to you the protection and freedom His plans and limits offer us. Meditate on Ephesians 1:17–19. Paul's desire for the Ephesian believers to catch a vision of the magnitude of God's love and power is the same desire God has for you and your students. Ask Him to show you and your students more and more of Himself, and pray for spirits that are willing to receive that truth.

Teacher's Preparation

Today's lesson centers on the concept of story, both in terms of general story structure and the specific story of the Bible. Your students have doubtless been taught about story structure in their English classes, so they should be familiar with the basics of this lesson. Yet they may never have thought of the Bible in relation to *plot* and *character*, the literary elements that are the focus of today's lesson. In *Poetics*, Aristotle articulated standards for literary forms, standards that are still widely held. Regarding plot, Aristotle noted that a proper plot should be complete and whole, containing a beginning, a middle, and an end. Another element of plot identified by Aristotle is that of unity, or the centering of all action of the plot around a central theme or idea. Often, that central theme will coincide with the goals or purposes of the main character and what he seeks to accomplish. And of course, every good story has conflict—a struggle between forces that makes the achievement of the main character's purpose difficult and complicated.

Word Play	
The following terms may be pretaught or used as the basis for a vocabulary assignment:	
climax	the turning point in the story, often the most suspenseful point (the point at which the reader will know whether the main character is successful in meeting his goal)
conflict	a struggle between opposing forces
denouement	a synonym for falling action
exposition	the plot's first segment, which often reveals the characters, setting, and situation of the story
falling action	the portion of the story revealing the characters' reaction to the climax; an unraveling of details related to the conflict
plot	the sequence of events or actions in a story (according to Aristotle, a complete whole containing a beginning, a middle, and an end)
protagonist	the main character of a literary work
resolution	the events or circumstances that reveal the end of the conflict
rising action	the buildup of events, including problems, complications, and conflicts faced by the characters
unity	the centering of all action of the plot around a central theme or idea

The story of the Bible certainly fulfills these elements. Unity of plot is found in the Bible's theme of the desire by God for intimate relationship with His creation. We will look further, in chapter 2, at this particular aspect of the story, but as you teach today's lesson it is appropriate to draw the students' attention to a line in Newbigin's book: "God will not leave us until he has won us back to be his children" (2005, 10; SE p. 10). This is the heart of the story of the Bible. Again and again we see God enacting a plan to bring us back into right relationship with Him. This is the mission that we are invited to participate in. And it is important to help students understand this unifying theme of the Bible, since we often view the Bible as a lot of small, similar but perhaps unrelated stories. Understanding the Bible as one story that continues to be told in our lives today can profoundly change our thinking.

The story of God's relational purpose is complicated by the continuous conflict that God encounters throughout the story of the Bible. Beginning with the Fall and continuing to the present day, people have been and are rebelling against God, choosing their own ways instead of His. The conflict of the Bible's story is the struggle between God's ideal for us and our own picture of what is best for us. Newbigin (2005) brings out this theme in many ways, particularly in descriptions of the Fall (SE pp. 9–10), the tower of Babel (SE p. 11), Moses' initial hesitation to accept God's invitation (SE p. 12), Israel and idolatry (SE p. 14), the chaos of Israel's judges and kingship eras (SE pp. 14–15), war between the two kingdoms of Israel (SE p. 16), the prophets' warnings to the divided kingdom of Israel (SE pp. 18–20), the varied hopes of Jesus' contemporaries for the establishment of God's kingdom (SE pp. 21–22), the events leading to Jesus' death (SE pp. 26–28), and the conflicts in the early Church about accepting the work of Jesus after His resurrection (SE pp. 30–32). Your students will certainly be able to identify contemporary examples from their own lives and the world around them that demonstrate the truth of the ongoing conflict between our desires and the desires of God. Helping students draw those parallels is one of the ways you can help them see how they are a part of the story that is told in the Bible, a story that continues to be written on the pages of history down through the ages.

Another way to help students see the unity of the Bible as one story is to show them that the Bible has a clear beginning, middle, and end, just as in any good plot. Newbigin says, "The Bible tells the story of the whole human race in terms of a particular story of one race—that of Israel—and of one person within that race—Jesus of Nazareth" (2005, 5; see SE p. 8). The story of Israel is central and foundational to the Bible's story, and it really gets going in Genesis 12 with the calling of Abraham and the establishment of the family that would ultimately be the nation of Israel. Breaking the plot of the Bible into a beginning, a middle, and an end would look something like the chart on the next page.

The climactic moment of the story of the Bible is the resurrection of Jesus Christ, which Newbigin identifies as a new act of creation that is "to recreate the whole cosmos according to his glorious purpose" (2005, 70; SE p. 29). From this moment, a new order is created, leading to the falling action of the Bible story and culminating in the resolution pictured in the book of Revelation.

Another key part of this lesson is in identifying whom the story of the Bible is about. Gerald Robison, coauthor of *Cat and Dog Theology*, says, "Christians are trained to read, preach, and teach the Bible for 'personal application.' We read our Bible as though it were about us. As a result we don't live for God" (2007). Newbigin notes that the hero, or protagonist, of the Bible is God: "The Bible interprets the whole of reality and the whole of history in terms of the actions, the doings, the speakings, the promises of God. And therefore the Bible is the way in which we come to know God, because we don't know a person except by knowing his or her story" (2005, 5; SE p. 8). The Bible does tell the story of the whole of humanity, and people are definitely characters in the story. But to approach the Bible as though it were something other than God's story will inevitably lead to a skewed reading. None of us, including the other human actors we find in the story, is the main character. God is the main character of the Bible.

But we do have a part in the story told by the Bible. Though we will examine more of this in chapter 2, today's lesson is designed to help

Beginning	Middle	End
Genesis 1–11	**Genesis 12–Revelation 4**	**Revelation 5–22**
Characters (God and human-kind) and setting (Earth; more specifically, the nation of Israel and its surroundings) are revealed. Exposition of the basic relationships and conflicts of the story is given. (See SE pp. 9–11.)	The work of the redemption of the nations is begun through the establishment of Israel and its ultimate king, Jesus of Nazareth. Complications and conflict continue as the rising action continues through the story of Israel. The climax, or turning point, of the story is the death and resurrection of Jesus. The falling action from this point leads to the resolution pictured in the end of the story. (See SE pp. 11–32.)	The final outcome or untangling of the events of the story is seen in the establishment of God's fully revealed kingdom of heaven. The enemies of God are not only defeated but banished. And the relationship of God with His created children is fully and permanently restored. (See SE pp. 32–35.)

students begin to think about their part in the ongoing story of God's desire to be in relationship with people, to redeem them, and to reconcile them to Himself. Newbigin says, "The Bible gives us the whole story of creation and of the human race and therefore enables us to understand our own lives as part of that story" (2005, 82; see SE p. 33). As Newbigin relates the ultimate end of the story—the restored fellowship of God's kingdom found in Revelation—he shows the purposefulness we can live with here and now. Newbigin describes the vision of a holy city in which face-to-face, personal relationship with God is found: "It is a vision that enables us to see the whole human story and each of our lives within that story as meaningful, and which therefore invites us through Jesus Christ to become responsible actors in history, not to seek to run away from the responsibilities and the agonies of human life in its public dimension. Each of us must be ready to take our share in all the struggles and the anguish of human history and yet with the confidence that what is committed to Christ will in the end find its place in his final kingdom" (84–85; see SE p. 35).

Helping your students see their place in the ongoing story of God in His mission to restore fellowship with His creation is the ultimate purpose of this course. Ultimately students should understand that their own lives each tell a story, and that story says something about God to the world around them. The journey of learning to submit ourselves to God's plans and leadership for the stories of our lives is one of ongoing revelation, learning, and reflection. It is a relationship journey. As we explore that journey in a specific way during this lesson, keep in mind that journeys are ongoing processes with times of understanding and times of questioning. Your students may have more questions than answers after today's lesson. But God will be faithful to guide and direct this journey you are helping them along, as He always has.

Objectives

- Students will identify God as the main character of the Bible's story.
- Students will identify the Bible as one story with a distinct beginning, middle, and end.
- Students will discover the overarching story of the Bible: God is on mission to complete His purpose.
- Students will identify the fact that they have a part in God's ongoing story.

Unpacking

Reading Quiz (5 minutes)

Using the following questions, quiz the students for a check of completion of the assigned reading:

1. According to chapter 1, story is the only way to communicate truth. True or false? (false; a good way but not the only way)

2. Who, according to Newbigin, is the hero of the Bible? (God)

3. Name one of the bearers of God's purpose, according to Newbigin. (any of these three: Israel; Jesus; later, the Christian church)

4. The Bible, according to Newbigin, is "a unique interpretation of universal history." True or false? (true; 2005, pp. 4, 83; SE pp. 8, 34)

5. Name one example of conflict that is found in the story of the Bible. (varying answers, though each should reflect a reading of the chapter)

Preparation for Learning (5 minutes)

Ask students to brainstorm and share answers to the following questions:

- What new things did you learn about the story of the Bible from the assigned reading?

- What did you learn about God in this reading?

List their answers on the board. Use this as a means of beginning a discussion about plot and character. You may wish to refer back to this list as you lead the next part of the lesson.

The Bible as One Story (15 minutes)

Using the material in the "Teacher's Preparation" section and in the graphic organizer found in **BLM 1.1 Plot Components**, discuss the following points with the class:

- The Bible is one narrative story that has a beginning, a middle, and an end. Identify the various portions of the Bible that represent each of these parts of the plot.

- The main character of the narrative is God.

- The plot of the Bible reveals the purpose of God and the conflict between His desires and the desires of the people He created.

Your Part in the Story (10 minutes)

Lead a discussion centering on the roles students are to play in God's ongoing story as revealed in the Bible. In their roles, which appear as part of the middle of this unfolding story, they are invited to participate, just as Israel was, as bearers of God's purpose. Use the graphic organizer in **BLM 1.1** to help students identify elements of the Bible story and to envision their own roles in the story.

Final Application (5 minutes)

Have students write a sentence or paragraph that summarizes the story of the Bible. After today's lesson they should be able to synthesize the story into a sentence similar to *The Bible is the story of God and His relationship with His creation.*

If Time Activities

Index Card Assessment

On one side of an index card, have students write the Big Idea for this lesson: The Bible, from Genesis to Revelation, tells the story of God's purpose. On the flip side of the card, have students write a question or statement that indicates either something they don't yet understand about this concept or more they would like to know about it. You can use these responses for further clarification and discussion, possibly small-group discussion.

Placing Yourself in the Story

Have students select from one of the sections of the assigned reading in which the conflict of the Bible's plot is developed. Some of these selections are listed with page numbers in the "Teacher's Preparation" section. After reading a selection, they should write a parallel version of the account that demonstrates conflict in their personal lives, or in our contemporary society, between the desires of God and the desires of man.

What's Next

Choose one of the activities in the "If Time Activities" section for homework.

Bearers of God's Purpose

Big Idea

The Bible, from Genesis to Revelation, tells the story of God's purpose.

Key Concepts

- Story is a powerful means of communicating truth.
- A person's perspective influences the way that person reacts to and responds to a story.
- The Bible is God's story.
- The Bible is an interpretation of the whole of history from beginning to end, and of the human story within that entirety.
- Though told in terms of one nation and one man within that nation, the story of the Bible reveals that God has a purpose regarding all nations.
- The story of the Bible reveals that we are invited to participate with God as bearers of His purpose.

Reflective Questions

- What have you learned about God by understanding the Bible as His story and understanding that He is the main character? Now that you know those things, what effect will they have on your life? (SE p. 90)
- Do you read the Bible differently after having studied this unit? If so, what difference does that make in the way you perceive the Bible? What about in the way you live your day-to-day life? (SE p. 90)
- Most of the time we don't think about the fact that our lives are telling a story to other people. What sorts of truths is the story of your life revealing to those around you? How can you be more intentional about the story your life is telling? (SE p. 90)

Teacher's Heart

I came across this quotation in a prayer calendar this morning: "Not knowing who God made us to be, trying to be who we are not, or even just *desiring* to be someone else, can only lead to a life of misery, frustration, and unfulfillment" (Omartian 2002). I remember well the anxiety of the last years of high school—spending so much time worrying about choices for my future, wanting to be sure I made the "right" ones. I had no idea that there is no such thing as a foolproof, twenty-year plan for our lives. In fact, just the opposite is true. Our lives are to be guided in moment-by-moment, day-by-day relationship with God. I often get my instructions on a need-to-know basis. As a result, I have had at least three or four careers. But God knew (and knows) that what I was doing as a twenty-three-year-old would also prepare me for the work I would do as a forty-year-old. He sees and directs the entire path.

It is comforting to know that when you are in a relationship with Him and desiring to serve His purpose, He is faithful to guide you. Nothing is wasted, and there is peace in the assurance that we are a part of His plan. Yes, there are major life decisions to be made, but not without guidance from the wonderful Counselor. Your students are probably experiencing some anxieties about their futures. Today's lesson points to a picture of purpose for every life. Pray that the hearts of your students will be open to the excitement in knowing that God guides their paths.

Teacher's Preparation

In chapter 1 Lesslie Newbigin uses the phrase "bearers of his [God's] purpose" to describe the role of Israel and Jesus as witnesses and testifiers to the greatness of God and to His plans (2005, 79; SE p. 32). This phrase is synonymous with the phrases "on mission with God" and "living missionally" used elsewhere in this book and in our title, *Missio Dei: Joining God on the Adventure of a Lifetime*. All these phrases relate to what should be the ultimate aim of our lives—joining God in His purpose.

Newbigin observes, "The Bible tells the story of the whole human race in terms of a particular story of one race—that of Israel—and of one person within that race—Jesus of Nazareth" (2005, 5; SE p. 8). In today's lesson, we will look to the Bible to reveal more about this specific thread of the story. After students explore both Israel and Jesus as the bearers of God's purpose, they will explore the Bible's post-Resurrection portrait of the bearers of God's purpose.

Newbigin says, "What happened on that Easter day was a kind of new creation, the beginning of a new era for the world. The first fruit of God's intention to recreate the whole cosmos according to his glorious purpose" (2005, 70; SE p. 29). The New Testament reveals that this new era includes an invitation for believers in Him to become the bearers of God's purpose. As Newbigin points out, the writer of Hebrews "shows that Jesus also fulfils all that is written in the Old Testament concerning the priestly ministry of the temple and the priesthood—that in Jesus, all that was prescribed in the Old Testament by way of offering, sacrifice and priesthood has been fulfilled so that the Christian Church is itself now in Christ a holy priesthood" (76; SE p. 32).

This invitation to become a bearer of God's purpose, or to join God in His purpose, is the new covenant that Jesus referred to during the Last Supper (see Luke 22:20)—a reference to the prophecy found in Jeremiah 31:31–34. More familiar to you

and your students might be Christ's instructions found in Acts 1:8, "You will be my witnesses," or the words of the Great Commission found in Matthew 28:18–20.

A theme in today's lesson is that of priesthood. The concept of priesthood in the Old Testament is clearly that of mediation between God and man. Israel as a nation was to serve as such a mediator between God and the nations (see Exodus 19:5–6). Educator and author Christopher J. H. Wright notes the following: "As Yahweh's priesthood, Israel would be the means by which he would be known to the nations and the means of bringing them to himself (performing a function analogous to the role of Israel's own priests between God and the rest of the people). As a holy people, they would be ethically (as well as ritually) distinctive from the practices of surrounding nations (Leviticus 18–19). Such visibility would be a matter of observation and comment among the nations (Deuteronomy 4:6–8). The question of Israel's ethical obedience or ethical failure was not, then, merely a matter between themselves and Yahweh, but of major significance in relation to Yahweh's agenda for the nations (cf. Jeremiah 4:1–2)."[1]

This mediation, or priesthood, can be seen at the heart of bearing God's purpose, and as Newbigin notes on SE page 32, Christ perfectly fulfills the role of priest (2005, 76; see also Hebrews 8–9). Through Him, we have access to this same calling as well as the empowering of His Spirit, which enables us to faithfully bear God's purpose to the world. This idea is often referred to as the priesthood of all believers.

Of course, throughout the remainder of this course we will be unpacking our invitation to participate on mission with God as bearers of His purpose, but today's lesson is designed to further extend what was started in lesson 3: the bridge between the story of the Bible and the story of students' own lives.

Objectives

- Students will identify those who have been called to bear God's purpose throughout the Bible.
- Students will discover what the bearers of God's purpose do.
- Students will investigate examples of Israel and Jesus as bearers of God's purpose.
- Students will discover their own invitation to be bearers of God's purpose.
- Students will assess the relationship between the story of the Bible and God's purpose for their own lives.

Unpacking

Directed Study (20–30 minutes)

Purpose bearers. Call your students' attention to this passage found on SE page 8: "God makes himself known to us in the context of our shared life as human beings because that is what our human life is. We therefore come to know God through one another—and specifically through the people whom he chose to be the bearers of his purpose" (Newbigin 2005, 6). Discuss briefly what the bearers of God's purpose do. (**They reveal God to those around them.**) Then ask students who the bearers of God's purpose are. (**Newbigin identifies the bearers of God's purpose as Israel and Jesus, and later, believers through Christ.**)

Direct the students' attention to SE page 32 and the quotation, "God has chosen Israel and Jesus to be bearers of his purpose for the whole of creation and of the human race" (Newbigin 2005, 79). Discuss with students what they know about this idea. Then give them time to read the following passages and list what each reveals about Israel or Jesus as bearers of God's purpose: Exodus 19:5–6; Deuteronomy 4:5–8, 28:9–10; Matthew 11:4–6; Luke 4:16–20; John 17:4.
(**The first three show that Israel was set apart by God to be a priesthood to the nations, that Israel demonstrated by obedience God's nearness, righteousness, and blessing. The last three passages concern specific ministries of Jesus and how He did the work God gave Him.**)

Connecting to the present. Call attention to this quotation on SE page 32: "Jesus also fulfils all that is written in the Old Testament concerning the priestly ministry of the temple and the priesthood—that in Jesus, all that was prescribed in the Old Testament by way of offering, sacrifice and priesthood has been fulfilled so that the Christian Church is itself now in Christ a holy priesthood" (Newbigin 2005, 76). Discuss how this new order created by the death and resurrection of Christ offers a different picture of the method God used to reveal Himself to the nations—through us.
(**In the Old Testament God was revealed through the Law and the priesthood, but now, because of the new covenant, God's laws are written on our hearts and minds and God is revealed through our lives: see Hebrews 7–10.**)

Instruct students to read the following passages and draw conclusions about what is revealed regarding the bearers of God's purpose following Christ's resurrection:

Hebrews 8:6–13 (**prophecy of the new covenant fulfilled by Jesus**)
John 17:20–26 (**Jesus' prayer for all believers**)
Matthew 28:16–20 (**the Great Commission**)
Acts 1:4–9 (**Jesus' pre-ascension words**)

Have students read and compare 1 Peter 2:4–10 with Exodus 19:5–6.

If Time Activity

Have students write an essay or create a chart to compare Israel's imperfection in carrying out this mission (although you should note the ever-present faithful remnant) with Christ's perfection in carrying out this mission. Challenge your students to cite Bible references to support their observations. Some suggestions for passages that might aid in this comparison are Old Testament prophecies concerning Israel's unfaithfulness to God (see next lesson for some specific references); Jesus' own words in the book of John regarding how Jesus fulfills His mission (doing only what He sees the Father doing); and Paul's description of Jesus in Ephesians, Romans, and Hebrews.

Extra Mile

Assign students an etymological study of the verb *bear* and its various connotations. Ask them to compare the meanings with the idea of being the bearer of God's purpose.

For further study of biblical teaching on Christ as the perfect priest, and of the relationship between Israel as the bearers of God's purpose under the old covenant and Christ and His believers as the bearers of God's purpose under the new covenant, have your students study Romans 9–11 and Hebrews 8–9 and look up commentary regarding these passages (possible commentaries included in the "Further Study" section).

Students may also wish to explore the prophecies concerning the new covenant found in Jeremiah 31:31–34 and later references to the new covenant in Luke 22:20, 1 Corinthians 11:23–26, and Hebrews 12:18–24.

What's Next

Ask students to complete **JE 4 Bearing God's Purpose**, in which they will write a short essay on the following question: What is the relationship between the passages you studied today and your life at the present time?

Further Study

Since the gospel, or good news, is a topic that runs throughout this course, we highly recommend Milton Vincent's *A Gospel Primer for Christians* (Bemidji, MN: Focus Publishing, 2008). This book provides a clear presentation of the gospel in several different narrative formats, complete with extensive referencing to the passages in the Bible from which each point is drawn. It is an excellent resource for reminding yourself and your students of the truths of God's love and grace toward us. You may wish to purchase a full version of the book for your personal use or for classroom use. A resource that might be ideal to purchase for individual students in your class is the sixteen-page booklet version, which excerpts the prose narrative section of the larger book. More information is available at http://www.focuspublishing.com.

Some general resources that cultivate Bible study skills are as follows:

Bible Gateway website. www.biblegateway.com (a website that provides many useful study tools, including commentaries).
Blue Letter Bible website. http://www.blueletterbible.org (an excellent resource for in-depth Bible study).

ᘒ

NOTE

1. Christopher J. H. Wright, "Christian Mission and the Old Testament: Matrix or Mismatch?" http://www.martynmission.cam.ac.uk/COldTest.htm (accessed July 18, 2007).

A Heart for All Nations

Big Idea

The Bible, from Genesis to Revelation, tells the story of God's purpose.

Key Concepts

- Story is a powerful means of communicating truth.
- A person's perspective influences the way that person reacts to and responds to a story.
- The Bible is God's story.
- The Bible is an interpretation of the whole of history from beginning to end, and of the human story within that entirety.
- Though told in terms of one nation and one man within that nation, the story of the Bible reveals that God has a purpose regarding all nations.
- The story of the Bible reveals that we are invited to participate with God as bearers of His purpose.

Reflective Questions

- What have you learned about God by understanding the Bible as His story and understanding that He is the main character? Now that you know those things, what effect will they have on your life? (SE p. 90)
- Do you read the Bible differently after having studied this unit? If so, what difference does that make in the way you perceive the Bible? What about in the way you live your day-to-day life? (SE p. 90)
- Most of the time we don't think about the fact that our lives are telling a story to other people. What sorts of truths is the story of your life revealing to those around you? How can you be more intentional about the story your life is telling? (SE p. 90)

Teacher's Heart

There is an old hymn that reminds me of this lesson, a hymn I've been humming while writing these materials. It is H. Ernest Nichol's "We've a Story to Tell to the Nations," and I clearly remember enthusiastic congregational singing of it during my childhood. But beyond its musicality, this hymn reminds us of a very simple but important truth: we do have a story to tell to the nations. It is a story of hope and healing, justice and mercy, and grace undeserved and overflowing. The chorus says, "For the darkness shall turn to dawning, and the dawning to noonday bright; and Christ's great kingdom shall come on earth, the kingdom of love and light." Can you think of anything our entire broken and hurting world needs more than to know the Lord Jesus Christ? As you prepare today's lesson, ask God to help you boldly inspire your students to search out how He is calling them to tell His story to the nations.

Teacher's Preparation

Christopher J. H. Wright says in *The Mission of God*, "The nations of humanity preoccupy the biblical narrative from beginning to end" (2006, 454). He identifies God's mission in relation to the nations as the theme "that provides the key that unlocks the biblical grand narrative" (455). God's heart for the nations is the heart of the story that the Bible tells. And it is this heart of the story to which we turn our attention today, though one short lesson will hardly do the topic justice. As a foundation for future lessons in this course, your goal today should be to begin to expose your students to the idea that God has been pursuing all the nations of the earth, not just Israel, throughout the entire biblical narrative.

We are building on the previous lesson's theme. As believers, we are bearers of God's purpose, and we stand in a lineage that, through Christ, can be traced back to Abraham (see Galatians 3:6–9, 29). The idea of mission to the nations didn't start with the New Testament any more than the Christian church is the first bearer of God's purpose to the world. Today, we will examine how the whole Bible tells the story of God's heart for all nations. Generally speaking, believers are more familiar with the New Testament teaching on mission to the nations. This lesson focuses more on the Old Testament teaching regarding the nations. Both the psalmists and prophets repeatedly offer a view of all the nations of the world coming to worship the true God, Yahweh. Newbigin notes the following:

> It was through the ministry of these great God-inspired prophets that the defeat and exile of Israel was to be interpreted: not as a defeat for God but as a manifestation of God's faithfulness to his covenant....
>
> ... And it is from this time that we have the vision of Israel as the suffering servant of the Lord, who fulfills the Lord's will not by winning military victories but by bearing the sin of the world. (2005, 38; SE p. 19)

Another way of examining the story of God's heart for the nations through the Bible is to look at two different "forces" that are at work in mission to the nations. In the book *Perspectives on the World*

Christian Movement, Jonathan Lewis outlines these two forces, specifically in terms of the nation of Israel:

> The first of these was an *attractive force*, symbolized first by the tabernacle and then by the temple in Jerusalem. These buildings were the places where God's name dwelt. They were holy places, the heart of Israel's religious ceremony and practice. Yet they were not intended just to serve Israel. When Solomon dedicated the temple, it was clear to him that the temple had a wider purpose.
>
> The Bible records several other foreigners who were attracted to Israel because of the evidence of God's blessing, including Ruth, a Moabite woman, and Naaman the Syrian. Hundreds of other unrecorded accounts are evidenced by the fact that on the day of Pentecost there were devout men from "every nation under heaven" (Acts 2:5) staying in Jerusalem. God's plan to reach the nations, however, includes much more than a passive attraction.
>
> A second force in operation was an active, *expansive force* which operated to send God's message beyond the borders of Israel. Some examples of Israelites who were used to proclaim God's message to other nations include captives such as Joseph and exiles such as Daniel and Esther. Or consider the prophet Jonah, who was commanded to preach repentance to Ninevah. Jeremiah was appointed as a "prophet to the nations," and it is speculated that he or other messengers may have traveled widely in delivering his many oracles. Nor did God use only the great in this role of bearing His message. It was a little Israelite slave girl who announced His healing power to Naaman, the mighty but leprous captain of the Syrian army.
>
> Some might argue that these cases are exceptions and would point out that many of these people were captives or otherwise ministered against their wills. However, volunteerism has never been the deciding factor in furthering God's mission. God will use His people to spread His message, whether they are willing agents or not. Israel's tragic history would have been considerably different if she had been a willing instrument of God's redemptive plan. She was not. God used captivity and exile both to judge Israel's disobedience and to extend her witness beyond her borders. (1994, 60–61)

Lewis has confined his examples to the nation of Israel as seen in the Old Testament. In today's lesson students will be exploring biblical examples of attractive and expansive forces of mission found in both the Old and New Testaments. You may wish to use some of the attractive and expansive forces the students wrote about in the Identifying Missional Forces activity (in the "If Time Activities" section) as a means of extending and personalizing for your students this lesson's idea of two forces of mission to the nations.

You may want to consult commentaries or other study aids to add depth to your study of the passages you will guide students through in this lesson. Several books offer rich and deep insights to the topics introduced here, including Wright's book mentioned above. Articles such as Johannes Verkuyl's "The Biblical Foundation for the Worldwide Mission Mandate" and Steven C.

Hawthorne's "The Story of His Glory," both of which can be found in *Perspectives on the World Christian Movement* (Winter and Hawthorne 1999a), also have good supplementary information you might find useful for this lesson. Another way of strengthening your understanding of the role of the nations in the Bible story is to use searchable Bible software (such as www.biblegateway.com or http://bible.crosswalk.com) to look at all the verses containing words such as *nations*, *peoples*, or *kings*. The book of Psalms alone has multiple references to proclaiming God to the nations, as the first activity of today's lesson indicates.

Since there are a number of passages to be examined in today's lesson, you may choose to present the lesson as described below, or you may wish to divide your class into several small groups and assign each group a set of passages to read and respond to, and to report on to the rest of the class.

Objectives

- Students will discover the Old Testament picture of God's heart for the nations.
- Students will conclude that the idea of mission to the nations is a theme of the entire Bible.
- Students will compare two different types of mission templates seen in the Bible story.

Unpacking

Psalms Choral Reading (10–15 minutes)

Explain briefly the idea of choral reading to your students—individual lines or stanzas of poetic works being read aloud by a student, a pair of students, or a group in unison. Divide students into two or three groups, and let each group prepare and present a choral reading of Psalm 96. Point out that this psalm is one of several that indicate an Old Testament perspective that all nations are called to worship God. Students should listen for the number of times *nations* is mentioned during the presentations of the readings. Or if you wish to challenge your students further, you might ask them to compose individually or in groups their own choral readings that combine several psalms about the nations. See Psalms 9, 47, 67, 96, 98, 117, and 148; or Psalms 22:27–28, 45:17, 46:10, 57:8–11, 66:1–4, 82:8, 102:15–22, 108:1–5, and 138:4–5.

Two Forces Directed Study (20 minutes)

Using Jonathan Lewis' material in the "Teacher's Preparation" section, explain to students the concept of attractive and expansive forces of mission. Then lead students through the following Bible passages:

Event	Attractive	Expansive
The temple that is established in Jerusalem; Solomon's dedicatory prayers	2 Chronicles 6:32–33 1 Kings 8:59–60	
Ruth the Moabitess' declaration of allegiance to Yahweh	Ruth 1:16–18	
Shadrach, Meshach, and Abednego's faithfulness to Yahweh before Nebuchadnezzar		Daniel 3:16–29
Daniel's faithfulness to Yahweh before Darius the Mede		Daniel 6:6–27
Jonah's obedience in preaching to the Ninevites		Jonah 1:1–2, 3:1–5
The temple's attracting of Jews from every nation for Pentecost	Acts 2:5–12	
Jesus' post-resurrection commissions to the disciples		Matthew 28:18–20 Mark 16:15–16 Acts 1:8
Paul's missionary journeys		Acts 13–28

The Nations in Old Testament Prophecy (10 minutes)

Guide students through the following passages in which various prophets picture people of all nations returning to Jerusalem, where the God of Israel is the God of all peoples: Micah 4:1–4; Isaiah 2:1–4 (note similarities between this passage and the one in Micah), 56:6–8, 60:1–12; Jeremiah 3:17; and Zechariah 8:20–23. These next passages show pictures of the nations in Old Testament prophecy: Ezekiel 36:22–23, Zephaniah 3:9, Malachi 1:11, and Haggai 2:6–9. (The last passage in particular indicates that, even in the rebuilding of the temple, God intended the temple to be a center to draw people from all nations; compare this concept with Jesus' words in Matthew 21:12–13 and Mark 11:17, which reference Isaiah 56:6–8.)

If Time Activities

Identifying Missional Forces

Using **BLM 1.2 Attractive and Expansive Forces**, ask students to identify different elements of attractive and expansive missional forces in their own lives.

Reflection

Share this quotation from Steven C. Hawthorne: "At times the people disregarded the worship of God so greatly that generations would pass without the slightest attention to the simple regimens by which God had invited Israel to meet with Him (the ordinances for worship in the books of Moses)" (1999, 42). Talk about how it is possible to draw an analogy between Israel's relationship with God and our own individual relationship with God. Propose that your students personalize and rewrite Hawthorne's sentence in the following manner as a means of reflection:

> At times [*student's name*] disregarded the worship of God so greatly that [*length of time*] would pass without the slightest attention to the simple regimens by which God had invited [*student's name*] to meet with Him (such as time in the Word, time in prayer, fellowship with other believers—see Acts 2:42–46).

Assign **JE 5 My Worship of God**, which is based on this activity.

History Connection

Students can make a time line that identifies the biblical events described in chapter 1 with the events of recorded world history, both inside and outside the region of the Bible's setting.

Art Connection

Students can do visual presentations using posters or PowerPoint to demonstrate some of the various art forms used to communicate the story of the Bible throughout history. Note in particular the connection between art and the means by which the story of the Bible was communicated to the masses before the invention of the printing press. See SE page 7 for some of Newbigin's thoughts on how the story was communicated.

What's Next

Have students read chapter 2 in preparation for the next lesson.

Relationships, Redemption, and Reconciliation: Part 1

Big Idea

God's purpose is relationship, redemption, and reconciliation.

Key Concepts

- God intended, from the beginning, to be in intimate relationship with His creation.

- Because of the Fall, our relationship with God is broken.

- Redemption, offered only through Christ, can reconcile this broken relationship between God and people.

- The Bible shows that God has been pursuing and will continue to pursue this purpose throughout history.

- The state of our individual relationships with God influences our daily lives and choices.

Reflective Questions

- Which relationships do you turn to first when you're looking for guidance and support? Does your relationship with God have the same sort of dynamic interaction as some of your other relationships? Should it? (SE p. 92)

- Would you describe yourself as someone who seeks reconciliation, whether for yourself—reconciliation between you and God or between you and other people— or for others whom you help reconcile with God? What are some situations you see in your world that could use reconciliation? (SE p. 92)

- What is the importance of relationship—both vertically with God and horizontally with others? Why do you need both? What are you doing in response to God's purpose? (SE p. 92)

Teacher's Heart

While I was researching and writing the material for chapter 2, a gunman opened fire on the campus of Virginia Tech, killing more than 30 people before finally killing himself. I immediately wondered whether the shooter's motives somehow involved a broken relationship with a student on campus, or perhaps the shooter was a disgruntled former employee of the campus. Ultimately it was revealed that he was a deeply disturbed young man whose violence in part appeared to stem from his perceptions of rejection by others. This, too, is a consequence of the fall of man recorded in Genesis 3. We all stand in need of redeemed, renewed, restored relationships—primarily with God but also with those around us. Your students may not be able to identify that the core of their hurting and restlessness stems from fractured relationship, but it does. All of us have a God-shaped hole in the middle of our souls that longs to be filled with intimate relationship with our Creator. Until that void is filled and intimacy with God is restored, we labor through daily life with the handicap of a deeply and significantly broken relationship. For some, it plays out publicly with an unthinkable magnitude; for others, it simmers on a more-private level.

As you prepare for this lesson, ask God for special insight into paths of reconciliation and relationship you may need to walk down in order to lead your students to consider any paths they may need to take. Ask for eyes to see into the hearts of those sitting in your classroom. Do some of your students need ultimate redemption through faith in Christ? Are others struggling with relationships in need of reconciliation and repair? Pray that God will use these lessons to reveal His plan for these needs in your students' lives. The heart of God is for a unified community under the headship of Christ. Our world is a desperate and dark place without it. Thank God for the opportunity through these lessons to share with your students His plan and purpose of relationship for them.

Teacher's Preparation

In chapter 1 Newbigin wrote, "God will not leave us until he has won us back to be his children" (2005, 10; SE p. 10). Indeed, that is the story of the Bible—God in pursuit of His children. And this purpose of God is the core of this lesson. Students will uncover that God's purpose is relationship, redemption, and reconciliation.

Chapter 2 begins with the story of Creation and the Fall—familiar themes that set the stage for understanding both the intention God had for intimate community and fellowship with His creation, and the rebellion of Adam and Eve that forever splintered the intended relationship between man and his creator (Romans 5:12–14). Today's lesson unpacks the Bible's teaching regarding relationship, redemption, and reconciliation—the three elements of God's one purpose. We first turn to the concept of relationship. The Bible teaches about God's relational nature, as well as man's relational nature by virtue of being created in God's image. Throughout the Bible, we see that God desires intimate relationship with humanity—from the Garden of Eden (Genesis 2–3), to His instructions to build the tabernacle (Exodus 25:8, 29:44–46), to the Incarnation (Matthew 1:23, John 10:17–18, Philippians 2:5–11), to His willingness to come and live within each of the redeemed (1 Corinthians 6:19–20, Revelation 3:20), culminating with the vision of the new Jerusalem (Revelation 21:1–5).

Chapter 2 turns from relationship to redemption—God's action through Christ that provides a means of restoration of the broken relationship between God and humankind. Through their study of the story of Boaz and Ruth, students are introduced to the idea of a kinsman-redeemer and the foreshadowing of the work of Christ to redeem humankind from sin and death. In Christ the ultimate redemption is made possible. As 1 Corinthians 1:30 reminds us, Christ is our righteousness, our holiness, and our redemption. Should you wish to emphasize this concept of kinsman-redeemer or to study the biblical doctrine of redemption more deeply, you may want to search an online resource, such as StudyLight.org or Crosswalk.com, that contains links to or includes a variety of respected reference materials. In this lesson our main focus is on the specific redemptive work of Christ, but there are many aspects to redemption, including the renewal that comes in confession and the future redemptive glory seen in Revelation 21. (See more aspects in the articles listed in the "Further Study" section.) In unpacking the concept of redemption (and specifically in all the material presented in chapter 2), there is a very natural link to making a formal presentation of the gospel to your students. Though not a prescribed activity in the lesson, this opportunity is one that you may want to take advantage of, particularly if you sense a specific need on the part of your students.

Chapter 2 then turns from redemption to reconciliation, making the point that it is by the redemptive process that we have the opportunity to be reconciled to God in a right relationship. Reconciliation, defined as harmony or friendship with God, is something that is renewed, strengthened, and maintained through our drawing near to Him (see James 4:8; Hebrews 7:18–19, 10:19–23). Although reconciliation and redemption are closely related and intertwined, make clear to your students that true reconciliation with God cannot take place without the intervention of the redemption God offers us. It is only by that redemption that our relationship with Him can be truly reconciled. You can think of the two lessons for chapter 2 as a progression from head knowledge to heart knowledge in that lesson 6 seeks comprehension and lesson 7 focuses on personal application.

Objectives

- Students will discover that God's purpose has three parts: relationship, redemption, and reconciliation.

- Students will investigate biblical teaching on the three elements of God's purpose.

- Students will explore the connection between redemption and reconciliation, and how these elements affect relationship with God.

- Students will compile examples of relationship, redemption, and reconciliation.

Unpacking

Reading Quiz (5 minutes)

Using the following questions, quiz the students for a check of completion of the assigned reading:

1. What example does chapter 2 name from Genesis that demonstrated the interest God showed in His creation? (**Adam's naming of the animals**)

2. What are the three elements of God's purpose? (**relationship, redemption, reconciliation**)

3. According to chapter 2, which Old Testament character acted as a kinsman-redeemer, foreshadowing Christ's actions for us? (**Boaz**)

4. According to chapter 2, what costly price is always associated with the biblical concept of salvation or redemption? (**the spilling of blood**)

5. "Restoring friendship or harmony" is the basic definition of which part of God's purpose? (**reconciliation**)

Relationship Statues (10 minutes)

Chapter 2 talks about different relationship scenarios, including both broken and whole relationships. This activity will visually demonstrate different types of relationships. Have a different pair of students come to the front of the room to act out each of the provided scenarios (or others you create), letting one student be *A* and the other *B*. The students should remain silent and simply use their posture to indicate the relationship between them. After each statue pose is struck, ask the rest of the class to describe the nature of the relationship that is being demonstrated by the two students.

1. Have *A* and *B* stand about two feet apart with their backs to one another. Each should cross their arms. (noncommunicative relationship; ignoring one another)

2. Slightly modify scenario 1 by having *A* look over his or her shoulder. (divided relationship but with *A* showing some interest in *B*)

3. Have *A* stand on the left and *B* kneel on the right. *A* should have hands on hips and be looking off to one side. *B* should have hands palms up and be looking up at *A*. (one person entreating another)

4. Slightly modify scenario 3 by having *A* open arms widely and look at *B*. (one person responding welcomingly to another)

5. Have *A* and *B* stand side by side holding hands or being arm in arm. (unbroken relationship)

Relationship Analogy (5 minutes)

Once the statue game establishes a picture of how many kinds of relationships we can be in, have students use the provided references, if necessary, to answer the following questions: What is the original relationship between God and man in the Bible? (See Genesis 1–2: the creation of man is "very good," God showed interest in Adam's naming of the animals, God cared for Adam's need for a suitable helper.)

What is the relationship between God and man after the Fall? (See Genesis 3:8–9: man is hiding from God, the relationship is already full of fear and distrust.)

Ask students to create analogies for each situation using the following analogy patterns: God is to man before the Fall as (a father) is to (a child), and God is to man after the Fall as (a father) is to (a rebellious child). Discuss these.

Redemption and Reconciliation (15–20 minutes)

- Discuss the various definitions of *redeem* (see SE p. 41 sidebar). Ask your students to consider the definitions in terms of how they enhance understanding of Bible teaching on redemption. Then have students read Romans 3:23–24, Colossians 1:12–14, 1 Timothy 2:5–6, and 1 Peter 1:18–19 to identify the ways in which Christ's work fulfills the various aspects of the definition of redemption. (Examples: 1 Peter 1:18–19 draws the picture of "buying back," or a payment of ransom; Colossians 1:12–14 uses the idea of rescue.)

- Discuss the definition of reconciliation. Guide your students through the following passages, instructing them to note the ways in which the verses show the means of reconciliation: Romans 5:9–11, 2 Corinthians 5:18–20, Galatians 4:4–7, and Colossians 1:20–22. Finally, ask students to explain the relationship between redemption and reconciliation. (**The two are related, our reconciliation with God comes as a result of redemption, and both are necessary to bring our relationship with God into harmony.**)

Brainstorming (5 minutes)

As a check for comprehension, ask students to brainstorm some stories from the Bible and maybe examples from their own lives that demonstrate each of the three elements of God's purpose studied in today's lesson.

If Time Activity

Using a reference such as *New Strong's Exhaustive Concordance of the Bible*, guide students through a study of the Hebrew and Greek words that are translated "relationship," "redeem," and "reconcile" in the Bible. Or assign this as independent or small-group study. A further study of the idea of kinsman-redeemer can be done by looking at the passages referenced in chapter 2 as well as reference materials such as Bible dictionaries and Bible studies on the book of Ruth.

Further Study

Stories of redemption. 2006. Special section, *Discipleship Journal*, no. 156:43–69 (a section that includes the articles "The Dinner Party" by Claudia Mair Burney; "How Rohani Met Isa" by Anonymous, as told to Jamie Winship; "Folly Happens" by Gordon Atkinson; "Falling Through Holes" by Adrian Plass; "The Test of Time" by Philip Yancey; "In Living Color" by Steven Mosley; "Bible Study: Stories to Tell").

Relationships, Redemption, and Reconciliation: Part 2

Big Idea

God's purpose is relationship, redemption, and reconciliation.

Key Concepts

- God intended, from the beginning, to be in intimate relationship with His creation.

- Because of the Fall, our relationship with God is broken.

- Redemption, offered only through Christ, can reconcile this broken relationship between God and people.

- The Bible shows that God has been pursuing and will continue to pursue this purpose throughout history.

- The state of our individual relationships with God influences our daily lives and choices.

Reflective Questions

- Which relationships do you turn to first when you're looking for guidance and support? Does your relationship with God have the same sort of dynamic interaction as some of your other relationships? Should it? (SE p. 92)

- Would you describe yourself as someone who seeks reconciliation, whether for yourself—reconciliation between you and God or between you and other people— or for others whom you help reconcile with God? What are some situations you see in your world that could use reconciliation? (SE p. 92)

- What is the importance of relationship—both vertically with God and horizontally with others? Why do you need both? What are you doing in response to God's purpose? (SE p. 92)

Teacher's Heart

Over and over again, the Bible tells us that God is gracious and compassionate. Isaiah 30:18 describes the Lord as longing to be gracious and as rising (taking action) to show compassion. He looks for every opportunity to be in relationship with us. The Bible also teaches us that God delights in His children—Psalm 18:19 is but one example. This reminds me of an experience I had with my son when he was about eighteen months old. We were in the car, and he asked if he could have some milk. I told him that when we got home he could have some chocolate milk. He was exuberant, clapping and chanting about chocolate milk all the way home. Seeing his excitement about this simple offering brought such joy to me. Similarly, God must receive great joy when He sees us delight in the gifts He gives us. This is a fact of relationship—we have the capacity to bring great joy to one another.

But as in any relationship, we also have the capacity to disappoint God greatly. I think of how often I turn away from Him, unwilling to engage Him in the ways He desires. It is like what happens when someone puts together a great gift, or surprise, for a friend who gets distracted or impatient and doesn't take the opportunity to receive. Those times are a disappointment for the giver and a missed opportunity for the one who would have been the recipient. They are also times of sadness and fracture. Pray that this lesson will be an opportunity for students to understand more about the dynamics of relationship with God and to honestly evaluate the nature of their own relationships with Him.

Teacher's Preparation

Ultimately, chapter 2 is about God's purpose. God is a relational God who desires fellowship with His creation. He has chosen relationship and community not only as a way in which He relates to us, but also as a means of revealing Himself to us. Newbigin noted in chapter 1, "God does not wish to make himself known to us in the isolation of our own individual souls…. We therefore come to know God through one another" (2005, 6: SE p. 8). You will recall from chapter 2 the study of the term *Elohim* and what it indicates about the nature of God and about our own relational natures that result from being made in His image. Take time to assess student understanding of these concepts today if you sense the need.

This lesson is primarily about prompting your students to think about their lives in terms of where they stand in relationship with God and their need for redemption or ongoing reconciliation. By the end of the lesson, they should be poised to begin thinking of the larger implications of this relationship in preparation for exploring in the next lesson their own participation in God's purpose. Since this lesson requires a degree of trust and honesty (especially if activities are done in class rather than completed independently), pray for your own willingness to be transparent and honest before your students and for insight into guiding students to move beyond pat answers.

Objective

Students will evaluate their own lives in terms of the biblical concepts of relationship, redemption, and reconciliation with God.

Unpacking

Reviewing and Discussing God's Purpose (5–10 minutes)

Ask students to share any questions they have that are related to the previous lesson. Then discuss the following questions:

- Which of the three parts of God's purpose is the easiest for you to understand? the most difficult? Why?

- What is the importance of relationship, both with God and with others?

- Did you see yourself in any of the illustrations in this chapter?

Journal Entry (5–7 minutes)

Assign students a reflective writing and use these prompts from **JE 6 Broken or Restored?**:

- What are the characteristics of your relationship with God?

- Is it more broken or more restored?

You could also ask your students, Which statue from the previous lesson best illustrates your relationship with Him?

Understanding Ongoing Redemption and Reconciliation (15–25 minutes)

Put the following quotations on the board:

- "Redemption is not limited to our salvation, but occurs wherever there is release from the effects of sin and the fall."

- "If we confess our sins, he is faithful and just and will forgive us our sins and purify us from all unrighteousness."

- "At some level, we all long for things to be different, healed, repaired."

Draw the students' attention to these quotations (respectively, from Redemption in the Day-to-Day 2006, 52; 1 John 1:9; and SE p. 42) and to **JE 7 Redemption Coupons**. Give students time to meditate on the quotations and to complete the journal entry.

Thinking Ahead (5–10 minutes)

Let students respond to the following in small-group discussion:

- When we receive the gifts of relationship with God, redemption, and reconciliation, we are charged with the mission and joy of working for reconciled relationships in the world around us (see SE p. 47).

- What does this look like when it is lived out in the lives of believers?

If Time Activity

If you haven't already used the reflection activity in the "If Time Activities" section of lesson 5, use it now or as homework.

What's Next

Have students read chapter 3 in preparation for the next lesson.

Lesson 8   # What a Blessing Is

Big Idea

God invites us to participate in His purpose; He blesses us so that we can bless others.

Key Concepts

- Blessing from God is not just for us to enjoy, but for us to use to bless others.

- Blessing comes in many forms; it isn't always what you think.

- Not only are we saved *from* something, but we are saved *for* something.

- Faith in God is what enables us to participate with God on His mission.

- As Christians, we stand in a line of faith that extends back to Abraham himself.

Reflective Questions

- What are some of the ways in which you are blessed? Do you see ways you can bless others out of the circumstances of your life? (SE p. 93)

- Are there hard circumstances in your life that you cannot possibly perceive as containing a blessing? Would you dare trust God to reveal to you His plan of blessing through those circumstances? (SE p. 93)

- Where are you on the proverbial racecourse mentioned in this chapter? Have you crossed the starting line? Are you jumping around, celebrating being a racer, but not taking a step farther? Are you running out the race? Do you need to be at a different point in your relationship with God? (SE p. 93)

Teacher's Heart

I had a great deal of joy and anticipation in taking on the project of writing this course material. It has been an experience in which I have had to lean fully on the Lord's provision. In the process, I have been so blessed to learn and understand more of God as I study and prepare for writing each chapter and lesson. But as much as that blessing of knowing Him more brings great joy to me, I was literally overwhelmed and brought to tears the day I finished writing the first chapter. It wasn't so much that a deadline was met or even that we were finally moving forward on the work. No, I was filled with an almost unspeakable joy that God had chosen to use me to help communicate His love and heart to teenagers. I am so humbled to be asked to participate in His plan to proclaim Himself and His purpose to young people. What a tremendous blessing and joy it is to get to share God's blessings with others. And it can be ours every day. God doesn't desire for us to hoard the blessings He pours out on us. We are blessed in order to be a blessing. What joy that brings!

As you prepare to teach this chapter to your students, thank God for the opportunity to bless them through your teaching. Thank Him for allowing you to share your experiences, your love for Him, and your unique gifts with your students each day. What a privilege to serve such a great God, who allows us to participate in His work!

Teacher's Preparation

Many of the concepts presented in chapter 3 may be new not only to your students but to you as well. You may wish to avail yourself of some of the additional reading resources in preparation for the next several lessons if you have questions that are not addressed in the lessons themselves. One of the first activities today gives students a chance to ask questions and discuss the Big Idea presented by the chapter. Keep in mind during the discussion that many of the concepts in the chapter are examined in more depth in this lesson and the next two. You may wish to wait until all the lessons have been presented before answering some of the questions your students ask. In today's lesson we will be looking both at the concept of "blessing" as well as the top-line and bottom-line approach to reading the Bible.

A critical understanding for students to take away from this lesson is that blessings don't always look as we expect or desire them to look. We are prone, both by nature and by cultural conditioning, to seek ease and comfort. It is not unusual for us to confuse *want* with *need*. Consequently our ideas of what constitutes a blessing are probably very narrow when compared with God's definition. Some of your students are likely to define blessing in terms of "stuff," happiness, and anything they would welcome into their lives. But the Bible shows us that sometimes blessing comes through trial, loss, and loneliness. Trusting and accepting the mysterious ways in which God works to bless us is a mark of spiritual maturity. Indeed, God's love for us, fortunately, is not limited to *our* definitions of what would make us happy. That is not to say, however, that God doesn't delight in bringing happiness to His children, but it is simply to remind us that His ways are not our ways (see Isaiah 55:8–9). Today, take the pulse of your students in terms of their understanding of the many dimensions of blessing. Then, as you guide them through the story of Abraham's willingness to obey God's command to sacrifice Isaac, help them see that even circumstances that we might not always describe as blessings can be used mightily, in the Lord's hands, to bless. An example of this is found in the life of Joseph and in his ability to ultimately say to his brothers, "You intended to harm me, but God intended it for good to accomplish what is now being done, the saving of many lives" (Genesis 50:20).

The lesson concludes with some guided practice of using the top-line/bottom-line approach to the Bible. **JE 9 Top Lines, Bottom Lines** is a template that will allow you to visually demonstrate this concept to your students. This tool helps us see that God's blessings are tied to a larger purpose—the desire God has to bring about His plans, to increase His fame and reputation among the nations so that many will be united in relationship with Him. The top lines may contain blessings, but the bottom lines contain a vision of the purpose of God, His intentions, and His invitation to us to participate. The bottom lines call for response. They give us a vision that is larger than our immediate comfort and ease—they offer us a window into God's far-reaching plans and our place in them. There is nothing wrong with top lines, but they are only part of the picture. Together, top lines and bottom lines paint the full picture of the purpose of God and His plans to bless us so that we might be a blessing to others. Ultimately, God seeks to have His plans for all nations fulfilled so that He might be glorified throughout the earth. Our blessings are merely a step on that path of purpose, not the destination. A goal of this part of the lesson is to begin to open students' eyes to seeing both top lines and bottom lines in the Bible.

Objectives

- Students will describe their concept of "blessing."
- Students will contrast their idea of blessing with a biblical view of blessing.
- Students will apply the top-line/bottom-line principle of Bible study to several passages.

Unpacking

Reading Quiz (5 minutes)

Using the following questions, quiz the students for a check of completion of the assigned reading:

1. What chapter of the Bible contains God's initial promise to Abraham? (**Genesis 12**)

2. God's promise to Abraham is sandwiched between a verse with a specific command and a specific _____. (**act of obedience by Abraham**)

3. What visual image of the future did God give to Abraham regarding His promise to give Abraham children? (**the multitude of stars**)

4. A _____ verse concerns a blessing that is promised or offered. (**top-line**)

5. A _____ verse concerns a responsibility or response that is required. (**bottom-line**)

Clarifying the Big Idea (5–10 minutes)

Draw the students' attention to the Big Idea for chapter 3: God invites us to participate in His purpose; He blesses us so that we can bless others. Ask students whether they understand this concept through their reading, and give opportunity for questions about portions of the reading that may require additional clarification.

Blessing Unpacked (15 minutes)

On the board, write the brainstorming prompt "Blessing is …" and solicit student responses. Record student answers and examine them with the entire class. It is likely the majority of the list will contain items that lead to safety, ease, and comfort. Have someone read aloud James 1:2–4. Discuss the implications of this passage. Ask students to think of Bible stories that illustrate that God's blessing sometimes comes through trials. If there's time, direct students to complete **JE 8 Abraham's Diary Entry**. This activity may need to be assigned as homework.

Finding the Bottom Lines (15 minutes)

Use **JE 9 Top Lines, Bottom Lines** as a guide for demonstrating how to identify top-line and bottom-line passages. You may also want to use Genesis 12:1–3 as an example with the class. Emphasize the locating of the bottom-line verses, since those verses have a big-picture orientation and often specifically state God's intention to bless all nations. Have students look at Exodus 15:13–14, 1 Samuel 17:45–49, and Psalm 46:10–11 to identify the bottom-line portions and what they reveal about God's purpose. (**bottom lines: Exodus 15:14, 1 Samuel 17:46–47, Psalm 46:10**)

If Time Activities

Passages Challenge

Challenge those students who tend to highlight or underline verses in their Bibles to examine the types of passages they have marked. Are more of the passages top-line verses or bottom-line verses? If your students are like many believers, there are more top lines highlighted. Discuss what this reveals about how the students view the Bible and their understanding of God.

Song Message Challenge

Challenge your students to begin the ongoing activity of identifying the emphasis (top-line or bottom-line) placed on the messages of contemporary Christian music and worship songs (those they hear on the radio or those they sing in their church or youth group). Have your students keep a log of the title and primary focus of the songs. Designate a day when this information will be discussed in class. Calculate and compare the percentage of songs whose primary message is top line and the percentage of those that include both. (You might be surprised by your findings!)

Extra Mile

A more in-depth alternative to the Blessing Unpacked activity is to have the students chart the story of Joseph told in Genesis 37–50, noting the various hardships in Joseph's life and the blessings that each of these hardships brought. Students could take this project on individually or in small groups, completing diary entries for different points in Joseph's life. Many other stories of the Bible lend themselves to an examination of the various sources of blessing God is able to use.

What's Next

Journal Entry

Have your students do **JE 8 Abraham's Diary Entry** if it was not completed in class.

Top-Line/Bottom-Line Practice

Provide your students with additional practice in finding top lines and bottom lines, using the following passages:

- 1 Kings 10:23–24 (**top line: v. 23; bottom line: v. 24**)
- Isaiah 61:9–11 (**top line: v. 10; bottom lines: vv. 9 and 11**)
- Daniel 6 (**many top lines; main bottom lines: vv. 25–27**)
- Matthew 10:18–20 (**top lines: vv. 19–20; bottom line: v. 18**)
- Luke 3:3–6 (**top line: v. 5; bottom line: v. 6**)
- Hebrews 5:8–10 (**top line: v. 10; bottom lines: vv. 8–9**)

Lesson 9 # The Faith of Abraham

Big Idea

God invites us to participate in His purpose; He blesses us so that we can bless others.

Key Concepts

- Blessing from God is not just for us to enjoy, but for us to use to bless others.
- Blessing comes in many forms; it isn't always what you think.
- Not only are we saved *from* something, but we are saved *for* something.
- Faith in God is what enables us to participate with God on His mission.
- As Christians, we stand in a line of faith that extends back to Abraham himself.

Reflective Questions

- What are some of the ways in which you are blessed? Do you see ways you can bless others out of the circumstances of your life? (SE p. 93)
- Are there hard circumstances in your life that you cannot possibly perceive as containing a blessing? Would you dare trust God to reveal to you His plan of blessing through those circumstances? (SE p. 93)
- Where are you on the proverbial racecourse mentioned in this chapter? Have you crossed the starting line? Are you jumping around, celebrating being a racer, but not taking a step farther? Are you running out the race? Do you need to be at a different point in your relationship with God? (SE p. 93)

Teacher's Heart

This morning I had the sad opportunity to lift up in prayer a family I know that is grieving the loss of a child. Again and again as I thought about this situation and prayed for the family members, I returned to the idea of the previous lesson: even the most difficult and trying situations can be vehicles for God's blessing in some form. As I cried out to God on behalf of my friends, I knew that the peace I was praying for them to have in the midst of their pain is a difficult thing to imagine. But I know that God sees the whole picture. It takes great faith to trust God with what is unseen.

Great faith is one of the truths of the life of Abraham, who showed that it does take great faith to trust God with what is unseen. Similarly, today we are often called to trust God with matters we can't see, understand, or control. But we can take comfort in knowing that the God who was faithful to His promise to Abraham is the same God who is faithful to His promise to us today. The person in whom Abraham placed His trust is our Abba Father, the Creator of the universe. May you and your students take great comfort today in the fact that the God of the ages is inviting us to walk intimately with Him so that all nations might be blessed.

Teacher's Preparation

Often we think of everything from the time of Christ forward as the central message of the Bible that is relevant for today. Many of your students will have a good understanding of New Testament teaching about the gospel and God's desires for the nations, but they may not have a very developed understanding of the Old Testament as a part of this same story. This limited viewpoint shortchanges our understanding of the greatness of God—a God who remains the same yesterday, today, and forever (Hebrews 13:8), a God who is fulfilling His long-established purpose. His love for the nations, as one can see from a search for the bottom-line truths of the Old Testament, was there from the beginning. His consistent and unrelenting pursuit of His purpose for His creation has been unfolding since the very earliest recorded events of the Bible. Even in Genesis 3 we find a foreshadowing of God's triumph over the evil and death that seek to separate humankind from God. He told the serpent, "And I will put enmity between you and the woman, and between your offspring and hers; he will crush your head, and you will strike his heel" (Genesis 3:15). The Bible is an epic story. And understanding its breadth and depth as one story of God's universal redeeming love that reaches back to the very moment of our breach from God in the Garden of Eden gives us a breathtaking picture of His greatness.

Today's lesson may feel different to you from any other so far in this course. The only activity for this lesson is a guided but open-ended discussion of the redemptive work that is at the heart of the story of the Bible, a redemptive work that began not with the Crucifixion but in the pages of Genesis. The idea of the gospel being something that is woven not only through the pages of the New Testament but throughout the Bible is perhaps a new concept to you. You should feel no pressure to guide your students to specific conclusions at this point; instead, think of this as an opportunity to introduce teaching that may take some time to fully develop in their minds and lives. This lesson seeks to give another lens through which to view the ongoing story of God. It offers another opportunity to dwell on the magnificent truths introduced in chapter 1.

In that chapter we discussed the idea that the Bible tells one story of God, and we identified the middle of this story as beginning in Genesis 12 and continuing on through Revelation 4. This is the part of the story that we find ourselves living in. Your students' realization that each of us is a part of the same working out of God's purpose that the familiar characters of the Bible were a part of can be tremendously powerful. More than just a sentiment from a children's song such as "Father Abraham had many sons.... I am one of them, and so are you" (written by Joseph W. Linn, Lillenas Publishing Company, 1988), this is a powerful truth of the Bible. In later chapters and units, we will examine how that story, which was begun so long ago, has continued unabated throughout history. God has always been at work to accomplish His purpose.

Today's lesson is shaped by several guiding questions and activities that progress through a series of ideas—ones that are the tips of several proverbial "icebergs" of theology that have been discussed and debated for centuries. Some students may wish to delve more deeply into these areas, and the "Further Study" section offers additional resources. In the next few paragraphs, we attempt to briefly summarize ideas to guide your students through. The first is the idea of the gospel, then justification by faith, followed by the Trinity. Rather than trying to provide definitive answers to questions that theologians have been wrestling with for centuries, we seek only to offer food for thought and to provide the basis for classroom discussion that spurs your students on to a deeper understanding of the one-story aspect of the Bible.

The Gospel

As the first activity will reveal, the concept of the gospel is abstract. In asking each student to define *gospel*, you will probably get a wide range of responses. The following information may serve to guide discussion with your class:

- "Identifying the gospel is both simple and challenging.... The gospel is Jesus himself. The New Testament's Gospels narrate the life, death, and resurrection of Jesus as the action of God that both reveals God's passion for the world and achieves God's purpose for that world" (Guder 1998, 87).

- The word translated "gospel" as found in the Bible comes from the Greek words *euaggelion* (a noun) and *euaggelizō* (a verb), both of which have a root meaning "good news" or "good message."[1] Jesus announced the good news as the arrival of the kingdom of God (Mark 1:14–15), which we will study further in the next chapter.

- Though the word *gospel* is found only in the New Testament, it was certainly a concept understood by Old Testament saints.[2] The Hebrew *basar* is the equivalent to the Greek *euaggelion* or English *gospel*.[3] This is the word found in verses such as Isaiah 52:7, which says, "How beautiful on the mountains are the feet of those who bring good news, who proclaim peace, who bring good tidings, who proclaim salvation, who say to Zion, 'Your God reigns!' " *Basar* is also the word found in Isaiah 61:1–2, the same passage Jesus read at the synagogue in Nazareth and proclaimed fulfilled in Himself (Luke 4:16–21).[4]

- As mentioned on SE pages 51 and 55, Paul describes God's promise to Abraham in Genesis 12:1–4 as a declaration of the "gospel in advance." You may wish to read all of Galatians 3 to prepare for this lesson.

Justification by Faith

Students will rightly equate the idea of gospel with the concept of salvation or justification. In a nutshell, justification is a "new standing" with God by which we are restored to God's favor. It is a verdict declared by God regarding man, just as an earthly judge would declare a verdict in a legal case. Paul writes in Romans 3:28, "For we maintain that a man is justified by faith apart from observing the law." Typically, ideas like this are thought of as New Testament concepts only, but the Bible has a "through-line" of thought on the role of faith in justification before God. Romans 4 outlines the roots of justification by faith going back to that pivotal encounter Abraham had with God. Reading Romans 4 together as a class might be a helpful part of your discussion in this lesson. Here are some additional considerations regarding the doctrine of justification by faith as a theme throughout the Bible:

- "The New Testament doctrine of justification is not an innovation; it is a truth already known in Old Testament times, and righteousness was obtained in the same manner in those days as in the New Testament dispensation," notes theologian Henry C. Thiessen (1979, 277). "It is evident that the Old Testament saints were justified as well as the New Testament believers" (278).

- From the *Matthew Henry Complete Commentary on the Whole Bible*, written in the early eighteenth century, we see that the above sentiment is not that of contemporary scholars only. Commenting on Galatians 3:6–18, Matthew Henry notes, "This argument of the apostle's may give us occasion to remark that justification by faith is no new doctrine, but what was established and taught in the church of God long before the times of the gospel. Yea, it is the only way wherein any sinners ever were, or can be, justified."[5]

For many of us, the idea of the mission of God to the nations has been taught to us as a primarily New Testament revelation. But as Christopher J. H. Wright notes, "The Old Testament presented YHWH as the God who wills to be known to the ends of the earth." As your students worked through the top-line/bottom-line exercise in the previous lesson, they found Old Testament examples of this fact that Wright speaks of, and there are literally hundreds more. Far from believing that Jesus Christ brought something new in terms of the mission of God, we see that He fulfilled and extended something old—God's promise to bless all nations through Abraham. Perhaps a truly shocking fact about the Bible is that Jesus' contemporaries did recognize Jesus as YHWH. Wright notes that "people who knew YHWH, the Holy One of Israel, to be *the* God and that YHWH was transcendently unique in all the rich dimensions of his scriptural identity, character and actions, constructed a careful, persistent, point-by-point identification of Jesus of Nazareth with this same YHWH" (2006, 106). It is perhaps not easy for us as believers in the resurrected Christ to remember that He is this same YHWH we first meet in the Old Testament. Jesus Christ is the same God, YHWH, who called Abraham to a covenantal, set-apart life of promise. Abraham's response to God in faith resulted in not only Abraham's justification before God but the opportunity for your justification before God. Genesis 15:6 tells us, "Abram believed the Lord, and he credited it to him as righteousness." Abraham's faith is affirmed in other places in the Bible, such as Romans 4:3, 17–22; Galatians 3:6; and Hebrews 11:8–10; and each time we are told that Abraham placed his faith in God. As believers, we place our faith in Jesus Christ, who is God; and this truth leads us into the next section on the Trinity.

Thoughts on the Trinity

Our faith is in the same thing that Abraham placed his faith in—the Creator, God of the universe, the indivisible Three-in-One. Paul understood and explained in his letter to the predominantly Gentile church at Rome that all believers in Christ are in the spiritual family of Abraham: "Therefore, the promise comes by faith, so that it may be by grace and may be guaranteed to all Abraham's offspring—not only to those who are of the law but also to those who are of the faith of Abraham. He is the father of us all. As it is written: 'I have made you a father of many nations.' He is our father in the sight of God, in whom he believed—the God who gives life to the dead and calls things that are not as though they were" (Romans 4:16–17). And again, Paul affirms this: "Understand, then, that those who believe are children of Abraham" (Galatians 3:7). As mysterious as the concept of the Trinity is, it is one worth pondering and holding on to, for it provides deeper understanding of the epic story of the Bible and the magnificence of the God whose story it is. What a long and storied line of faith we stand in as believers in the Lord Jesus Christ. And just as Abraham's life was called out to be a blessing to all nations, so we are called to be set apart to bless the nations with our lives in Christ.

Objectives

- Students will examine the nature of Abraham's faith and compare it with their own.

- Students will integrate (or relate) their understanding of the gospel of the New Testament with the faith of Abraham in the Old Testament.

- Students will assess the continuity of the story of the Bible.

- Students will identify their relationship to Abraham as an heir.

Unpacking

Defining the Gospel (10–15 minutes)

Ask students to define *gospel*. Keep a list of responses on the board to point out the variety of responses defining this concept. Discuss any themes that emerge, and tie them to the points made in the "Teacher's Preparation" section under "The Gospel" heading.

Discussing the Gospel (30–35 minutes)

Use the material in the "Teacher's Preparation" section as a guide to lead students in discussing the gospel, the biblical concept of justification, and the unity of the story of the Bible and God's purpose. Some questions that might guide your discussion include the following:

- What is the gospel? Is the gospel found in the Old Testament?

- What did Paul mean in Galatians 3:8 about the "gospel in advance"?

- What did Abraham's faith result in? Who did Abraham place his faith in? What is the relationship between the object of Abraham's faith and the object of your faith?

- What does the song "Father Abraham" really affirm? What difference does it make to understand that you are an heir of Abraham?

What's Next

Have your students write a journal entry, **JE 10 Reflection on the Lesson**, in which they react to what they learned in today's class discussion. Have them record any questions they have and instruct them to make a plan to find the answers.

In preparation for class discussion in the next lesson, ask your students to reread "The Parable of the Race" and to respond to the questions (**JE 11 "The Parable of the Race"**).

Further Study

Deffinbaugh, Bob. An Old Testament illustration of justification by faith (Romans 4). http://www.bible.org/page.php?page_id=1170.

Glasser, Arthur F. 2003. *Announcing the kingdom: The story of God's mission in the Bible.* With Charles E. Van Engen, Dean S. Gilliland, and Shawn B. Redford. Grand Rapids, MI: Baker Academic (see especially pp. 369–72).

Wright, Christopher J. H. 2006. *The mission of God: Unlocking the Bible's grand narrative.* Downers Grove, IL: InterVarsity Press (see particularly chaps. 2 and 3).

❧

Notes

1. James Strong, *New Strong's Exhaustive Concordance of the Bible* (Nashville, TN: Thomas Nelson, 1990), s.vv. "euaggelion," "euaggelizō."

2. Jim Gilbertson, *PC Study Bible for Windows*, CD, version 3.1 (Seattle, WA: Biblesoft, 2000), s.v. "gospel."

3. Septuagint.org, "LXX Greek Text," http://septuagint.org/ (accessed March 25, 2008).

4. Strong, s.v. "basar"; Gilbertson, s.v. "basar."

5. *Matthew Henry Complete Commentary on the Whole Bible*, s.v. "Galatians 3," http://bible.crosswalk.com/ (accessed July 11, 2007).

Cats, Dogs, and Footraces

Big Idea

God invites us to participate in His purpose; He blesses us so that we can bless others.

Key Concepts

- Blessing from God is not just for us to enjoy, but for us to use to bless others.
- Blessing comes in many forms; it isn't always what you think.
- Not only are we saved *from* something, but we are saved *for* something.
- Faith in God is what enables us to participate with God on His mission.
- As Christians, we stand in a line of faith that extends back to Abraham himself.

Reflective Questions

- What are some of the ways in which you are blessed? Do you see ways you can bless others out of the circumstances of your life? (SE p. 93)
- Are there hard circumstances in your life that you cannot possibly perceive as containing a blessing? Would you dare trust God to reveal to you His plan of blessing through those circumstances? (SE p. 93)
- Where are you on the proverbial racecourse mentioned in this chapter? Have you crossed the starting line? Are you jumping around, celebrating being a racer, but not taking a step farther? Are you running out the race? Do you need to be at a different point in your relationship with God? (SE p. 93)

Teacher's Heart

A great Christian folk song called *Pass It On* (written by Kurt Kaiser, Bud John Songs, 1969) talks about how it takes only a spark to start a fire that will warm everyone around it. The song compares that concept to what happens when someone experiences God's love and then spreads it on to everyone else. The idea captured in this simple song is the same idea as our calling to join God's mission to the world. We have been blessed with the love of God so that we in turn can bless others. As you prepare to challenge your students with this call today, pray that God would show you how to model this concept to your students. Ask also for insight into ways you can encourage this outlook and practice in their lives.

Teacher's Preparation

Since the previous lesson was fairly deep and theological, here's some lighthearted teaching to brighten your day. Let's consider some pet theology that conveys the differences between cats and dogs:

> A dog says, "You pet me, you feed me, you shelter me, you love me, you must be God."
> A cat says, "You pet me, you feed me, you shelter me, you love me, I must be God."
> (Sjogren and Robison 2003, back cover)

Are you smiling? If you have ever spent any time around a cat, you probably are. We all know that dogs and cats can have quite opposite personalities. Bob Sjogren and Gerald Robison, authors of *Cat and Dog Theology* (2003) propose that Christians can find themselves in one of two camps—dog theology, which is focused on God and His plans, or cat "me-ology," which is focused on self and one's own plans. Bob Sjogren notes, "Although most Christians say, 'God is the main character of the Bible,' they live and act as if *they* are the main character. Cats basically focus on *themselves* in their Christianity. Dogs basically focus on *God* in their Christianity" (2000, 6; words in italics inserted). This is just another way of thinking about the concepts we have been talking about in this course.

"Cats" and "dogs" are also found in "The Parable of the Race" (McLaren and Campolo 2003, 26–27) on SE pages 56–58. Notice that cats and dogs, as described above, both represent Christians, just as the people who cross the starting line in the parable are all Christians. The difference is in their orientation toward God. The racers who just step over the starting line and celebrate are a lot like cats. Those spectators who join the race to run it out are a lot like dogs. The activities in today's lesson will use both "The Parable of the Race" and the concept of cat and dog theology to challenge students to evaluate their own orientation toward God, the blessings of God, and the invitation to participate on mission with Him.

Objectives

- Students will examine "The Parable of the Race" to identify the various analogies present in it.

- Students will identify the things they consider to be blessings in their lives.

- Students will identify which of their blessings they use to bless others.

- Students will construct an application plan detailing two steps they could take to enact the idea of "blessed to be a blessing."

Unpacking

Cats and Dogs (5 minutes)

Have students look at **JE 12 Cat and Dog Theology**. Point out the differences between cat theology and dog theology. Discuss reactions and conclude by pointing out that we should aspire to have dog theology.

Parable Study (15–20 minutes)

Put students in small groups and give them the task of completing the identification analogies found in **BLM 3.1 Unpacking "The Parable of the Race."** Groups should be prepared to present their answers to the class. (See possible answers in the answer key, **BLM 3.1K**.)

Students should also discuss their responses to the following questions from **JE 11 "The Parable of the Race"** that they completed before class:

1. Which part of the parable resonates most with you? Why do you think that is?

2. What do you believe is the overall message of this parable?

3. Explain the following statement in relation to missio Dei: "Not only are we saved *from* something, but we are saved *for* something."

Inflow/Outflow Examination (15–20 minutes)

Spend a few minutes reviewing the idea of blessing. Remind students that blessings can be not only material possessions, but also gifts and talents, things they enjoy, relationships, and even difficult circumstances. Then have students individually work through the inventories in **JE 13 Inflow/Outflow Inventory**.

If Time Activity

Ask students to share some of the results from their completed inventories of inflow and outflow of blessings. Give students the opportunity to encourage classmates by having the students write or speak about ways they have seen their classmates bless others. Lead in a time of prayer for students and yourself, asking for enlightenment about ways to share our blessings.

What's Next

Journal Entry Examination

Challenge students to spend some time prayerfully examining their completed **JE 13**. Have them create an application plan that lists at least two ways they might be able to bless others by using some of the blessings they identified.

Reading

Have students read chapter 4 in preparation for the next lesson.

The Kingdom: Now and Not Yet

Big Idea

God's story is unfolding as we see and participate in God's kingdom throughout the earth.

Key Concepts

- The kingdom of God is the living reality of God's presence surrounding us here and now.

- The kingdom is both *now* and *not yet*.

- We must cultivate "eyes to see" the kingdom of God.

- We are invited to participate—to enter in and receive God's kingdom.

- We should accept Christ not only as our Savior, but as our King.

Reflective Questions

- What are the most puzzling aspects of the kingdom of God? What are some ways you can deepen your understanding of the kingdom of God? (SE p. 95)

- How much does dualistic thinking influence the way you think about your life and how you live it? How does considering your faith a private matter affect your interaction with the world around you? (SE p. 95)

- Does it make a difference if you view the world as "sacred and secular"? If Christians are isolated in a separate so-called sacred culture, what does that say about how they view "secular people"? Is that different from how Jesus views people? (SE p. 95)

Teacher's Heart

In his book *This Beautiful Mess*, Rick McKinley describes how we begin to see in a new way as we let the present reality of the kingdom of God come into focus: "We notice the kingdom dimension of life, but slowly. It's like when you walk from a completely darkened room out into the blazing light of noon. At first you squint and draw back. The whole world seems blurred by sun rays. But after a few seconds you see normally. In fact, you see more clearly than you did back in that dark room" (2006, 64). Seeing the kingdom, he says, may take a few seconds—or a few days, weeks, or months, perhaps even years. Just as with the adventure of walking with God, there is always more to be revealed.

McKinley's example above may describe just how you're feeling right now. It is possible you are overwhelmed by new ideas, more of God, truths previously unconsidered. Maybe you feel as if you are squinting hard and you want to draw back. You and your students both may have some of that reaction to this chapter on the kingdom of God. But give God the time it takes to help your eyes adjust to the light. He is faithful to draw you into deeper and deeper understanding of Himself and His purpose. May He be your guide as you lead students through this lesson.

Teacher's Preparation

Obviously there is a lot of content in chapter 4 that may be quite new and unfamiliar to both you and your students. For that reason, you may need to take an additional day to discuss the chapter and ensure deeper student understanding before moving on. You might also want to look ahead to chapter 5 because its description of the conflict between the kingdom of God and its enemies is very helpful in understanding the material in chapter 4. Additional resources for further study are listed at the end of this lesson plan. One thing to keep in mind is the last line of chapter 4: "Consider this chapter just the first layer of the onion we are peeling together as we discuss the mission of God, His kingdom, and your place in it" (SE p. 75). We are touching on themes in this chapter that we will return to again and again in this course.

Today's lesson seeks to give students the opportunity to process and discuss this material. While some of it is aimed in a specific direction, much of it will be up to your discernment. To facilitate a discussion of the major points of the chapter, we have pulled the summary quotations below from the chapter, and we've included page numbers for reference. Your discussion with students should seek to, at a minimum, touch on all these major points. There is a specific activity, **JE 14 Blinders**, that guides students through the portion of the chapter that emphasizes false ideas that might obscure our understanding of what the Bible says about the kingdom of God. This activity should be thought of as a support for the overall discussion of the chapter. It may turn out that you have a rich and lengthy class discussion, which would necessitate assigning **JE 14** as homework.

Chapter 4 Key Points

To guide your discussion in this lesson, here is a list of the key points of the chapter, presented on the pages in which they appear in the text:

- The kingdom of God is the presence and person of Jesus Christ (SE p. 63).

- A king has authority and deserves allegiance (SE p. 64).

- "God has all authority and deserves our allegiance" (SE p. 65).

- "The kingdom of God is the living, breathing presence and purpose and reign of God on our planet. It's beautiful *and* irreducible" (McKinley 2006, 21 [*This Beautiful Mess*]; SE p. 65).

- There are "things that we can see about God's kingdom, which in turn enable us to participate in it" (SE p. 66).

- "Understanding the kingdom of God in terms of the presence of Jesus not only makes it more accessible to us perhaps, but also rightfully centers attention on the person and work of Jesus Christ as the turning point in the work of God to bring about His purpose" (SE p. 67).

- "God's kingdom is both present *now*, and *not yet* fully present" (SE p. 67).

- "There is a realm of spiritual blessing into which we may enter today" (Ladd 1959; SE p. 68).

- There are blinders to the kingdom—beliefs or ideas that may stand in our way of understanding the Bible's teaching on kingdom (SE pp. 69–73). These blinders are enumerated in **JE 14**. You may want to discuss them in the first half of the lesson as well.

- "Without living as though Christ is King of our lives, we are missing the part about allegiance. We are missing the invitation to participate more deeply and fully in the adventure God has for us" (SE p. 69).

- "Kingdom life is a team sport!" It takes place not only individually, but also in the context of community (SE p. 75).

One of the key points from chapter 4 is the *now* and *not yet* aspect of God's kingdom. To understand the present, real, *now* aspect of the kingdom of God, your students may find it helpful to think in terms of an "alternate universe" or a "parallel universe" to the world we live in. That concept is likely to lead them to consider analogies from popular culture that highlight the fact that a "pretend" world can seem very real indeed, just as the seen world around us can appear to be the true world. Yet, the Bible teaches that the true world is God's kingdom—a very real supernatural realm that exists right now. Even a simple analogy can help, such as using a pilot's flight-training simulator compared to flying a real plane, a comparison in which our visible world would be analogous to using the simulator, and God's kingdom to flying the real plane. Other analogies are found in ideas such as the holodeck in *Star Trek: The Next Generation*; the Matrix, a computer-programmed reality in the movie *The Matrix* (Wachowski and Wachowski 1999); and the virtual reality video games and video game rides that simulate everything from NASCAR driving to riding a roller coaster. Even though these analogies may not correspond exactly, they can certainly aid students' understanding of God's kingdom as a *realm*.

Objectives

- Students will examine the kingdom of God as discussed in chapter 4.
- Students will be introduced to the concept that God's kingdom is both *now* and *not yet*.
- Students will reflect on the types of obstacles that keep them from seeing the kingdom.
- Students will consider the nature of God's kingdom and its present reality.

Unpacking

Reading Check (5 minutes)

Have students use the information they've learned from chapter 4 to write three "reading quiz" questions and an answer key without using the book as a guide. (Answers will vary, but they should reflect a reading of the chapter.)

Guided Discussion of the Kingdom (15–20 minutes)

Using the major points of the chapter, which were outlined in the "Teacher's Preparation" section, guide students in a discussion of chapter 4, allowing time for student questions.

Blinders (20 minutes)

Have students complete **JE 14 Blinders**. You may choose to use this as a homework assignment or as the basis for further class discussion.

If Time Activity

Our tendency, even as believers, is to prefer to think of God's kingdom in terms of measurable levels of achievement rather than as a dimension of reality. Share and discuss with your students the following quotations taken from Rick McKinley's book *This Beautiful Mess* (2006):

- "I have spent my life trying to get to the next level. You work hard and you save money so you can get through school, buy a better car, buy a house, or have kids. But every level requires that you try to get to the next level.... Spiritually we tend to think in levels too. Everything depends on what we *do*.... I like thinking in terms of levels of achievement because it gives me a sense of power and control" (55–57).

- "We're so inclined to try to make things happen for God. Every week we're tempted to get out a measuring stick…. And we figure that God is measuring too. But God isn't measuring anything. He only wants us to live in a dimension that is already there. Week after week, He is simply inviting us to be a part of what He is *already* doing" (61–62).

- "It has brought me back to a key verse in the book of Colossians [1:13], which says that Jesus has rescued us out of the kingdom of darkness and transferred us into the kingdom of the Son. We've been taken from one dimension and moved to another. No levels, just transferred by the King" (62).

- "The kingdom is a dimension I acknowledge, I live in, I participate in. Yet it's never a level I achieve. It is a lot less like building the business of Christianity and a lot more like slipping into the matrix of Jesus" (63).

What's Next

Reflection

Assign a reflective writing, **JE 15 Assess Yourself**, using these prompts:

- What questions do you have about material in chapter 4?

- What would help you understand that information better?

Journal Entry

If students did not complete **JE 14** in class, assign it as homework.

Further Study

Bell, Rob. 2005. *Velvet Elvis: Repainting the Christian faith*. Grand Rapids, MI: Zondervan (see particularly pp. 107–16 and 147–52).

McKinley, Rick. 2006. *This beautiful mess: Practicing the presence of the kingdom of God*. Sisters, OR: Multnomah.

Willard, Dallas. 1998. *The divine conspiracy: Rediscovering our hidden life in God*. New York: HarperCollins (see particularly chap. 1).

Our Need for Eyes to See

Big Idea

God's story is unfolding as we see and participate in God's kingdom throughout the earth.

Key Concepts

- The kingdom of God is the living reality of God's presence surrounding us here and now.
- The kingdom is both *now* and *not yet*.
- We must cultivate "eyes to see" the kingdom of God.
- We are invited to participate—to enter in and receive God's kingdom.
- We should accept Christ not only as our Savior, but as our King.

Reflective Questions

- What are the most puzzling aspects of the kingdom of God? What are some ways you can deepen your understanding of the kingdom of God? (SE p. 95)
- How much does dualistic thinking influence the way you think about your life and how you live it? How does considering your faith a private matter affect your interaction with the world around you? (SE p. 95)
- Does it make a difference if you view the world as "sacred and secular"? If Christians are isolated in a separate so-called sacred culture, what does that say about how they view "secular people"? Is that different from how Jesus views people? (SE p. 95)

Teacher's Heart

Here's more from Rick McKinley's book *This Beautiful Mess*: "When Jesus talked about the kingdom, He never talked about us building or advancing it. Never. He said, 'The kingdom is …' He simply invited His followers to see it, embrace it, believe in the unfading reality of it—and join in what His Father was already doing in the world" (2006, 57). It is only by God's Spirit that spiritual desire is created in us. It is only by the grace of God that we can cease from *doing for Him* and simply *be in Him*. Pray the following prayer with me:

God of Grace, help me to have eyes to see Your nearness. Grant that I may enter and receive Your kingdom moment by moment. Show me the blinders that I may wear unknowingly. Make me a clean, useful vessel through which You may flow to those around me. May I practice the presence of the kingdom this day. Amen.

Teacher's Preparation

"Repent, for the kingdom of heaven is near" (Matthew 4:17). These are the words of Christ. Notice what is first—*repent*. Repentance is simply a turning away from a previous behavior or way of thinking. Repentance moves you in a different direction from the one you were headed in. But what was Jesus talking about when He made this announcement at the beginning of His public ministry?

The Israelites were looking for Messiah—the king who would come and rescue their nation from its oppressors, the king who would set up a triumphant rule that would bring national prosperity and peace. As Newbigin reminded us in chapter 1 (2005, 45–48; SE pp. 21–22), there are several different ways this hope for the kingdom was expressed. When Jesus showed up, the people who had been longing for the Messiah's appearing almost missed it. Some did, completely. But others embraced the truth of Jesus as the Messiah, and *it changed the world.* It is impossible to overstate the impact of that embracing of the truth of who Christ is. Compellingly, it is the same for us today. We can embrace Jesus and what God is doing in His kingdom right now, and change the world.

But the first step to entering and receiving the kingdom is to repent. Just as in a twelve-step program, the first step is to admit that you have a problem. But we aren't talking about only the repentance that leads to salvation. We are talking about the steps of turning away from false ideas and perspectives that obscure our ability to see the reality of God's present kingdom. The first step in helping students participate fully in the kingdom of God is to help them understand that God's kingdom may not look as they had expected it to look and that they may be somewhat blinded to its present reality at this point. The previous lesson highlighted some of the perceptions we may hold that can obscure the present reality of the kingdom of God and His invitation to us to participate. We are not just saved from hell, but we are saved for His purpose, for His glory. He is so much greater than our imaginations that we shouldn't be surprised when His ways are not what we anticipate—and the ways of His kingdom *are* beyond our anticipation! Indeed, Jesus came that we "may have life, and have it to the full" (John 10:10) and, praise God, that abundance is of His choosing and not ours. He is not held back by our limited vision (see Ephesians 3:20–21).

Today's lesson is designed to help cast a wider vision for your students of who God is and what He is up to. The lesson centers on two activities. The first is an exploration of some Bible passages

on the kingdom, starting with Isaiah 61 and Luke 4. This pairing paints a wonderful picture of not only the shocking revelation by God of His fulfilling of ancient promises, but the shock of that fulfillment not looking at all how people had expected it to look. Stan Nussbaum describes it this way in *A Reader's Guide to "Transforming Mission"*:

> In Luke 4 …, Jesus reads to his hometown synagogue from Isaiah 61 and then stuns his hearers by announcing that Isaiah's very down-to-earth messianic prophecy was fulfilled that day. Before they can recover from the first shock, he delivers a second one, implying that the messianic wonders would somehow come without God taking vengeance on the enemies of Israel as expected. In fact, in this messianic kingdom God would bless outsiders, possibly even in preference to his own people Israel! (Luke 4:23–27). The crowd would not bear that reinterpretation of Isaiah's prophecy, and they almost killed Jesus for daring to suggest it (Luke 4:29–30). (2005, 26–27)

Nussbaum explains that Jesus stopped reading in the middle of Isaiah 61:2, "omitting the phrase all his hearers knew by heart and cherished as their national hope, 'and the day of vengeance of our God'" (2005, 26). And in *This Beautiful Mess*, Rick McKinley points out, "Yes, they believed in the *idea* of the kingdom of God, but the *person* of Jesus didn't meet their expectations. They saw not a king but a bad risk, and they rejected Him" (2006, 48).

If you read through verse 37 of Luke 4, however, you see that not everyone rejected the claims Jesus made. Many hearers were intrigued by His authority. Even demons were subject to Him (and recognized Him for who He was). What was different? Why did some accept His claims and teaching and others reject them? It has to do with the receptivity of the hearer. Jesus' teaching about the kingdom of God took into account the fact that some would be prepared to hear the good news, and others would not. Students will examine Jesus' parable of the sower (Matthew 13:1–23) for a window into this truth. You may wish to share with students this summary from Rick McKinley in *This Beautiful Mess*: "The soil in His parable, as Jesus explains it, stands for different types of welcome and responsiveness in the hearer of His message. Some don't understand; some do but don't act on what they've heard; some fall away once worldly distractions or hard times come. In these three kinds of people, the truth of the kingdom produces little or nothing. But some receive the message like deep, fertile soil. These hearers receive, understand, and reproduce the kingdom seed many times over" (2006, 72). You may wish to challenge students, if you sense it is appropriate after discussing Matthew 13, to consider the condition of their own "soil" with respect to accepting the invitation to receive Christ not only as Savior but as King and thus participating more fully in the real dimension of kingdom living that surrounds us.

The second activity gives students additional time to process and respond to the many ideas and themes of chapter 4 and God's kingdom. **JE 16 Consider This About the Kingdom** provides a list of quotations from various sources on the kingdom of God. These quotations may be used as either discussion prompts, writing prompts, or a combination of the two. If your students are struggling to understand the basic concepts of chapter 4 discussed in the previous lesson, you may want to use these prompts for discussion. If the atmosphere of your class suggests that students are ready to begin personal reflection and application, you may use the material in **JE 16** as writing prompts for in-class reflective writing that could be extended into further writing for homework.

Objectives

- Students will synthesize information from the Bible regarding God's kingdom.

- Students will connect their own experiences to those described in the Bible.

- Students will compare statements about the kingdom of God.

- Students will compare these statements with their own understandings.

- Students will reflect and respond in writing to the invitation to enter in and receive God's kingdom.

Unpacking

Seeing the Unexpected (10–15 minutes)

Have students read Isaiah 61:1–3. Ask them to identify what expectations of action they might have based on this passage, making sure they understand it as a prophecy written during a difficult period in Israel's history. (**possible answers: a powerful rescuer, a mighty ruler for Israel, a compassionate leader**) Then have them read Luke 4:14–37. Using the material in the "Teacher's Preparation" section, lead students to see the dynamics of how this announcement failed to meet the expectations some hearers had of a messiah, yet how others saw great authority in Jesus. Draw attention to several key points:

- Luke 4 announces that the arrival of Jesus marked the ushering in of His kingdom on earth in fulfillment of prophecy.

- Because it wasn't what they expected, many failed to see this kingdom.

- But because of the authority Jesus showed, others were willing to hear His message of the kingdom.

Next, have students turn to Matthew 13:1–23. They should discuss this parable and what it says about the effects one's receptivity can have on acceptance of new teaching. The discourse about the parable, particularly McKinley's quotation, in the "Teacher's Preparation" section can guide this discussion.

Considering the Kingdom of God (25–30 minutes)

Using **JE 16 Consider This About the Kingdom** as a guide, provide time for students to continue reflecting on the nature of the kingdom of God. Depending on the needs of your students, you may wish to assign this time as an individual reading and reflective writing activity, a small-group activity, a discussion with a partner, a class discussion, or some combination of these ideas. The ultimate goal is for students to begin to assess their lives in relation to the call to participate in God's kingdom.

Making It Personal (5–7 minutes)

Ask students to look at the quotations in **JE 16** and to select the one that is the most thought-provoking or striking to them. Give them two or three minutes to write as much as they can about why that quotation resonates with them.

What's Next

Have students read chapter 5 in preparation for the next lesson.

Further Study

Nussbaum, Stan. 2005. *A reader's guide to "Transforming mission."* American Society of Missiology Series, no. 37. Maryknoll, NY: Orbis Books (read particularly chaps. 2 and 3).

Lesson 13 Who the Enemy Is

Big Idea

The spread of God's kingdom takes place in the context of warfare with Satan.

Key Concepts

- God's authority is above all, yet we live our present lives in enemy territory.
- Though ultimately defeated, Satan attempts to anger God by attacking the apple of His eye—humankind.
- Believers in Christ are equipped by the power of the Holy Spirit to defeat the schemes of the enemy.

Reflective Questions

- One of the ways Satan tries to turn our thinking away from God is through tempting us with the things of this world. What are some prevailing cultural messages that take your thinking away from God's desires for you? How can you lessen your exposure and vulnerability to these temptations? (SE p. 97)
- What are some areas of your life that are particularly vulnerable to manipulation by Satan? Do you have strategies in place (such as memorizing Bible truths, praying, and being accountable to someone) to defend against such attacks? If not, why not? (SE p. 97)

Teacher's Heart

You may recall the animated film *The Incredibles* (Bird 2004)—the story of a family of superheroes that struggle with the tension of trying to live normally under the cloak of the mild-mannered identities they have assumed. Mr. Incredible can't do it, and he spends the whole movie trying to live out who he really is—a superhero who wants to battle the forces of evil, do good, and rescue people. There is a deep spiritual truth here, embedded in the lives and adventures of superheroes in a comedic animated film. As Christians, we aren't to settle for our mild-mannered alter egos that allow us to go undetected, blending in with the world. We are to embrace our identities in Christ, with the full glory and power that He longs to reveal in us to the world around us. This is the only way we join with God in fulfilling His purpose on the earth. To live kingdom lives, we must suit up in our true identity in Christ rather than settle for a mild-mannered alternative that seems safe and comfortable, doesn't attract a lot of attention, and falls far short of God's intentions for us.

Today's lesson is the first of three that unpack the dimension of the kingdom of God that is embroiled in the realities of warfare with an enemy who, though defeated, seeks to tear down as much of God's creation as he can. God has chosen us to be instruments in that battle, to help reveal the truth of God's kingdom to the blinded world around us. Remembering how Mr. Incredible longed to be able to live in His true identity, we need to realize that God longs for us to live in our true identities in Christ. One of the biggest weapons the enemy has is to tell us the lie that if we don't don a mild-mannered alter ego, there will be trouble. Pray that God will reveal to you and your students your true identities in Christ and the truth of His victory over darkness as you study chapter 5, and may the Light of the World shine brightly in and through you as you teach this material:

Lord, I pray that the eyes of my students will be opened to know the hope to which they are called, to know the riches of their glorious inheritance, and to know the incomparably great power for those who believe. Let each of them know Christ and the power of His resurrection at work in them.* Amen.

*Ephesians 1:18–19, 2:6–9; Philippians 3:10

Teacher's Preparation

Unfortunately, we don't live in a world that is absent of conflict. As Newbigin noted in chapter 1, "To be the place where God is made known in history, is to be chosen for suffering, for agony, for conflict" (2005, 6; SE p. 8). Christ modeled the way of the suffering servant in the face of the ultimate conflict—not even crying out (Isaiah 53:7). Indeed, we are called, as Paul was, "to know Christ and the power of his resurrection and the fellowship of sharing in his sufferings" (Philippians 3:10). And though suffering is what God allowed His Son to experience and what He allows us to experience as well, it is not without purpose in either case. Christ's sufferings paid the price for our sin and bought for us righteousness before God (2 Corinthians 5:21). Our experiences of suffering of trials have a purpose as well. James 1:2–4 teaches the following: "Consider it pure joy, my brothers, whenever you face trials of many kinds, because you know that the testing of your faith develops perseverance. Perseverance must finish its work so that you may be mature and complete, not lacking anything." God does not desire that we would drown or be overcome in our trials and temptations; He will always offer us a way to stand firm in Him (1 Corinthians 10:13, 1 Peter 5:10). The way to stand firm is to put on Christ—affirming our identity in Him and seeking the protection God offers us from the onslaught of the enemy.

Chapter 5 shows us that, in this present age, we are living between D-Day and V-E Day. This is the *now* and *not yet* aspect of the kingdom of God. And in this interim period, we will face attacks from the enemy. "Satan and the kingdom of darkness over which he rules pose a constant challenge and threat to the effectiveness and stability of believers," writes Mark I. Bubeck in *The Adversary* (1975, 68). However, we are not to be overcome with dread and fear regarding the enemy or the trials that we experience. "The great emphasis of the Word of God is upon the accomplished victory which is ours to appropriate and claim through our Lord Jesus Christ," notes Bubeck (68–69). It is this last idea that these next lessons seek to emphasize.

The following sentences from the article by Charles H. Kraft outline the progression of the three lessons for the chapter: "Our part in this war is first to receive the Holy Spirit's empowerment. Then we must imitate Jesus' obedience and intimate relationship with the Father. This enables us to follow his example in warfare against the kingdom of Satan" (2000, 27; SE p. 86). Lesson 13 corresponds to the first sentence and conveys Bible teaching about the kingdom, battle, Satan, and our own identities in Christ. These truths are part of the Holy Spirit's empowerment of each believer. Lesson 14 corresponds to the second sentence, and it is concerned with developing our relationship with the Lord. Lesson 15 shows Bible truths about engaging in battle.

This lesson is concerned with the empowerment that comes from knowing the truth. First, we will examine the contents of chapter 5, and students will have the opportunity to identify and discuss the major points of the chapter. Then you will guide students through truths of the Bible that teach us not only the limitations of the enemy but, more important, the true identities of those who are in Christ.

Chapter 5 Key Points

The following outline of the key points of chapter 5 (from the student edition text, including the excerpts by Ken Blue [1987] and by Charles Kraft [2000, 18–29]) will help guide you through a discussion with your students:

- God's kingdom and the enemy's pseudokingdom are not equals (SE pp. 78, 83). Humans ceded their authority over creation to the enemy at the time of the Fall (SE p. 81), but this does not create equal kingdoms. God is sovereign.

- The incarnation of Christ established God's authority in the history of earth (SE p. 78).

- "The kingdom of God has already gone through its darkest night" (Blue 1987; SE p. 78). The victory is won, but we live in enemy territory. This ties to the ideas spoken by C. S. Lewis (SE p. 77 epigraph) and to the quotation by Kraft: "We live as aliens amid the forces of Satan's kingdom" (2000, 20; SE p. 82).

- "When we participate with Jesus in taking back territory from the enemy, we are not establishing a part of the kingdom that wasn't there before; we are simply helping to reveal God's kingdom that is already present but unseen by many who are blinded by the lies of the enemy" (SE p. 80).

- We as believers are involved in the battle in two ways: Our lives are a battlefield, whether we like it or not, and "we are soldiers in Jesus' army," which is a matter of choice (Kraft 2000, 20; SE pp. 81–82). God has given us, His followers, the role of living out the kingdom of God in enemy territory and shining light on as much of the enemy's territory as we can. This is done through the leadership of the Holy Spirit, our guide (SE p. 83).

- "If Satan cannot attack God himself or ascend to his throne, his uncontrollable jealousy and hatred drive him to attack and destroy those on whom God has fixed his love" (Kraft 2000, 21; SE p. 83).

- The enemy can only pervert; he cannot create. The characteristics of God's kingdom are the opposite of those of Satan's (SE pp. 83–84).

- "There are three primary aspects to God's strategy to counter enemy schemes: God restricts, God protects, and God attacks" (Kraft 2000, 23; SE p. 84).

- "It is God's strategy for humans to play a major part in the defeat of Satan and his hosts" (Kraft 2000, 25; SE p. 86) through the use of both offensive and defensive strategies (SE p. 87). More specifics regarding strategy will be developed in lessons 14 and 15.

As you prepare to present the chapter 5 lessons to your students, keep in mind the balance called for by Bubeck: "As believers consider their warfare against Satan, two extremes must be carefully avoided. The first extreme is the tendency to ignore this enemy and to treat the whole subject of demonology lightly. One of Satan's clever strategies against us is to keep us in ignorance of his power and working.… The other extreme to be avoided is a fearful preoccupation with Satan and his kingdom. It is a strategy of Satan to make us more conscious and aware of Satan and his kingdom than we are of the heavenly Father, the Lord Jesus Christ, and the blessed Holy Spirit" (1975, 68).

Objectives

- Students will identify the analogy between D-Day and V-E Day and relate it to the Big Idea for this chapter.

- Students will examine and respond in writing to Bible passages regarding truths about the enemy.

- Students will list Bible truths about Christ and the identity of those who are in Christ.

Unpacking

Reading Quiz (5 minutes)

To check for reading completion and comprehension, quiz students with the following prompt: In a paragraph, explain the concept of D-Day and V-E Day as it relates to the kingdom of God as described in chapter 5. The analogy from the chapter is in the following quotation: "In God's war with evil, 'D-Day' occurred with the death and resurrection of Christ. Ultimate victory is now assured; yet the fight rages on till 'V-E Day,' the glorious return of Christ" (Blue 1987; SE p. 78).

Review of Chapter Highlights (15–20 minutes)

Using the key points outlined in the "Teacher's Preparation" section, lead a class discussion of chapter 5. Allow time for questions and explanations of other concepts that may not be clear to students. As you talk through each point, you may wish to ask for a show of hands of students who agree with the statement "I understand this material."

Bible Study (20–25 minutes)

Using **JE 17 Christ and the Counterfeiter** and **JE 18 A Believer's True Identity** (see answer keys **BLM 5.1K** and **BLM 5.2K**), guide students through Bible passages regarding who Christ is and who the enemy is, then passages that affirm the believer's identity in Christ. Students can individually complete these journal entries and turn them in as assessment pieces. Or you can have students complete them in pairs or small groups so that they can discuss each truth as they read it. Time constraints may make it necessary for the students to complete one journal entry in class and one as homework.

Extra Mile

Assign presentations on WWII history regarding the details of D-Day (when, where, how accomplished), and have students compare it to the Crucifixion and the Resurrection (when, where, how accomplished). Students should then examine V-E Day (when, where, how accomplished) and compare it to the victory pictured in the book of Revelation.

What's Next

Index Card Assessment

Students should each complete an index card for homework. On one side they should write a concept from the chapter that was particularly meaningful or surprising to them, explaining why this is so. On the other side, they should write at least one question they still have about the chapter material. These can be collected and used as the basis of further discussion, if needed.

Journal Entry

Complete the pages from the Bible Study activity (**JE 17** and **JE 18**) if these were not finished during class.

Further Study

Anderson, Neil T. 2001. *Who I am in Christ*. Ventura, CA: Regal.

Anderson, Neil T., and Dave Park. 2003. *Overcoming negative self-image*. The Victory Over the Darkness Series. Ventura, CA: Regal Books.

Arthur, Kay. 2000. *Lord, is it warfare? Teach me to stand*. Colorado Springs, CO: WaterBrook Press.

Bubeck, Mark I. 1975. *The adversary: The Christian versus demon activity*. Chicago, IL: Moody Press.

Kraft, Charles H., ed. 2000. *Behind enemy lines: An advanced guide to spiritual warfare*. With Mark White. Eugene, OR: Wipf and Stock.

Kraft, Charles H., and David DeBord. 2005. *The rules of engagement: Understanding the principles that govern the spiritual battles in our lives*. Eugene, OR: Wipf and Stock.

Abiding in Christ

Big Idea

The spread of God's kingdom takes place in the context of warfare with Satan.

Key Concepts

- God's authority is above all, yet we live our present lives in enemy territory.

- Though ultimately defeated, Satan attempts to anger God by attacking the apple of His eye—humankind.

- Believers in Christ are equipped by the power of the Holy Spirit to defeat the schemes of the enemy.

Reflective Questions

- One of the ways Satan tries to turn our thinking away from God is through tempting us with the things of this world. What are some prevailing cultural messages that take your thinking away from God's desires for you? How can you lessen your exposure and vulnerability to these temptations? (SE p. 97)

- What are some areas of your life that are particularly vulnerable to manipulation by Satan? Do you have strategies in place (such as memorizing Bible truths, praying, and being accountable to someone) to defend against such attacks? If not, why not? (SE p. 97)

Teacher's Heart

In the previous lesson, students were led through Bible verses that indicate that a characteristic of Satan is to deceive. He is the father of lies, who seeks to blind people to the truth of Christ. I think this is one of the reasons that human beings can be so arrogant. Does that sound like a harsh description? Think of it from God's perspective. God is able to *speak* an entire universe into existence. We cannot make anything from nothing, not by speaking, wishing, or jumping up and down. Even our most prized creations are made from "recycled materials" that God gave us. The Lord knew me as I was being knit together in my mother's womb. I cannot even control the beating of my own heart. We are so easily deceived into thinking we don't need the Lord—particularly in a culture that preaches self-sufficiency and that abounds with material comforts and luxuries beyond our wildest dreams. It's evident that even believers are able to be deceived into thinking we can manage things on our own; otherwise, we wouldn't need so much counsel in the Bible regarding our choices, behaviors, and thoughts. Nor would we need to be exhorted to stand firm against the schemes of the enemy.

It is good to realize our true need for the Lord. He gives us everything, including our next breath. Even our faith is a gift from God (Ephesians 2:8). It is from this perspective that we realize how critical it is for us to remain in Him. As you prepare to present this lesson on abiding in Christ, pray for both yourself and your students to have receptive hearts to the truth of our dependency on Him. It is a truth the enemy would like to keep concealed from us for as long as possible.

Teacher's Preparation

Today's lesson is about standing firm in Christ against the attacks of the enemy. At the core of standing firm is abiding, or remaining, in the Lord Jesus Christ. The term *abide* is all but unused in our current speech, but it is a strong word. The Greek word translated "abide" in many translations of John 15, and "remain" in the New International Version, is the verb *meno*, which means "to stay (in a given place, state, relation or expectancy)." It can also mean "continue, dwell, endure, be present, … stand."[1] This same word is used in John 14:17 to describe the Holy Spirit living in us. The main thrust of this lesson is to encourage your students to "stay in Christ" and to help them recognize anything that can pull us away from abiding in Christ.

We begin with the passage in John 15—the last teaching of Christ to His disciples, which took place after the Last Supper and before His arrest in the Garden of Gethsemane, according to Orville E. Daniel's *A Harmony of the Four Gospels* (1996). In this passage we see Christ imploring His followers to abide, or remain, in Him, for apart from Him they would be able to do nothing of any value. This same concept of remaining firmly in Christ is communicated in a different way in the classic warfare passage of Ephesians 6:10–18, in which believers are encouraged to stand firm against the schemes of the devil, putting on the full armor of God—a concept we will investigate further in the next lesson. **BLM 5.3K Abide in Him (Answer Key)** shows the truths about abiding in Christ that students will encounter in today's lesson.

Imitating Jesus' obedience and intimate relationship with the Father is a key element to maintaining firm footing when we face attacks from our own flesh or from the enemy. This obedience pictured in John 15 has a transforming effect in two different ways. First, *we* are transformed as we dwell in Him. Paul speaks of this transformation in 2 Corinthians 3:18: "And we, who with unveiled faces all reflect the Lord's glory, are being *transformed* into his likeness with ever-increasing glory, which comes from the Lord, who is the Spirit" (emphasis added). There is an intimacy with God that transforms us into His likeness. And that is what leads to the second effect of abiding in Christ: we bear much fruit to the Father's glory (John 15:8). As Jesus taught in Luke 6:43–45

and Matthew 12:33, the fruit of a tree reveals its true identity. The fruit we bear reveals our true identity to the world around us. And that fruit can have a transforming effect on others, either drawing them to Christ or pushing them away. As you lead students through the exercise of making a comparison between the fruit of intimacy with the world and the fruit of intimacy with Christ, be conscious of the tendency to fall into legalism and to become judgmental when using such labels. Teenagers particularly cling to black-and-white representations that may or may not portray the whole story in a given situation. Be careful to avoid references to specific people as you compose the first list. Ask for God's grace as you bathe this activity in prayer.

Connected to this idea is the principle of garbage in, garbage out (GIGO). In other words, what we surround ourselves with manifests itself in the behaviors and attitudes of our life. The Bible teaches this same truth in Luke 6:45: "The good man brings good things out of the good stored up in his heart, and the evil man brings evil things out of the evil stored up in his heart. For out of the overflow of his heart his mouth speaks." Some "garbage" that gets into our thoughts and lives may be fairly innocent to begin with, though other garbage might be an outright embracing of false teaching and lies. As you complete the Recognizing a Tree by Its Fruit activity, talk about the GIGO concept and ask students to consider the impact of the different inputs in their lives. If you have time in class to complete **JE 20 Garbage In, Garbage Out**, use that activity at this point. Otherwise assign it for personal reflection.

One aspect of abiding in Christ is being intentional about pursuing silence and stillness before God so that we can hear His voice above all the other noises that clamor for our attention. Busyness, distractions, and the cares of this world—whether good things in and of themselves or outright strategies of the enemy—can sometimes shout so loudly in our ears that we have no chance to hear God's voice, much less obey it. Students will conclude this lesson by exploring the principle of garbage in, garbage out, identifying both the types of "voices" that compete with time for developing intimacy with God, and the products of voices other than God's voice.

Objectives

- Students will examine John 15 and synthesize the teaching of Jesus regarding relationship with Him.
- Students will identify the transformation possible when they abide in Christ.
- Students will make a comparison between the fruit borne by intimacy with the world and the fruit borne by intimacy with Christ.
- Students will identify those things that distract them from intimacy with Christ, and they will plan strategies to help them abide in Christ.

Unpacking

Abiding in Him (10–12 minutes)

Using **BLM 5.3 Abide in Him**, have students work through John 15:1–11 either in partners or in small groups. They should be prepared to briefly share their thoughts with the class.

Recognizing a Tree by Its Fruit (15–20 minutes)

Use the "Teacher's Preparation" section as a guide to share the idea of transformation with your students. Draw attention to the idea of a tree being recognized by its fruit. Do the following to help students make a comparison between the fruit borne by intimacy with the world and the fruit borne by intimacy with Christ: First, brainstorm as a class to determine symbols of success that are validated by the world (**wealth, popularity, cool boyfriend, cool girlfriend; students will have plenty more answers**), and list them on the board. Assign students the following passages to look up and use as a basis for composing a contrasting list of fruit borne by abiding in Christ:

Galatians 5:22–23 (**fruit of the Spirit**)
Philippians 2:3–8 (**humility, looking out for the interest of others, surrender**)
1 John 2:3–6 (**obedience**)
John 13:34–35 (**love for others**)

As you discuss the differences between the lists, have students copy them down as the basis for a homework assignment. In discussing the differences between the lists, bring in the GIGO concept and challenge students to consider the nature of what is put into their lives and the effects of what we choose to abide in.

Silence and Stillness (10–15 minutes)

Read Exodus 14:14, Psalm 37:7, and Psalm 46:10 to students. Ask them what the imperative is in all three verses. (**Be still.**) Ask students to identify how many minutes a day they are still, not counting the time they are asleep. Discuss the role of silence and stillness before the Lord by looking at the example of Christ in Mark 1:35 and Luke 5:15–16. Despite the crowds' needs for healing and teaching, Christ withdrew for times of intimacy with His Father. He was intentional about seeking solitude. Give students some time to be still before the Lord and to capture, in **JE 19 Be Still**, any thoughts they have about what they hear. Share what you have learned about cultivating time alone with God in your life. Challenge them to be intentional about formulating a plan to be alone with God regularly.

If Time Activity

JE 20 Garbage In, Garbage Out has a diagram that students can use to consider the effects of various "inputs" in their lives. This journal entry can be completed by each student as homework or as a self-assessment piece in class.

Extra Mile

Word Play

Have students investigate the use of the word *abide* in hymns, to give the students a window into the rich teaching of previous generations of believers regarding this term.

GIGO Transformation

Some examples of the GIGO principle at work in characters from popular culture may resonate with your students. One example is the transformation of Anakin Skywalker into Darth Vader in 20th Century Fox's *Star Wars* movies. Another is the Gollum character from Tolkien's Lord of the Rings series. Have students examine the negative transformation of a character from literature or film, such as Anakin or Gollum (or others they might suggest). They could view movie clips or examine passages to identify subtle turning points in the character's journey from good to evil. They should then compare this to the subtle temptations of the enemy as evidenced by the initial temptation of Adam and Eve in the Garden (Genesis 3). Satan's tactic there, as always, is misinformation and lies. The goal of this activity is for insight into the types of temptations and tactics the enemy might use to draw us away from intimacy with God.

What's Next

Journal Entry

If the GIGO journal entry (**JE 20**) is not completed in class, challenge students to complete it on their own.

Journal Entry

Using James 4:4–5 and the fruit lists generated in class, have students complete **JE 21 What Fruit?** to reflect on what the fruit of their own life reveals about where their heart is.

Music

Ask students to identify several praise and worship songs that draw them into God's presence. You may wish to have them bring in CDs and play the songs during the praise and prayer portions of lesson 15.

☙

NOTE

1. James Strong, *New Strong's Exhaustive Concordance of the Bible* (Nashville, TN: Thomas Nelson, 1990), s.v. "meno."

The Weapons of War

Big Idea

The spread of God's kingdom takes place in the context of warfare with Satan.

Key Concepts

- God's authority is above all, yet we live our present lives in enemy territory.
- Though ultimately defeated, Satan attempts to anger God by attacking the apple of His eye—humankind.
- Believers in Christ are equipped by the power of the Holy Spirit to defeat the schemes of the enemy.

Reflective Questions

- One of the ways Satan tries to turn our thinking away from God is through tempting us with the things of this world. What are some prevailing cultural messages that take your thinking away from God's desires for you? How can you lessen your exposure and vulnerability to these temptations? (SE p. 97)
- What are some areas of your life that are particularly vulnerable to manipulation by Satan? Do you have strategies in place (such as memorizing Bible truths, praying, and being accountable to someone) to defend against such attacks? If not, why not? (SE p. 97)

Teacher's Heart

This morning I made my coffee as usual—except for the part about grinding beans and putting them in the basket of the coffeemaker. I didn't discover this fact until I had poured the very last of my half-and-half into a travel mug full of hot water. There was no way to retrieve the half-and-half for the new cup of coffee I was going to have to make. Situations like this are real attacks on my attitude and heart before God.

To combat my mounting frustration with everything that was not going well in my morning, I put on an old Jars of Clay CD. Pretty soon my two-year-old and I were dancing around the room, and my heart was praising God. The lyrics of the song "Sinking" struck me: "But you see through my forever lies,… you are forever healing" (CD titled *Jars of Clay*, Essential Records, 1995). God sees through the lies we want to hold on to—lies like your day is wrecked if your coffee doesn't start out right. Or that no one likes you. Or that you cannot survive the weight of depression. Or that you fall short in a thousand different ways. God is forever healing. He heals us from the sting of minor annoyances. But even more, He heals us from the crushing weight of sin, warfare, and everything else that seeks to separate us from His love.

Pray that you can embrace God's "forever healing" of you today—whether you need healing from a small annoyance that threatens your attitude or a huge weight that threatens your well-being. Ask God to reveal the depths of His love, power, and healing to your students as well.

Teacher's Preparation

Whereas chapter 5 involves attack by a supernatural enemy, teenagers can too easily explain away all sin in their lives by adopting a "devil made me do it" attitude. Students need to understand that not all struggles, bad decisions, and temptations can be blamed on Satan. In *The Handbook for Spiritual Warfare*, Ed Murphy draws from James 4 to identify three dimensions of attack against believers—the flesh, the world, and evil supernaturalism (1992, 508). The chart below walks through the teaching on these battlegrounds and battle strategies found in James 4:1–8 and elsewhere.

Of course, the list of strategies given in the chart is not comprehensive, but it offers samples of the Bible's teaching regarding the various areas of struggle. You may want to spend additional time exploring the differences between the attacks of Satan and the struggles we experience because of our own sin nature and friendship with the world. Obviously, the distinctions between these areas can blur. If you sense a need to spend more time on this material, you can develop some study and discussion based on the chart, which we will only briefly touch on in today's lesson plan.

This lesson primarily will focus on Bible teaching regarding both "defensive" and "offensive" weaponry that can be taken up in the battle with the enemies of God's kingdom (Kraft 2000; see SE p. 87). Not only are these tools from the Bible to combat the rulers, authorities, powers of this dark world, and the spiritual forces of evil in the heavenly realms (Ephesians 6:12), but they are also effective strategies to use in struggles with the flesh and the temptations of the world.

The previous lesson's focus on abiding in Christ is at the heart of a defensive posture toward the enemy (as well as struggles with the flesh and the world). God has provided a refuge and armor for us in the person of Christ. In Him we find truth, righteousness, the gospel of peace, faith, salvation, and the Word of God spoken of as pieces of armor (belt, breastplate, shoes, shield, helmet, and sword) in Ephesians 6:14–17. This armor is our defense against the lies and deceptions of the enemy. Of course, confession and repentance (1 John 1:9, Revelation 3:19–20) are profoundly important truths of the Word that we must employ as defenses against the enemy as well.

In terms of offensive weaponry, this lesson briefly reviews three strategies: proclaiming the Word, praise and worship of God, and prayer. Each strategy has suggested application activities for students. Depending on time constraints, you may choose to present the activities as an out-of-class application option. On the next page is a brief summary of each of the three offensive strategies, along with passages for each.

Spiritual Warfare as Described in James 4

Passage	Battleground	Strategy
James 4:1–3	**The Flesh** Desires battling within you (v. 1) Self-reliance (v. 2) Wrong motives (v. 3)	Confess (1 John 1:9) Persevere (James 1:12–15) Trust in God's provision (1 Corinthians 10:13) Take thoughts captive (2 Corinthians 10:5)
James 4:4–6	**The World** Friendship with the world being hatred toward God (v. 4)	Recognize that we are citizens of another kingdom (Galatians 4:3–7) Cling to intimacy with Christ (John 15, 2 Peter 2:20)
James 4:7–8	**Supernatural Evil** The devil (v. 7)	Resist the devil (James 4:7, Ephesians 6:10–18) Draw near to God (James 4:8, John 15)

Chart adapted from Murphy 1992, 508–20.

- *Proclaiming of the Word.* Ephesians 6:17 refers to the Word of God as the "sword of the Spirit"—the only item in the Ephesians 6 arsenal that can be wielded both offensively and defensively. Second Timothy 3:16–17 teaches that the Word equips us for every good work. The prime example of the power of the Word to defeat the lies of Satan is found in Jesus' wilderness temptation, in which Christ defeats each temptation with a passage of Scripture. This event is recorded in detail in Matthew 4:1–11 and Luke 4:1–13.

- *Praise and worship of God.* Whereas praise and worship, particularly musical praise, can be a powerful encourager to focus our thoughts on God (see the "Teacher's Heart" section), it can also have tremendous power to shake our opposition. The account in Acts 16:25–34 of Paul and Silas in prison shows not only the effect of praises on their situation, but the declaration of the gospel that came as a result.

- *Prayer.* The instructions given in Ephesians 6:18 involve the role of prayer in warfare. Jesus instructed us to pray that God's kingdom would come "on earth as it is in heaven" in Matthew 6:10—an indication that prayer enables more and more of God's kingdom to be revealed on earth. The Bible abounds with portraits of the power of prayer in accomplishing the Lord's will, and it even encourages us in that if we do not know what to pray, "the Spirit intercedes for the saints in accordance with God's will" (Romans 8:27).

If you asked your students to bring in CDs of praise music as part of their homework for lesson 14, you may choose to use it in different ways: you could have some songs playing as soft background music during the lesson, or you could play one or two as part of a concluding worship segment of class (see the "If Time Activity" section).

Objectives

- Students will examine three different battlegrounds that believers face—the flesh, the world, and supernatural evil.

- Students will integrate what they have learned about abiding in Christ with the armor described in Ephesians 6.

- Students will explore three different offensive tactics in doing battle with enemies of God's kingdom.

Unpacking

Battlegrounds (10–15 minutes)

Using the chart in the "Teacher's Preparation" section as a guide, read and discuss James 4:1–8 and what it reveals about the three battlegrounds on which we will face struggles as believers. You may wish to put the chart on the board and have students take notes about the strategies for each battleground. Discuss the roles of confession and repentance as they relate to abiding in Christ and wearing the armor of God.

Standing Firm in Christ (10 minutes)

Have students read Ephesians 6:10–18. Ask them to describe how this passage relates to the previous lesson on abiding in Christ. If needed, guide them to see that abiding in Christ accomplishes putting on the armor. Discuss this as a defensive strategy.

Going on Offense (15–20 minutes)

Using the "Teacher's Preparation" material as a guide, present the offensive strategies of the Word, praise, and prayer. Have students look up relevant Bible passages for each strategy. Then challenge students with some (or all) of these application ideas:

- *The Word.* Refer to the Scripture truths from lesson 13 (**JE 17 Christ and the Counterfeiter** and answer key, **BLM 5.1K**), and challenge students to identify one or two to memorize and speak into the circumstances of their lives.

- *Praise.* Refer to the songs of praise and proclamation that students identified or brought in as homework for the previous lesson. Let students explain what makes their songs significant to them. Challenge students to speak or sing words of praise to God regularly. Challenge them in their music listening to consider only songs with lyrics that glorify God or that edify and challenge them as believers. Have them record the effect such an exercise has on their thought life over a period of time.

- *Prayer.* Let students have a time of intercessory prayer with one or more partners in class. Create a class prayer box where written prayers can be deposited and prayed over. Challenge students to keep a prayer journal in which they write out their prayers for themselves and others each day. Challenge students to find verses of promise pertaining to areas of struggle to pray for themselves and others, particularly those who don't know Christ.

If Time Activity

Play a couple of praise songs—particularly ones that affirm our position in Christ. Invite students to sing along or to pray while the songs are playing. Conclude a worship time by having intercessory prayer or by having students read Bible verses that proclaim a truth about who they are in Christ (see lesson 13).

What's Next

Have students read chapter 6 in preparation for the next lesson.

Further Study

Barrett, Lois. 1999. The church and the powers. The Gospel and Our Culture Network. http://www.gocn.org/.

Murphy, Ed. 1992. *The handbook for spiritual warfare.* Nashville, TN: Thomas Nelson (see particularly chap. 63).

Robb, John D. 1999. Strategic prayer. In *Perspectives on the world Christian movement: A reader*, ed. Ralph D. Winter and Steven C. Hawthorne, 145–51. 3rd ed. Pasadena, CA: William Carey Library.

Silvoso, Ed. 1999. Prayer evangelism. In *Perspectives on the world Christian movement: A reader*, ed. Ralph D. Winter and Steven C. Hawthorne, 152–55. 3rd ed. Pasadena, CA: William Carey Library.

Wells, David. 1999. Prayer: Rebelling against the status quo. In *Perspectives on the world Christian movement: A reader*, ed. Ralph D. Winter and Steven C. Hawthorne, 142–44. 3rd ed. Pasadena, CA: William Carey Library.

Review: God's Purpose and Mission

Teacher's Heart

Do you feel as if you've gone through the wringer with this textbook so far? There has been a lot of material covered in this unit, and it may seem a bit overwhelming. You may feel as though you've started a lot of discussions that you didn't get to finish. Well, there are two pieces of good news: First, the next unit shifts gears a little and moves to a new lens through which to view what God is doing to fulfill His purpose in the world. This shift will allow you and your students to pick up the threads of conversations introduced in this first unit. Second, God is able to accomplish what concerns you every single day, and He is the guiding force behind the study and the work you and your students are doing through this course. I am filled with joy when I think of these materials in your hands and before your students:

"I thank my God every time I remember you. In all my prayers for all of you, I always pray with joy because of your partnership in the gospel from the first day until now, being confident of this, that he who began a good work in you will carry it on to completion until the day of Christ Jesus."* Amen.

*Philippians 1:3–6

Teacher's Preparation

Chapter 6 itself should serve as a guide for discussing the highlights from the chapters in this unit. You can review lesson plans and any notes you may have taken from teaching the material in this unit to revisit issues that may require additional review or clarification before formal end-of-unit assessments.

One key assessment piece will result from assigning The Story of the Bible: Version 2, a repeat of the assignment in lesson 1 to write the story of the Bible in the students' own words. You can compare this second pass with the first version of the assignment to assess what your students have learned in this unit. You may also ask them to discuss with you whether it was easier to write the assignment at this point or previously, and why they think that might be the case.

You may also wish to compile review facts to use as the basis for an in-class review game to prepare for the written unit test. If you choose to use an alternative form of assessment, you may need to set aside some additional review and preparation time for that as well.

Objectives

- Students will review concepts from chapters 1–5 in preparation for a unit assessment.
- Students will write the story of the Bible in their own words.
- Students will complete other assessment activities.
- Students will apply the truths from chapters 1–5 to their lives.

Unpacking

Discussing the Impact of His Story (10–15 minutes)

Guide a class discussion on chapter 6, and as a basis, use the following question from that chapter: What difference does it make in your reading, in your daily life, and in your relationship with God when you approach the Bible as His story? (SE p. 92).

The Story of the Bible: Version 2 (10–15 minutes)

Have students repeat in class the project from TE lesson 1, The Story of the Bible. As before, they should write a brief narrative of the Bible in their own words, and the length should be no longer than a page.

Comparing Stories (15–20 minutes)

Compare in class the two student versions of The Story of the Bible. Have students examine how their most recent version varies (if any) from their earlier one. Have students share insights and new understanding they gained about the Bible over the course of the unit.

Formal Assessment

Formal assessment could be administered by using one or more of the following:

- Unit 1 exam
- The Story of the Bible: Version 2
- A sampling of What Difference Does it Make? questions (found on SE pp. 90, 92, 93, 95, 97) for an essay test

What's Next

Have students read chapter 7 in preparation for the next lesson.

Culture Unit
unit two

Culture Unit Introduction

Student Edition Introduction

In this unit, we are going to pick up some binoculars and take a fresh look around us. We'll examine how God views culture and how cultural differences have an impact on the way we live with one another. The viewpoint of God always starts with people—the pinnacle of His creation and the apple of His eye. The children's song "Jesus Loves the Little Children" reminds us of this fact: "Red and yellow, black and white, they are precious in His sight." At the heart of living missionally is the task of learning to see the world the way God does—looking through His binoculars, if you will. In the next chapters, we hope to begin to do just that.

Big Ideas

- Effectively communicating God's story requires an intimate understanding of culture and God's view of it.

- The incarnation of Jesus is the model for reaching out to all people, whether within one's own culture or across cultural boundaries. Jesus tells us not only what to communicate but how to communicate it.

- The process of reaching out across cultures can be enhanced by a study of people.

- God's people must learn to connect incarnationally with others in significant cross-cultural relationships.

Memory Verses

Genesis 1:28

God blessed them and said to them, "Be fruitful and increase in number; fill the earth and subdue it. Rule over the fish of the sea and the birds of the air and over every living creature that moves on the ground."

Psalm 67

May God be gracious to us and bless us and make his face shine upon us,… that your ways may be known on earth, your salvation among all nations. May the peoples praise you, O God; may all the peoples praise you. May the nations be glad and sing for joy, for you rule the peoples justly and guide the nations of the earth … May the peoples praise you, O God; may all the peoples praise you. Then the land will yield its harvest and God, our God, will bless us. God will bless us, and all the ends of the earth will fear him.

1 Corinthians 9:19–23, The Message

Even though I am free of the demands and expectations of everyone, I have voluntarily become a servant to any and all in order to reach a wide range of people: religious, nonreligious, meticulous moralists, loose-living immoralists, the defeated, the demoralized—whoever. I didn't take on their way of life. I kept my bearings in Christ—but I entered their world and tried to experience things from their point of view. I've become just about every sort of servant there is in my attempts to lead those I meet into a God-saved life. I did all this because of the Message. I didn't just want to talk about it; I wanted to be *in* on it!

John 1:1–9, 14

In the beginning was the Word, and the Word was with God, and the Word was God. He was with God in the beginning. Through him all things were made; without him nothing was made that has been made. In him was life, and that life was the light of men. The light shines in the darkness, but the darkness has not understood it. There came a man who was sent from God; his name was John. He came as a witness to testify concerning that light, so that through him all men might believe. He himself was not the light; he came only as a witness to the light. The true light that gives light to every man was coming into the world.

The Word became flesh and made his dwelling among us. We have seen his glory, the glory of the One and Only, who came from the Father, full of grace and truth.

Web Resources

Link to more resources in our community at www.missiodei-thejourney.com.

Optional Enrichment Extension Projects for the Culture Unit

The following are some ideas for ongoing projects your class could undertake related to the topics studied in this unit on culture.

Cross-cultural immersion field trip. Plan a field trip that will fully involve your students in the sights, sounds, and experiences of another culture. Depending on what is available in your area, you could plan an experience ranging from dining in an ethnic restaurant, to attending a mosque or temple, to shopping in an open-air market where English is not the predominant language of trade. Students could journal both pre– and post–field trip reactions.

Cross-cultural emphasis week. Plan and host a missionary speaker day in class, or set aside a week of celebrating different cultures by having ethnic foods, speakers from different countries, and presentations of various elements of different cultures (e.g., music, dance, art, traditional clothing). You could combine this activity with your school's regularly scheduled chapel presentations or mission emphasis programs.

"Get out of your comfort zone" activity. Challenge students to participate in an activity that has a cross-cultural emphasis during a specified period of time. The activity should be something that they normally wouldn't do. Ideas include shopping in an ethnic neighborhood, attending a worship service in a different cultural setting, journaling about international events after reading a newspaper or watching a newscast daily for several days, learning to prepare an ethnic meal, learning some basic phrases in a foreign language, inviting someone from another culture into their home, and visiting the home of someone from another culture. Be creative about challenging your students. Assign journaling throughout the activity to capture their reactions.

Ongoing class cultural studies. Use the Looking Outside project format from lesson 22 (or parts of it, such as **BLM 10.2 Culture Analysis Template**) to create ongoing projects for cross-cultural research. You could have students bring in a news article every month and complete a culture analysis on it. These articles and culture analysis sheets could be kept in a notebook in the classroom. Locations of researched people groups could be tracked on a classroom world map by using thumbtacks, pins, or color coding of countries.

Adopt a people group. Your class could adopt an unreached people group for prayer, study, and mission projects. Joshua Project's website (www.joshuaproject.net) is a good place to find information on people groups. Adopt-A-People Clearinghouse (www.adoptapeople.com) is a clearinghouse for mission agencies and churches that are interested in formally adopting an unreached people group, with the ultimate goal of planting a church among that group. While your school may not be able to commit to the larger scope of adoption described on this website, you can glean ideas for an informal classroom adoption of an unreached people group. Resources for prayer and links to other similar organizations can be found at this site.

Culture and God's View of It

Big Idea

Effectively communicating God's story requires an intimate understanding of culture and God's view of it.

Key Concepts

- God's purpose is not limited to the bounds of one culture.

- God is glorified through unity within diversity.

- Our culture and worldview, which shape us, can cause us to clash with those who have cultural backgrounds or worldviews different from ours.

- God is above culture, and He works through culture to bring about His purpose.

Reflective Questions

- Which of Kraft's five views of God and culture best describes your own view? Is it difficult for you to see that God values all cultures and can work through them? (SE p. 160)

- How aware are you of the different cultural influences that shape you? What are some of the most predominant cultural influences in your life? (SE p. 160)

- What are some evidences of cultural diversity that you see in your own community? Is there more or less diversity surrounding you than what you thought? (SE p. 160)

Teacher's Heart

When I was in fourth grade, I had two best friends. One was from Great Britain, and the other was from Africa. Having these types of friendships was certainly not very typical for a southern girl from Alabama. But we lived for a few years in suburban Washington, D.C., and I was surrounded by children whose parents were a part of various foreign diplomatic staffs. My environment was a rich way to be introduced to the great diversity of the world. Very often I was confronted in unexpected ways with even the simple differences in cultures. The first time I ate supper at the house of my British friend, I recall being shocked that the British don't drink anything with their meals. It was difficult for me to imagine how you could eat without something to drink, because I had never met anyone who did so! I believe these friendships in my childhood profoundly shaped my interest in and love for people from other parts of the world. But not every child has the opportunity to spend time among such diversity. It may be that you or your students have never had the opportunity to experience much in the way of cultural diversity. May God give you eyes to see the richness of this world with the love He has for it. As you study the lessons in this unit, pray that He will soften your students' hearts and open them to His love for all people.

Teacher's Preparation

This lesson for chapter 7 seeks to clarify a few basic terms and ideas. We will use author Charles H. Kraft's definitions of culture and worldview (1998, 385; SE p. 106):

culture "a peoples' way of life, their design for living, their way of coping with their biological, physical and social environment"

worldview "included in culture as the deepest level presuppositions upon which people base their lives"

An example from chapter 7 helps distinguish both the difference and the relationship between these two terms. Paul G. Hiebert notes an "obsession with platforms" for sleeping (beds), sitting (chairs), and eating (tables) as an example of a behavioral preference that is part of the American culture. The worldview assumption that lies behind these behaviors is an assumption that floors are dirty and therefore we should stay off them (1999, 377). Worldview can be thought of as the foundation that shapes the choices people of a culture make in how to live and cope with their environment.

Chapter 7 Key Points

A major portion of chapter 7 is devoted to understanding a biblical view of the relationship between God and culture. Note the following key points:

• God is above all culture—in other words, culture didn't create God; God created culture (SE pp. 109–10).

• God works through culture. This stands in contrast to views that assume that God either hates culture, is indifferent to culture, or is aligned with only one particular culture (SE p. 111).

The chapter details five general positions regarding the relationship between God and culture (Kraft 1996, 92–93). Four are inconsistent with the whole story of the Bible. One of these four that is easy to assign credence to and that bears mentioning here

is the third position outlined by Charles H. Kraft (SE pp. 108–9), which says that God endorses a particular culture or subculture. It is easy to see how some Christians work to create an alternative "Christian culture." Examples of this abound: Christian cruise lines offer vacation packages; Christian media offer alternatives to mainstream publications, videos, and music; Christian food companies market diets that are based completely on ingredients found in the Bible. Though there is nothing wrong with alternatives to objectionable offerings of American culture, it is critical to avoid using these alternatives as a "Christian culture litmus test." Not only does such thinking establish a false view that God prefers only one sort of cultural form (so-called "Christian culture"), but it can isolate Christians from the people and the cultures they are called to bear witness to. This may be an area in which your students have difficulty. It may be particularly hard for them to grasp the difference between living a life that is obedient and honoring to God and living a life that imposes certain (often very American or Western) behavioral standards as part of a "superior Christian culture." Jesus battled this same difficulty when speaking with the Pharisees. An excellent resource you may want to consult for further explanation of the biblical view of this tension is Sherwood Lingenfelter's book *Transforming Culture* (see the "Further Study" section).

As further study in chapter 7 shows, God can and does work through any culture to achieve His purpose. Diversity in culture is not something that was created as a by-product of punishment (as some believe, on the basis of Genesis 11), but it is an intentional creation of God, allowing for a greater expression of His glory. Unity within diversity is the desire of God. Note the difference between unity and uniformity. Unity in Christ doesn't mean everyone is the same, but it does mean that they are united under the headship of Christ (Colossians 1:15–20).

Objectives

- Students will be able to define and explain the concepts of culture and worldview, and how these concepts relate to each other.

- Students will identify a view of God and culture that is consistent with the Bible, and they will explain why other views fall short.

- Students will explore the theme of scattering and the idea of unity within diversity as they are described in the Bible. Students will draw conclusions about God's view of culture on the basis of this study.

Unpacking

Prediscussion Check on Terms (7–10 minutes)

As a reading check, have students define the terms *culture* and *worldview* in their own words. Briefly discuss their answers. Present the definitions as they appear in the chapter, and discuss the relationship between the terms (see the "Teacher's Preparation" section). Near the end of class time you may wish to do a further check of understanding and ask students again to define the two terms and explain their relationship.

Five Views Discussion (15–20 minutes)

Using **BLM 7.1 Five Views of God and Culture** and its answer key, **BLM 7.1K**, discuss with students the five predominant views of God and culture as presented in chapter 7. Guide students as they fill in the missing information, and give them time to write their reaction to each position.

Examining the Word (15–20 minutes)

Below are three different Bible study activities for students to complete. You may want to lead these activities in class or assign them as homework or as small-group or independent work in class. Each activity explores an element of culture described in chapter 7.

- Read 1 Corinthians 9:19–22. Discuss the context and teaching of the passage. What is revealed about God's view of culture and about our own approach to other cultures? (**Paul demonstrates that we have to be willing to engage other cultures. In verse 23, Paul writes, "I do all this for the sake of the gospel, that I may share in its blessings."**)

- Discuss the theme of scattering as presented in chapter 7. What are some occurrences in the Bible in which you see a theme of God-ordained scattering? (**Possible answers include the tower of Babel incident, the conquest of Palestine, the captivity and exile of Israel, the persecution of the early Church.**) What could be the purpose of such scattering?

- Explore the theme of unity within diversity by reading Acts 2, Revelation 7:9, Isaiah 11:1–10, and Isaiah 2:1–4 or Micah 4:1–3. Note the similarities between these last two passages. How does unity within diversity demonstrate God's glory and power? (**Remind students that unity doesn't mean that everyone agrees; rather, unity is an intentional mind-set of working together for a greater purpose. God celebrates diversity [His creation], as demonstrated by the great multitude in Revelation 7:9.**)

What's Next

Journal Entry

Assign a reflective writing (**JE 22 A Sketch of My Culture**) using these prompts:

- What are some of the habits of your particular culture?
- Aside from sleeping on platforms, what are some things you regularly do?
- What might be the worldview assumptions that underpin those behaviors?

Reading

Have students read chapter 8 in preparation for the next lesson.

Looking Ahead

Following the introduction to the Culture Unit were optional activities, a list of enrichment extension projects. If you plan to have students participate in a cross-cultural field trip or experience during this unit, start making the necessary arrangements (e.g., reservations, permission slips).

Further Study

Lingenfelter, Sherwood G. 1998. *Transforming culture: A challenge for Christian mission.* 2nd ed. Grand Rapids, MI: Baker Books.

Misunderstandings, Ethnocentrism, and Premature Judgments

Big Idea

Effectively communicating God's story requires an intimate understanding of culture and God's view of it.

Key Concepts

- Effective cross-cultural communication can be hampered by misunderstandings, ethnocentrism, and premature judgments.

- Our beliefs, feelings, and values can either hinder or help effective cross-cultural communication.

- We must rely on God's perspective rather than our own for ultimate insight into cross-cultural communication. Cultural relativism can be a very tempting pitfall.

Reflective Questions

- How willing are you to learn about different cultures, particularly ones that are very different from your own? (SE p. 161)

- Do you recognize your own ethnocentrism? What specific areas of your culture do you think of as being superior to others? Why? Do these views square with the Bible? (SE p. 161)

- Do you try to make God fit into your worldview, or are you open to fitting into His? (SE p. 161)

Teacher's Heart

You may recall Duane Elmer's quotation at the beginning of chapter 8: "Among the hardest tasks in life is to divest ourselves of the culture we wear so comfortably" (2006, 19). Today's lesson puts a spotlight on some of the blindness that can come through the lenses of our own cultural prejudices, preferences, and presuppositions. Becoming aware of our own ethnocentrism can be uncomfortable. Today's discussion may resonate deeply with you and your students in areas very close to home. Ask the Spirit of God to bathe this lesson with His presence. "But when he, the Spirit of truth, comes, he will guide you into all truth. He will not speak on his own; he will speak only what he hears, and he will tell you what is yet to come. He will bring glory to me by taking from what is mine and making it known to you" (John 16:13–14).

Teacher's Preparation

This lesson begins with time set aside to clarify three of the main points from chapter 8. The diagram in **JE 23 Cultural Pitfalls** summarizes three areas of cultural pitfalls as presented in the chapter. Though each of these pitfalls can appear in isolation, there is a progression found among them. Just as beliefs can inform our feelings, which in turn can affect our values, misunderstandings can feed ethnocentrism, which can lead to premature judgments about other cultures. Similarly, the solutions represented on the diagram are also related in a progression: learning more about a culture can lead to the ability to develop empathy with its members. This in turn can develop into deeper understanding and appreciation of the culture.

The second activity in today's lesson deals with cultural relativism. Your students are of a generation that is saturated by a way of thinking that rejects most (if not all) boundaries, including the assertion of any absolute truth. They are surrounded by a culture that questions traditional ways of finding meaning, including faith in God in some cases. This generation is most adept at embracing fragmentation, ambiguity, and relativism. As it relates to a study of culture, this sort of thinking would say that truth for one culture could be (and most likely is) different from truth for another culture. Chapter 8 defines cultural relativism as "the belief that all cultures are equally good—that no culture has the right to stand in judgment of others" (Hiebert 1999, 379; SE p. 123). You may find that some of your students struggle with the concept of maintaining biblical truth in the face of relativism. It is a matter for much prayer and wise counsel, as contemporary teenagers are generally not satisfied with pat answers.

There is a fine line between expressing a biblically sound cultural sensitivity and slipping into the murky waters of cultural relativism. This tension is all the more heightened by the prevalent thinking of our times. Paul G. Hiebert notes, "This position of cultural relativism is very attractive. It shows high respect for other people and their cultures and avoids the errors of ethnocentrism and premature judgments. The price we pay, however, in adopting total cultural relativism is the loss of such things as truth and righteousness. If all explanations of reality are equally valid, we can no longer speak of error, and if all behavior is justified according to its cultural context, we can no longer speak of sin" (1999, 379; SE p. 123). This idea is at the forefront of what students should take away from today's discussion and activity. Help students evaluate cross-

cultural interactions and the students' personal attitudes in light of the truth of the Bible rather than the prevailing trends of relativistic thought.

Keep in mind that today's lesson is not designed to *solve* the problem of balancing the tension between cultural sensitivity and cultural relativism. It is designed to bring these issues to light for students. During the remainder of the unit and the course, we will explore the complexity of biblical cross-cultural interaction, and the material will continue to highlight the need for students to cling to a relationship with God to guide them in all matters. Think of this lesson as a first step in broadening students' view of these challenges.

Today's homework assignment prepares students for the next lesson, in which students will explore more about ethnocentrism by studying a paper presented in the 1950s by Horace Miner (1956). It is an ethnography of a fictitious culture called the Nacirema. Students are to read the Miner article in their student journals, note any significant or puzzling behaviors, and then answer some questions about their own attitudes toward befriending the Nacirema or living among them. Only after these things have been discussed in class during lesson 19 should you reveal that the Nacirema are a fictional tribe based completely on the behavior of Americans in the 1950s (the word *Nacirema* is *American* spelled backward). Keeping the true identity of the Nacirema a secret until lesson 19 is essential to maintaining the effectiveness of this activity. There are several terms that may be unfamiliar to your students as they read. You may wish to define the following for them: *ablution* (washing of the body or a part of it) and *thaumaturge* (performer of miracles). Also the term *font* is used with its 1950s' connotation, as a receptacle for liquids. Students today will probably think instead of a computer term. Rather than sending your students to online resources to find definitions of terms that are unknown to them, encourage them to keep a list of unfamiliar terms so that the terms can be discussed during the Examining the Nacirema activity in the "Unpacking" section of lesson 19. Many online resources disclose the true identity of the Nacirema.

Objectives

- Students will be able to define and give examples of cultural misunderstandings, ethnocentrism, and premature judgments. Students will identify the relationship between each of these three cultural pitfalls.

- Students will identify and assess the tension between cultural sensitivity and cultural relativism.

- Students will consider ways to avoid the cultural pitfalls described in chapter 8.

Unpacking

Studying the Three Main Points (15–20 minutes)

Using **JE 23 Cultural Pitfalls** and material from the "Teacher's Preparation" section, guide students through the three areas of cultural pitfalls discussed in chapter 8—misunderstandings, ethnocentrism, and premature judgments. Discuss how each relates to the others. Particularly draw attention to the three solutions depicted on the diagram and challenge students to brainstorm ways to learn more about other cultures, develop empathy with people of other cultures, and avoid premature judgments by gaining an understanding and an appreciation of another culture.

Exploring Cultural Relativism (10 minutes)

Use the "Teacher's Preparation" material as a guide to discuss the ideas of relativism, cultural relativism, and cultural sensitivity. Draw attention to the last paragraph in Hiebert's excerpt, beginning with the phrase "As Christians, we claim another basis for evaluation" (1999, 379; SE p. 123). Read and discuss that paragraph in preparation for the next activity.

Time in the Word (15–20 minutes)

Give students time to read and study Romans 14:1–8, 13–21 and 1 Corinthians 10:23–11:1. You may want to provide commentaries or background information on the circumstances Paul was speaking about in these passages. After the students complete this reading, ask them to explain how Paul addresses the tension between cultural sensitivity and cultural relativism.

What's Next

Journal Entry

Assign the reflective writing **JE 24 Empathy** that covers the following questions:

- What are some means of developing empathy?

- In your own life, what situations have caused you to have an understanding or appreciation for something new or different?

- Is there a way to cultivate empathy for others?

Reading

Students should read **BLM 8.1 Excerpts from "Body Ritual Among the Nacirema"** and underline or highlight interesting or important characteristics of that culture. Have them keep a list of terms that are unfamiliar to them. They should be prepared to discuss in class tomorrow the Nacirema culture and what strategies could be used to build relationships with them.

Looking Ahead

If you plan to have students participate in a cross-cultural field trip or experience during this unit, continue making the necessary arrangements (e.g., reservations, permission slips).

Further Study

Elmer, Duane. 2002. *Cross-cultural connections: Stepping out and fitting in around the world.* Downers Grove, IL: InterVarsity Press.

Elmer, Duane. 2006. *Cross-cultural servanthood: Serving the world in Christlike humility.* Downers Grove, IL: InterVarsity Press.

The Nacirema and Ethnocentrism

Big Idea

Effectively communicating God's story requires an intimate understanding of culture and God's view of it.

Key Concepts

- Effective cross-cultural communication can be hampered by misunderstandings, ethnocentrism, and premature judgments.

- Our beliefs, feelings, and values can either hinder or help effective cross-cultural communication.

- We must rely on God's perspective rather than our own for ultimate insight into cross-cultural communication. Cultural relativism can be a very tempting pitfall.

Reflective Questions

- How willing are you to learn about different cultures, particularly ones that are very different from your own? (SE p. 161)

- Do you recognize your own ethnocentrism? What specific areas of your culture do you think of as being superior to others? Why? Do these views square with the Bible? (SE p. 161)

- Do you try to make God fit into your worldview, or are you open to fitting into His? (SE p. 161)

Teacher's Heart

Here are a couple of humorous examples of ethnocentrism: The executives of General Motors couldn't understand why the Chevy Nova was not selling well in Latin America until they were told that *no va* in Spanish means "it doesn't go." And a U.S. napkin company used the following phrase in an advertisement in Great Britain: "You could use no finer napkin at your dinner table." Sales were hardly brisk given that, to the British, *napkin* means "diaper." Though we find these examples easy to laugh about and we assume we could never make the same sorts of mistakes, the truth is, we are all capable of not recognizing our own biases and cultural blind spots. Think of your students. Are there cultural pitfalls you fall prey to as you interact with them? generational gaps? ethnic differences? political differences? As you prepare this lesson, ask God to give you a heart to see your students (and other people) through His eyes, not simply through the viewpoint of your own cultural bias.

Teacher's Preparation

The revelation of the true nature of the Nacirema that will come during today's lesson should provide your students with some sort of "Aha!" moment regarding their own ethnocentrism and cultural bias. Some may be disbelieving that the culture described in "Body Ritual Among the Nacirema" could be in any way related to their own lives. Even though the piece was written in the 1950s, many of the rituals described are even more defining of American society today. Much of the punch in this lesson will come from the simple revealing of the true identity of the Nacirema. As you teach about the Nacirema and about the short story by Duane Elmer in the Cross-Cultural Silliness activity, push your students to really consider and identify what their own ethnocentrism is, how it aligns with God's perspective on culture and humanity, and what the potentially dangerous consequences of unchecked ethnocentrism are.

To aid in revealing the true identity of the Nacirema, you may want to consult this chart, which explains some of the key terms in the order they appear in the ethnographic essay:

Terms Used in "Body Ritual Among the Nacirema"	Translations
Shrine (ritual center) devoted to body ritual and ceremony	Bathroom
Box or chest, also called a charm-box, built into the wall of a shrine	Medicine cabinet
Charm or magical potion	Prescription or other medication
Medicine man	Doctor
Herbalist	Pharmacist
Small font beneath a charm-box	Bathroom sink
Ablution	Washing of the body or a part of it
Holy-mouth-man	Dentist
Latipso, or temple	Hospital
Thaumaturge	Performer of miracles

Objectives

- Students will begin to identify their own cultural biases and feelings of ethnocentrism.

- Students will evaluate the power of cultural bias to shape our feelings, beliefs, and values.

Unpacking

Examining the Nacirema (15–30 minutes)

Begin by asking students to share their impressions of the Nacirema. Then discuss the following questions: Which of this group's customs did you find the most absurd or the most primitive? Which seemed the most advanced? Could you see yourself living among this people group? Why or why not? What might be the biggest challenge to effective communication with them? How would you share the gospel with this group? What might be some challenges to doing so?

After students have had a chance to fully explore their responses and reactions to this people group, reveal to them that the Nacirema are in fact the people we label as American (*Nacirema* spelled backward). Give as much background of the original piece of writing as you desire. You may want to use the charted information above to help show the different facets of American culture outlined in the Nacirema ethnography. Complete this activity by listing on the board the students' reactions to the real group profiled in the ethnography.

Cross-Cultural Silliness (5–7 minutes)

To reveal the potential consequences of ethnocentrism and cultural bias, read to your students the following story by Duane Elmer:

> A typhoon had temporarily stranded a monkey on an island. In a secure, protected place, while waiting for the raging waters to recede, he spotted a fish swimming against the current. It seemed obvious to the monkey that the fish was struggling and in need of assistance. Being of kind heart, the monkey resolved to help the fish.
>
> A tree precariously dangled over the very spot where the fish seemed to be struggling. At considerable risk to himself, the monkey moved far out on a limb, reached down and snatched the fish from the threatening waters. Immediately scurrying back to the safety of his shelter, he carefully laid the fish on dry ground. For a few moments the fish showed excitement, but soon settled into a peaceful rest. Joy and satisfaction swelled inside the monkey. He had successfully helped another creature. (2002, 14)

Ask students to evaluate the actions of the monkey and the misunderstandings that led the monkey to do the opposite of his intention with the fish, and then to write a moral to this story.

Journal Entry (10–15 minutes)

Give students time to write a reflective essay, **JE 25 Discoveries**, on the lessons found in today's activities. Some guiding questions could include the following:

- What did the stories about the Nacirema (Miner 1956) and the monkey and the fish (Elmer 2002, 14) reveal to you about your own cultural bias or ethnocentrism? about the power of ethnocentrism?

- Is it easier to identify the ethnocentrism of the monkey than the ethnocentrisms you have? Why or why not?

- What are some of the consequences of unchecked cultural bias and ethnocentrism?

- What are some of your feelings, beliefs, and values that should be submitted to closer examination in light of the Bible?

Extra Mile

As a connection to a history class or a current events class, you may want to assign students the task of finding historical or contemporary events that are examples of the consequences of ethnocentrism. An event such as the Holocaust, and ethnic tensions and strife in places such as the former Yugoslavia, Rwanda, the Middle East, and the Sudan are all examples of world events in which ethnocentrism plays a central role.

What's Next

Have students read chapter 9 in preparation for the next lesson.

Lesson 20   # The Incarnation

Big Idea

The incarnation of Jesus is the model for reaching out to all people, whether within one's own culture or across cultural boundaries. Jesus tells us not only what to communicate but how to communicate it.

Key Concepts

- The incarnation of Jesus was a crossing of the largest cultural divide there is—from the infinite to the finite.

- Jesus was sent to the earth to proclaim His purpose of relationship, redemption, and reconciliation. As followers of Christ, we also are to proclaim this purpose to the world around us (John 17:18, 2 Corinthians 5:17–19).

- Jesus did not shy away from the "other"; He sought out and embraced the marginalized and rejected of society.

Reflective Questions

- What do you think is the most puzzling aspect of the Incarnation? Why? (SF p 162)

- Do you think of yourself as being "sent" into the world to be God's ambassador of love, just as Jesus was sent to the world to demonstrate God's love? (SE p. 162)

- What particular elements of Jesus' example do you believe are the most significant for your spiritual journey at this point? Are you willing to seek to understand them and live them out more fully? (SE p. 162)

Teacher's Heart

As I write this, I am pregnant with my second child. One of the things that stuns me about new human life is the miraculous growth that takes place in the first twelve weeks of a baby's life. From the first spark of life in impossibly small cells, there quickly develops an embryo that has all the same parts as you and I have—only tremendously in miniature and unable to survive without the nourishing and protective environment of the womb. I find it interesting to contemplate all this as I write about the incarnation of God. One of the things that strikes me is the intense vulnerability of Jesus on His journey to the earth. He was once an unborn child in His mother's womb! I don't know about you, but if I were all comfy and ensconced in heaven, I wouldn't be very inclined to humble myself to the point of becoming a few small cells—just to bring love to a bunch of folks who didn't even want to see me or who didn't like me that much.

In preparation for today's lesson, look at some pictures of a fifteen-to-twenty-week-old embryo or hold a baby. Think about the God of the universe. Let your mind be blown away in worship and adoration.

Teacher's Preparation

Today's lesson is designed to give students an opportunity to reflect on the glory of the Incarnation and to consider the model and example that this event gives to those who would be Christ-followers. Jesus calls us to a life of discipleship and imitation of His example. In Matthew 11:29, Jesus says, "Take my yoke upon you and learn from me." We are to be so closely aligned with Jesus that it is as though we are yoked together with Him in the same way that partnering oxen are yoked together. We are to learn from Him so that our lives can speak the truth of Him and so that we can say with Paul, "Follow my example, as I follow the example of Christ" (1 Corinthians 11:1).

This lesson is designed to set the stage for some worshipful reflection and personal response on the part of your students. For some, it may be a time of confronting the depths of Christ's love in a fresh way. There may even be some who, in the experience of reflecting on the incarnation of Jesus and His life, realize they need to commit to a relationship with Him for the first time. The lesson plan offers a variety of suggestions rather than specifically ordered activities, and it includes an initial time of setting the tone for the reflective experiences that will follow.

You may use a variety of resources and techniques to stimulate reflection. The simplest may be to play some of the suggested music and give students time to reread the chapter and jot down their reactions and questions. You may wish to provide creative outlets, such as drawing or writing, for the students as they listen to music. More mature classes might be able to have small-group discussion and sharing at the end of the class period. You may wish to close class in an open-ended prayer time, inviting students to respond to the experience of this lesson.

Students may have questions from the chapter, particularly regarding the "200 percent man" concept. A resource for further information on that is listed in the "Further Study" section. If you sense a need, you can have students submit written questions about the chapter at the beginning of this lesson, and address these questions either individually throughout the class period or at the beginning of the next lesson. Submitted written questions are a way to assess student understanding.

Objectives

- Students will reflect on the Incarnation and respond to its meaning as they interact with a variety of media.
- Students will assess the power of the story of the Incarnation in their own lives.

Unpacking

Setting the Tone (5–10 minutes)

Using **JE 26 Responding to the Incarnation**, ask for student reaction to chapter 9. Ask them to identify elements of the Incarnation that are the most puzzling or the most striking to them. If you sense that students have struggled with any of the information in chapter 9, have them submit written questions about the material. (This is a good way to check for comprehension.) You can address student questions sometime during this lesson or the next.

Explain that today's activities will give them a variety of ways to reflect on and respond to the Incarnation. Give them any specific guidance needed for the activities that will follow.

Creatively Hearing and Responding to the Incarnation (20–40 minutes)

You may choose to do several of the following activities in the order given, or you could set up several "centers" in your classroom to allow students to quietly move at their own pace from one activity to the next. Background music, such as a compilation of hymns celebrating the Incarnation or music from any of the following suggested CDs, will help keep the attitude worshipful and reflective: *Behold the Lamb of God* by Andrew Peterson; *Your King Has Come* by various artists; *The Music of Christmas* by Steven Curtis Chapman; *Christmas: An Irrational Season* by Carolyn Arends; *New Irish Hymns #3: Incarnation* by Margaret Becker, Kristyn Getty, and Joanne Hogg; and *Savior: Celebrating the Mystery of God Become Man* published by Sovereign Grace Music.

Here are some activities and experiences for your class today:

- Provide pastels and drawing paper so that students can create an image in response to music about the Incarnation.

- Have paints and paper or modeling clay available for students to work with while they listen to music about the Incarnation.

- Read aloud the "Twenty-five Questions for Mary" sidebar in chapter 9 or have the students silently read it.

- Provide written copies of the lyrics for music played during class so that students can read and reflect on the words.

- Present a slide show or a PowerPoint presentation of classical pieces of artwork that depict Christ's birth or events surrounding it. (An online search of images related to Madonna and child, baby Jesus, or Christ's birth may lead you to some appropriate images.)

- Challenge students to write poetry about the Incarnation.

- Ask students to read a selection of Bible passages such as John 1:1–18 or Isaiah 9:6–7 and to write responses to them.

- Have students rewrite the story of Christmas and the Incarnation in their own words.

- Ask students to write or draw a response to the following questions: What does it mean to be sent? What does it mean to you that Jesus was sent to us?

- Have students write an essay on what the Incarnation means to them.

- Have students write prayers of response as they listen to the music.

- Let students reread chapter 9 as they listen to music related to the Incarnation.

You may want to close with an open-ended time of sharing or response, or in prayer.

Looking Ahead

In lesson 22, students will be assigned a cross-cultural research project that will extend over the course of several days and that will culminate in a written report containing several elements. You may want to begin looking at this assignment now for planning purposes (see **BLM 10.1 Looking Outside: A Cross-Cultural Research Project** and **BLM 10.2 Culture Analysis Template**).

Further Study

Lingenfelter, Sherwood G., and Marvin K. Mayers. 2003. *Ministering cross-culturally: An incarnational model for personal relationships.* 2nd ed. Grand Rapids, MI: Baker Academic.

Lesson 21

Going to the Margins in Love

Big Idea

The incarnation of Jesus is the model for reaching out to all people, whether within one's own culture or across cultural boundaries. Jesus tells us not only what to communicate but how to communicate it.

Key Concepts

- The incarnation of Jesus was a crossing of the largest cultural divide there is—from the infinite to the finite.

- Jesus was sent to the earth to proclaim His purpose of relationship, redemption, and reconciliation. As followers of Christ, we also are to proclaim this purpose to the world around us (John 17:18, 2 Corinthians 5:17–19).

- Jesus did not shy away from the "other"; He sought out and embraced the marginalized and rejected of society.

Reflective Questions

- What do you think is the most puzzling aspect of the Incarnation? Why? (SE p. 162)

- Do you think of yourself as being "sent" into the world to be God's ambassador of love, just as Jesus was sent to the world to demonstrate God's love? (SE p. 162)

- What particular elements of Jesus' example do you believe are the most significant for your spiritual journey at this point? Are you willing to seek to understand them and live them out more fully? (SE p. 162)

Teacher's Heart

I have often felt like an outsider. I imagine that from time to time you probably have also. Other people can deeply wound us, and when this happens, we often put up walls of "protection" to keep people from getting close enough to hurt us like that again. Being invited into a life of community and deep fellowship with others, such as the life Christ calls us into, can help us break down those walls. I can really identify with the response of the woman at the well—her shock that Jesus would speak to her, much less offer forgiveness and acceptance rather than harsh judgment or rejection. She was, after all, a marginalized person. Perhaps you can identify with her also. In some way or another, we, including your students, have all been people of the margins. Perhaps no other period in life makes us feel so marginalized as the teen years. Pray for insight into how you can use this lesson to meaningfully reach out to the hearts of your students.

Teacher's Preparation

Today's lesson focuses on the second part of the Big Idea for chapter 9: Jesus tells us not only what to communicate but how to communicate it. Of course, there are many events and incidents in Jesus' life and ministry that can be studied as models for our own life, but in terms of cross-cultural relationships, the John 4 story of the Samaritan woman is particularly relevant. That story is also a parallel to the Incarnation itself, depicting what Jesus' being sent to the world was all about—an invitation to a new life of forgiveness in the kingdom of God. You may wish to help establish the tone for this lesson by discussing the universal nature of wanting to feel loved and accepted. It might be appropriate to share from your own experiences what a blessing it is to know acceptance in Christ.

To help your students view the John 4 narrative with fresh eyes, you may choose from two different writing assignments that are designed to give students the opportunity to personalize the story and cast it in a more-contemporary light. The first option is for students to recast the story in contemporary terms, identifying elements of their world that might match the prejudices of the ancient world in which this story was told. For example, a modern-day, drug-addicted single mother might stand in place

of the woman at the well. A believer might stand in place of Jesus in the story. The chart below identifies several key elements of the John 4 narrative that students would need to update into contemporary terms. The possible contemporary equivalents are provided to aid in the thinking process. You could use these suggestions as a basis for brainstorming, but you should in no way feel limited by them.

A second writing option is to give students the assignment of writing a monologue in the voice of the woman at the well. The monologue should describe the woman's reaction to this encounter with Jesus. You may have them write from her point of view in the ancient world, or let them write from a contemporary point of view. If you have a longer class period, you might want to assign both activities. Regardless of which of these two writing assignments you choose, the goal is to challenge students to analyze the story and develop a deeper empathy for the woman—and especially for the type of marginalized person that she represents. As the course unfolds, you will be guiding your students to begin thinking about the places they may be "sent" (as Jesus was sent) to minister to those who might be very different from them. Today's lesson is a foundation to help them begin to see those needs.

Elements from John 4	Possible Contemporary Equivalents
Jesus chooses to go through Samaria (v. 4).	Travel through an unsavory part of town.
Tired, Jesus sits down at a well (v. 6).	Take a rest; have a vehicle break down.
The disciples leave Jesus alone (v. 8).	Have travel companions go for help.
A woman comes to the well; Jesus asks her for a drink (v. 7).	Have a marginalized woman approach; ask her for help.
The woman is puzzled by Jesus' speaking to her (v. 9).	Have the woman be skeptical that you're approaching her.
Jesus continues the conversation, revealing that He knows her and promising that He will meet the woman's deepest needs (vv. 10–26).	Continue speaking and discover that she is not a believer. Explain to her Christ's love and forgiveness.
The woman's testimony and Jesus' continued stay in the area lead to many finding salvation (vv. 39–42).	Have the woman be transformed by the gospel, and have her invite you to share the good news with her friends.

Objectives

- Students will analyze the story of the woman at the well, and they will compose a contemporary version of those events.

- Students will identify their own feelings of being the outsider, and they will evaluate the power of acceptance and forgiveness in those types of situations.

- Students will reflect on the universal desire to feel accepted and understood, and they will examine how this desire relates to cross-cultural communication.

Unpacking

Contemporary Parallels (20–25 minutes)

Brainstorm with students to find some potential contemporary parallels to the John 4 story of Jesus' reaching out to the woman at the well. You might wish to give students a copy of the chart in the "Teacher's Preparation" section to help them identify portions of the story they need to update. Then give them time to write their own contemporary versions of this Bible passage.

Woman at the Well Monologue (15–20 minutes)

Explain to students that a monologue is a speech made by one person sharing his or her thoughts directly to an audience. Assign a written monologue from the point of view of the woman at the well in the story described in John 4. The monologue should contain her reaction to meeting Christ and being accepted by Him. Students can write from her perspective as described in the Bible, or they may imagine her in a more-contemporary setting and write from that perspective.

Discussing an Outsider's Perspective (7–10 minutes)

Divide the class into groups of two or more students, and have them discuss and react to the following questions: What kinds of things make you feel like an outsider? How do you feel as the outsider? When you've been the outsider, how does it feel to be reached out to? Whom do you identify with most in the "woman at the well" story: Jesus (reaching out in love), the woman (in the margins and skeptical that anyone could know her and love her), the disciples (unsure of what Jesus was doing and why He would minister to a Samaritan woman)?

If Time Activity

Plan a time to have students share with the class either their contemporary versions of the John 4 story or their monologues. You may wish to challenge them to memorize and perform their monologues for their classmates.

What's Next

Journal Entry

Assign a reflective writing, **JE 27 Reaching Out**, that covers the following questions:

- What are some conclusions you can draw from the last two lessons?

- How can you relate these lessons on the Incarnation and Jesus' reaching out to a marginalized woman to your own missional invitation to a life of reaching out to the "others" of the world?

- Do you think the desire to feel accepted and understood is universal among people?

Reading

Have students read chapter 10 in preparation for the next lesson.

Lesson 22 | # A Big, Big World

Big Idea

The process of reaching out across cultures can be enhanced by a study of people.

Key Concepts

- We live in a world that is much larger than we typically realize, and Americans are not in the majority when compared to the world population.

- Christ reached out to all, regardless of their "other-ness." Believers are called to do the same.

- Understanding cultural distance and people blindness can help us see beyond our cultural comfort zones. We must be intentional about living missionally and reaching out to all people.

Reflective Questions

- Do you notice those in your community who are from people groups that differ from yours, or are they largely invisible to you? How do you feel about people from other groups? (SE p. 163)

- How intentional are you about getting to know people who are different from you? Have you ever taken the time to try to bridge the cultural distance between you and another person? Why or why not? (SE p. 163)

Teacher's Heart

It is easy to assume that the rest of the world is just like us. This is particularly true in America, because so much of our culture is exported to other countries—I've eaten at a McDonald's in Moscow and a Pizza Hut in Ecuador, and I've never been too far from either a Coke product or a Pepsi product on any trip overseas. Of course, the reality is that Americans are not in the majority culturally when compared with the rest of the world's population. Nor are Christians in the religious majority around the world. But this fact is no different from what Jesus experienced in His day. He was certainly in a minority group, as was the early Church. Understanding that there are many people who are different from us shouldn't discourage us. Learning about the rest of the world—particularly in light of the relative wealth and ease we enjoy here in the United States—can begin to change our perspective about how we live, the choices we make with our time and money, and the effort we are willing to put into living as though we are sent to the whole world. Pray that as your students begin to learn more about the world, they will develop empathy and appreciation for those who are different from them. Pray that they, rather than fearing the "other," will be energized and inspired to know more about the rest of the world that God loves.

Teacher's Preparation

This lesson and the next are designed to unpack the contents of chapter 10. Today's lesson centers on expanding your students' understanding of how large and diverse the world is. The next lesson will focus specifically on your students' own cultural contexts and on identifying people who are removed from that context by varying degrees of cultural distance.

Today's lesson introduces a two-phase research project that will be an ongoing homework assignment. In phase 1, students will identify international current events that interest them, and then, in phase 2, they will choose an event to research in more detail. Assign a due date for each of the phases of the project. Phase 1 will need one or two days outside of class for completion; phase 2 will probably require four or five days of out-of-class research. The emphasis is on their gaining an understanding of the cultural context of the

news story they have chosen. They will use templates provided in **BLM 10.1 Looking Outside: A Cross-Cultural Research Project** and **BLM 10.2 Culture Analysis Template** to guide their research and allow for independent work. You will want to incorporate some in-class reminders and checkups in the coming days. You may also wish to schedule a day for in-class presentations at the conclusion of their research.

This project, which should be completed before the end of this unit, is detailed in the lesson plan below and on **BLM 10.1** and **BLM 10.2**. Feel free to adapt this basic format to the needs of your classroom. Many resources exist for researching current events, people groups, and geopolitical facts. Some are listed in the "Further Study" section, and many others exist, particularly online. You may also want to enlist the help of a librarian or a current events or history teacher for cultivating additional research options for students.

Objectives

- Students will answer questions about the scope of the world population and how their own culture fits into that big picture.

- Students will explore other cultures through a study of current events.

- Students will research one or more people groups and evaluate cultural differences that exist between those groups and their own culture.

Unpacking

Reading Quiz (5 minutes)

Use the following questions to check for completion of the assigned reading:

1. Which group is greater in number: nations or people groups? (people groups)

2. In the illustration of the world as a group of 1,000 people (in **JE 28 A Global Village**), what ethnic group tops the list? (the Chinese)

3. What is people blindness? (blindness to separate peoples within countries)

4. According to the E-Scale of cultural distance, a person with whom you have the least in common would be what sort of relationship? (E-3)

People Blindness Discussion (7–10 minutes)

Discuss these questions related to chapter 10:

• Why do you think Ralph Winter says that people in the United States are particularly susceptible to people blindness?

• How would you rate your knowledge of other cultures? Is there a particular area of the world you are interested in learning more about? Are there parts of the world you don't want to know anything about? If so, why?

Graphing It Out (10 minutes)

Using Duane Elmer's statistical snapshot about the world population and religions (2002, 19–20; SE p. 136 and sidebar), challenge students to create graphs on the templates provided in **JE 28 A Global Village**. Discuss any conclusions that this visual representation leads to.

Looking Outside: A Cross-Cultural Research Project (15–20 minutes)

Introduce students to the cross-cultural research project. Explain the various phases and requirements of the project. Assign due dates, suggest resources, and answer questions regarding the project. It has two phases—current events identification and culture analysis research based on people groups—with assignments for each phase:

• *Phase 1 (1–2 days)*. Students should read global news coverage of current events and select two or three events of interest to them that are taking place outside the United States. Encourage them to consider many sources for their stories. The Internet Public Library News and Currents Events page at www.ipl.org/div/subject/browse/ref55.00.00/ provides links not only to major American news organizations but to international ones as well. Students should bring in several different stories (articles or transcripts of reports) on the due date for phase 1. Assist students in evaluating and selecting one story to concentrate on for phase 2 research. You may want to work toward a diverse global distribution of stories among your class members and thus enhance your discussion.

• *Phase 2 (4–5 days)*. Using the guidance provided in **BLM 10.1 Looking Outside: A Cross-Cultural Research Project** and **BLM 10.2 Culture Analysis Template**, students should prepare the different research elements required for the final report portfolio that will be turned in (a three-ring binder or a folder works well for this type of project). You can specify format and length requirements for each element of the report, adding to or adapting as needed. We suggest that the final report portfolio include the following ten elements, in this order: (1) title page, (2) table of contents, (3) copy of any original news articles, (4) map detailing the area of the event, (5) geographic description of the area in which the news event takes place, (6) student-written summary of additional information relating to the news event, (7) profile of any people groups involved, (8) cultural difference essay, (9) personalization essay, and (10) response to the project.

At the end of the research project, students should turn in a notebook with all the required research components. You may wish to schedule in-class presentations or discussions on what the students learned from the project.

If Time Activities

Film Presentation

Show the documentary film *Paper Clips* to your students (Fab 2003; see www
.paperclipsmovie.com/synopsis.php for more information). The film chronicles a
Tennessee middle school's study of the Holocaust and how the ongoing project
allowed a very homogeneous community to broaden its understanding of other
cultures.

Current Events Locations

Post a world map in your classroom and use tacks or pins to indicate the various
locations of the current events being researched by your students for the cross-
cultural research project.

What's Next

Allow for ongoing work on the research project.

Further Study

Johnstone, Patrick J., Robyn J. Johnstone, and Jason Mandryk. 2001. *Operation
    world*. 6th ed. Waynesboro, GA: Paternoster USA.

Joshua Project. http://www.joshuaproject.net (a website devoted to people group
    research and evangelism).

Mission frontiers: The bulletin of the U.S. Center for World Mission. http://www
    .missionfrontiers.org (a bimonthly publication focused on helping followers of
    Christ worldwide take the gospel to every people group).

Operation World Web links. http://www.operationworld.org/updates/bldlnks.php (a
    website with links to online sites that provide detailed country profiles).

Smith, David J. 2002. *If the world were a village: A book about the world's people*.
    Tonawanda, NY: Kids Can Press.

Identifying Cultural Distance

Big Idea

The process of reaching out across cultures can be enhanced by a study of people.

Key Concepts

- We live in a world that is much larger than we typically realize, and Americans are not in the majority when compared to the world population.

- Christ reached out to all, regardless of their "other-ness." Believers are called to do the same.

- Understanding cultural distance and people blindness can help us see beyond our cultural comfort zones. We must be intentional about living missionally and reaching out to all people.

Reflective Questions

- Do you notice those in your community who are from people groups that differ from yours, or are they largely invisible to you? How do you feel about people from other groups? (SE p. 163)

- How intentional are you about getting to know people who are different from you? Have you ever taken the time to try to bridge the cultural distance between you and another person? Why or why not? (SE p. 163)

Teacher's Heart

If you grew up during the 1980s (as I did), you probably remember hearing about a movie called *The Breakfast Club* (Hughes 1985). Or perhaps you've seen its cleaned-up version in one of countless reruns on TV. The movie chronicles a few hours in the lives of five students assigned to Saturday detention at their high school. They are each from very different segments of high school society, initially skeptical and hostile toward one another. But over the course of the morning they realize they have more in common than they had thought initially. A voice-over at the close of the movie shares their new perspective: "You see us as you want to see us: in the simplest terms, in the most convenient definitions. But, what we found out is that each one of us is a brain … and an athlete … and a basket case … a princess … and a criminal." The movie's simple point is that we are much more than our labels imply and there can be a little bit of many "types" in each of us.

Pray that your students will have this insight about themselves, their peers, and the many different people of the world whose paths will cross theirs during their lifetime.

Teacher's Preparation

Even though today's lesson includes several activities that involve classifying people, it is important to steer yourself and your students away from the tendency to define people solely in terms of neat, one-size-fits-all labels. All of us are far more complex than that. Exercises such as identifying one's own cultural context and determining cultural distance are simply tools for helping develop a larger worldview. They are not the stopping point but the starting place toward greater understanding. Ultimately, our goal is to see with the eyes of Christ. As highlighted by the Bible story from Luke 7:36–50 (mentioned at the end of chapter 10), Jesus sees and loves *people*—regardless of their labels, regardless of their "other-ness." This is the example we are to follow and the example to which you should always direct your students' focus.

The first activity of this lesson invites students to identify their own cultural context. **JE 29 Uncovering My Cultural Context** is a tool that will help students identify themselves in terms of cultural context and people group. You may discover through this activity that your classroom is homogeneous culturally, or you may discover a range of diversity.

The second activity uses **JE 30 E-Scale Thoughts** to guide students in identifying people or groups of people who, though they may be near neighbors geographically, are culturally distant. This activity is designed to help you and your students think through the various types and E-Scale levels of people groups (Winter and Hawthorne 1999b) that may be represented in your school, your community, or your state. If you live in a more urban area or in a town with a university campus that has international students, or if you have an international population within your school, you will probably be able to identify many different levels of the E-Scale present in your area. If you live in a more rural area, identifying E-2s and E-3s geographically nearby may be more difficult. If your immediate geographic area is not very culturally diverse, direct students to identify the geographically nearest examples of E-2s and E-3s that they can think of. Since this portion of the lesson focuses on the idea of cultural distance and E-Scale, you may wish to read about it in more detail than what is in chapter 10. Ralph Winter's full article, which provided the basis for the material in chapter 10, is referenced in the "Further Study" section.

Word Play	
Here are several terms and definitions used in today's lesson:	
cultural distance	a term that refers to cultural and worldview factors that may create difficulty in communication between two people groups regardless of other proximity
E-Scale	a form of measurement used to describe the varying levels of cultural distance ranging from no cultural distance (E-0) to extreme cultural distance (E-3)
people blindness	the phenomenon of not recognizing different peoples within countries or geographical boundaries
people group	a group that shares the same ethnicity and language and a common self-identity; a group in which members can communicate well without barriers of understanding or acceptance; a group whose members think of themselves as "us" and those outside their group as "them"

Objectives

- Students will outline the distinctives of their own cultural contexts and will evaluate the cultural similarities and differences they have with their classmates.

- Students will identify different spheres of cultural distance as the spheres apply to the students' individual contexts.

Unpacking

Uncovering Cultural Context (20–25 minutes)

Using **JE 29 Uncovering My Cultural Context**, direct students to spend 5–10 minutes to complete the personal inventory and then another 2–3 minutes to brainstorm and find adjectives that describe their own cultural context. After students have completed these tasks, you may wish to collect the pages and assemble a cultural profile of your class to share (e.g., sixteen students are native English speakers, four are not; ten students are African American, three are Hispanic, and seven are Caucasian). Discuss the makeup of your classroom:

- Are there significant cultural differences among your students, or is your class largely from very similar cultural contexts?

- Broaden the discussion to include the cultural context of your community: How is your particular area homogeneous? How is it diverse?

- Think of your community in terms of your school, your church community, your larger community, your state.

Identifying Cultural Distance Around You (20–25 minutes)

Direct students to **JE 30 E-Scale Thoughts** and guide them through identifying an example of people or groups of people in your community that fall into each of the areas of cultural distance represented on the diagram. Students may need to refer to material in chapter 10 to refresh their memory about what each level of the E-Scale means. This activity should be completed as a class, although individual answers will vary to some degree. As you work through each level of the E-Scale, discuss the presence of different levels of cultural distance in your particular geographical area.

Extra Mile

Challenge students to read *Jesus Freaks*, a book describing contemporary martyrs for faith in Christ. This book, whose publishing details are in the "Further Study" section, offers a portrait of believers in a wide range of cultures (showing how Christians live in different cultures), and it gives a glimpse of the cost associated with their belief and faith in Jesus Christ. It is not only challenging and thought-provoking but very teen reader-friendly.

What's Next

Journal Entry

Assign a reflective writing to address the questions included in **JE 30**:

- How can you learn more about the cultures and people groups you identified in your personal E-Scale diagram?

- What specific steps could you take to learn more about one of those people groups, to develop empathy for them, and to gain an appreciation and an understanding of them?

- In what ways can the use of an E-Scale to identify cultural distance be harmful?

- In what ways can this exercise be beneficial? For what purpose should it be used?

Reading

Have students read chapter 11 in preparation for the next lesson.

Looking Ahead

Continue to work with students on completion of the cross-cultural research project assigned in the previous lesson.

Further Study

Create International. 2006. *Global purpose*. DVD. http://www.createinternational. com/ (a summary of many missio Dei themes on this well-produced twenty-minute video; the full-length video for purchase and a preview sample also available at this website; and a number of podcasts focusing on various cultures and Christian mission available at http://createit.podomatic.com/).

DC Talk and the Voice of the Martyrs. 1999. *Jesus freaks: Stories of those who stood for Jesus; The ultimate Jesus freaks.* Tulsa, OK: Albury Publishing.

Winter, Ralph D. 1999. The new Macedonia: A revolutionary new era in mission begins. In *Perspectives on the world Christian movement: A reader*, ed. Ralph D. Winter and Steven C. Hawthorne, 339–53. 3rd ed. Pasadena, CA: William Carey Library.

Lesson 24 # Incarnational Living

Big Idea

God's people must learn to connect incarnationally with others in significant cross-cultural relationships.

Key Concepts

- Incarnational living emphasizes living out the example of Christ in any and all situations and contexts.

- Significant cross-cultural relationships can be challenging to our way of thinking and our way of life.

- We must learn to connect in significant relationships with others. This requires being both intentional about it and yielded to the Holy Spirit.

Reflective Questions

- What does Paulson's experience demonstrate to you regarding the difference between studying about cross-cultural ministry and really living it out? (SE p. 165)

- Do you agree with Paulson's perspective? How does it differ from your own way of thinking? How does it compare with Jesus' life and ministry? (SE p. 165)

- Explain how well the interaction described by Paulson demonstrates the idea of incarnational living. (SE p. 165)

Teacher's Heart

Following Christ can shake us down to the core, and it probably has many times. I find that I am sometimes challenged to reconsider some of the most basic and deeply seated assumptions I hold, needing to reexamine them in light of God's Word rather than my cultural views. Today's reading may have stirred such feelings in you or your students. Some of the things Elliot Paulson (2003) had to say in his article "Between a Rock and a Hard Place" may have put you on the defensive; perhaps you would accuse him of being unpatriotic or of being timid in proclaiming his faith. But the piece is significant precisely because it calls to light so many challenges that await us when we seek to live incarnationally before the whole world—particularly in those parts of the world that seem tremendously foreign to our own cultural lens. As we have noted in previous chapters, it is very difficult to recognize our own ethnocentrism or to rise above it. Pray that God would focus your thoughts today on the distinctives of following Christ's example of mission and love to all people. Pray for a heart that sees and loves all people of the world as God sees and loves them—especially for those people we might consider our enemies.

Teacher's Preparation

Some of your students may have harsh or even closed-off reactions to reading the article "Between a Rock and a Hard Place" in chapter 11. Be sensitive to this possibility, but remember, the focus of this lesson is not to debate the correctness of

98   Missio Dei: Joining God on the Adventure of a Lifetime

Paulson's actions or attitudes based on our personal standards. Also, try to avoid debates about the war in Iraq, U.S. policy in the Middle East, and similar topics. Focus should be maintained on the cross-cultural experience and the difficulties in communicating with someone from a culture that misunderstands yours. Ultimately we are called to live out the love of Christ regardless of the circumstances or the reception.

Focus the lesson on developing wider vision that encompasses kingdom values rather than our own specific cultural values. Living on mission with God often calls us to some tricky places, and our own ethnocentrism can be difficult to overcome. Paulson is a veteran of two decades of living and working in the Middle East and, as his writing indicates, is no stranger to the culture. This piece demonstrates the value of understanding the cultural context in which you are communicating, especially if it is significantly different from your home culture.

Before discussing the article in any depth though, make sure your students understand the basic concept of living incarnationally, which is another way of talking about living missionally, or living on mission with God. Jesus came as one of us, and He lived His earthly life as part of His Father's mission. Believers are sent on mission just as He was. John 20:21–22 reminds us of this: "Again Jesus said, 'Peace be with you! As the Father has sent me, I am sending you.' And with that he breathed on them and said, 'Receive the Holy Spirit.'" Notice in this passage both a commissioning and an equipping. Jesus *sent* His disciples, and He *equipped* them with the Holy Spirit. We cannot be on mission with God without utter dependence on His leading and His Spirit. This is a key point to emphasize with your students, and it's one that we will look at again in the next lesson.

Living incarnationally is, simply put, living out the example of Christ in any and all situations and contexts. It is about living out the kingdom of God (recall the teaching in chapter 4). By its very nature, living on mission with God is about *others* rather than *self*. Pastor and teacher Michael C. Voigts notes that "our dynamic relationship with Christ is *for those who do not yet have this relationship*."[1] Underscoring this idea are two key points from chapter 11: that of moving into the neighborhood and that of being intentional about seeking people out rather than waiting for them to come to you (see SE pp. 145–46). The first portion of the lesson is devoted to unpacking the idea of living incarnationally. During this, you will wish to review the four aspects Michael Frost introduces (2006, 55; SE p. 146) and to give students time to read and reflect on the passages found in **JE 31 Kingdom Culture**.

The second portion of the lesson deals with discussing the anecdote Elliot Paulson wrote about his encounter with a Middle Eastern taxi driver (2003; SE pp. 147–51). In order for students to better see the big picture of this story, help them understand the perspective from which Paulson views the conversation. One way to do this is to examine the encounter through the lens of Frost's four aspects of living incarnationally (2006, 55) and the Bible passages found in **JE 31**. One thing that is clear is that Paulson had indeed *moved into the neighborhood*. He had gone to the people and had committed time and effort to understanding them during his many years as a resident of the Middle East. He *actively shared in their lives*, and he *was sensitive to their fears, frustrations, and afflictions*. Too, Paulson *knew the language and thought forms* of his host culture. He spoke to the taxi driver in terms of places and references the taxi driver knew and understood (like the reference Paulson made to his own nose as an indication that he was from Anchovy Province).

Word Play	
living incarnationally	living out the example of Christ in any and all situations and contexts; living out the kingdom of God; living missionally, or living as sent on mission and as equipped by the Holy Spirit

He knew to anticipate the feelings of anxiety, "other-ness," and perhaps hostility that his American heritage would bring to the mind of his Arab companion. He also knew that to describe himself as a "follower of Jesus the Messiah" rather than as a "Christian" is a way to describe the same thing without bringing the instant skepticism and hostility that the label *Christian* brings to the mind of a Muslim. Finally, you get a sensing that Paulson was confident that this ordinary taxi ride conversation could have a kingdom meaning. Did he win the taxi driver to Christ? He doesn't say, but probably not. Did he build some bridges or shatter stereotypes of Christianity for this one man? Yes. Did he offer a loving relationship to the driver? Yes, as indicated by the affectionate words exchanged as he exits the taxi.

Paulson's story does show the need to "die" to being primarily identified by an earthly cultural identity in favor of rising to the higher standards of God's kingdom life. Remember some of the distinctives of kingdom life discussed in chapter 4 (from the "Teacher's Preparation" section of lesson 11): The kingdom of God is the presence and person of Jesus Christ. God has all authority and deserves our allegiance. The kingdom "is a realm of spiritual blessing into which we may enter today" (Ladd 1959). Without living as though Christ is King of our lives, we are missing the invitation to participate more deeply and fully in the adventure God has for us. These distinctives are at the heart of incarnational living—living out the example of Christ in any and all situations and contexts.

Objectives

- Students will summarize what it means to live incarnationally.

- Students will examine Bible teaching on what it means to follow Christ and live as His disciple.

- Students will evaluate the difficulties of cross-cultural communication.

Unpacking

Living Incarnationally (20–25 minutes)

Using the information from the "Teacher's Preparation" section, discuss briefly what it means to live incarnationally. Students may have their own ideas to add, especially based on their activities from lessons 20 and 21. You may also want to review and discuss Frost's four aspects of incarnational living from SE page 146. Finally, give students time to read through **JE 31 Kingdom Culture**, which presents some passages for study and reflection.

Living Between a Rock and a Hard Place (15–20 minutes)

Lead a discussion with your students about the conversation between Elliot Paulson and his taxi driver. Use **JE 31** and material from the "Teacher's Preparation" section to guide the conversation.

Reflection (10 minutes)

Assign **JE 32 "Between a Rock and a Hard Place" Response**, choosing one or more of the following prompts:

- In your opinion, was Paulson guilty of not being a good American? Why or why not?

- How did Paulson live incarnationally in his interaction with this taxi driver?

- Which Bible passage from the journal entry on kingdom culture (**JE 31**) stands out to you most? Why?

What's Next

Have students read chapter 12 in preparation for the next lesson.

Looking Ahead

If students are still working on the cross-cultural research project from lesson 22, check on their progress and schedule any remaining deadlines.

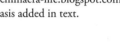

NOTE

1. Michael C. Voigts, "The Incarnational Life, Part 2," Chimaera Life, comment posted April 30, 2006, http://chimaera-life.blogspot.com/2006/04/incarnational-life-part-2.html (accessed October 14, 2007); emphasis added in text.

Evaluating Case Studies

Big Idea

God's people must learn to connect incarnationally with others in significant cross-cultural relationships.

Key Concepts

- Incarnational living emphasizes living out the example of Christ in any and all situations and contexts.

- Significant cross-cultural relationships can be challenging to our way of thinking and our way of life.

- We must learn to connect in significant relationships with others. This requires being both intentional about it and yielded to the Holy Spirit.

Reflective Questions

- In what ways do you encounter similar tricky situations while living out your faith in your own context? Do you have peers who misunderstand your choices? (SE p. 166)

- Is your relationship with God deep enough to help you weather a difficult encounter with a nonbeliever? What strength do you draw on at such a time? (SE p. 166)

Teacher's Heart

Oh, for eyes to see how big the heart of God really is! We are often so limited in our vision. One of the beautiful aspects of the Body of Christ is that in Christ unity is possible within such diversity. Nowhere is that fact more precious than in the cross-cultural ministry setting. As students work through the ambiguity of some case studies today, pray that their hearts will begin to beat with the bigness of God. Living on mission with Him is a dynamic adventure, one that Dwight J. Friesen, an associate professor at Mars Hill Graduate School, reminds us "will always find unique expression through each follower of Christ and each cluster of Christ-followers—so much so that one person incarnating Christ out of his or her uniqueness may appear to be in direct conflict with another person incarnating Christ out of his or her uniqueness. But fear not, God is big enough to handle such occasional differences."[1] You may see some of those differences in the discussions in your classroom during this lesson. Pray that God may be glorified through a spirit of unity despite a diversity of opinions and viewpoints today.

Teacher's Preparation

One of the undergirding themes of missio Dei is the fact that the relationship between a believer and Christ is the essential starting point of any endeavor. Perhaps that is nowhere more evident than in today's lesson. Any strategy, any decision of action, must be made with God's leading. The cornerstone of Christian life is Christ. Christ is what makes mission Christian. We truly cannot do things for God; we are to join what He is already doing. Vibrant relationship is essential. If you need to underscore this point, you may wish to begin this lesson by reminding students of the study they completed in chapter 5 regarding the need to abide in Christ. Also, John 14:16–17, 23–27; 15:26–27; and 16:7–15 are good reminders of the Holy Spirit's role in our lives. Dwight Friesen writes, "When Christ is incarnated through you and me, we will be looking for ways to empty ourselves in the service of the Father by serving others as the Holy Spirit guides us. We become active participants in a divine dance through which all of creation is being reconciled to Christ."[2]

Today's lesson concerns the case studies presented in chapter 12. There are two facets to the lesson: The first is a small-group discussion of one or more specific case studies, during which the group ultimately comes to a conclusion regarding what action should be taken. The second is a class presentation, in which each group presents a summary of their discussion and conclusions. You may want to spread this lesson out over two days to give adequate time for discussion and reflection on the complexities of the case studies or to allow time for each group to tackle more than one case study.

Below are specific talking points for each case study. To help guide discussion and keep it on track, each group should have a copy of **BLM 12.1 Case Study Talking Points** and should use the talking points that apply to its case study. Of course, you will want to circulate throughout the room and observe the discussions, helping keep things focused. Remind students that throughout their discussion they should keep the tone of the conversation cordial and open-minded rather than combative. There are no simple cut-and-dried answers to these case studies, though there may appear to be on the surface. You might share with your students the quotation by Dwight Friesen in the "Teacher's Heart" material. Though students are to wrestle with these issues, the point of the lesson isn't as much arriving at the "right" solution as it is recognizing the need to trust God in the face of ambiguity.

As a follow-up to the case studies, have students reflect on some of the shorter vignettes presented in **JE 34 Imagine This**. Students should journal their responses and provide their own difficult challenge based on situations they are aware of in their own lives or community. Students may have trouble identifying with the difficult choices faced by believers in other cultures, or they may object if they can't think of scenarios that are quite as dramatic as those in this exercise. Reassure them that regardless of the details of difficult choices, God is interested in equipping His people to stand firm in their faith and to respond in Christian love to whatever challenges they face.

Talking Points for Case Study 1: Food Offered to Idols (Hiebert and Hiebert 1987, 38–39; SE p. 154)

- What is the central choice Rajasekaran faces in this situation? (The central choice is whether to accept food sacrificed to idols so as not to offend his friend Mani or not to compromise his own faith by accepting such food.)

- How would accepting the food compromise Rajasekaran's faith? Or would it? (Answers will vary, but they may include reference to the Ten Commandments or to Paul's instructions in 1 Corinthians 8.)

- In terms of an ongoing relationship with Mani, what are the dangers if Rajasekaran refuses to accept the food? What opportunities for discussion of Christianity might occur in refusing to accept the food? (Answers will vary.)

- If you were Mani, how would you feel if Rajasekaran rejected your offer? if he accepted it? (Answers will vary.)

- If you were Rajasekaran and you did accept the food, what would you feel you needed to say to Mani about your Christian faith? How would accepting the food affect your relationship with God? (Answers will vary depending on each student's experience.)

- What other factors are there to consider? Is it possible that the actions of Rajasekaran might have repercussions in terms of his job at a Christian magazine? If he accepted the food, would others besides those present ever find out? (Answers will vary.)

Talking Points for Case Study 2: Honor Your Mother and Father (Egeler 2000; SE p. 155)

- What is the central choice Suji has to make? (Suji must decide whether to bow down to shrines of ancestor worship or to refuse to bow down to an idol—just as Shadrach, Meshach, and Abednego refused to do—and thus dishonor her parents.)

- What are the possible repercussions if she refuses to bow down to images of her ancestors? Obviously in Suji's culture, honoring one's elders is highly valued. What might the act of dishonoring her parents mean in terms of the Christian witness Suji has to them? (Answers will vary.)

- What guide do you use when faced with a choice that seems to require you to break at least one of God's commandments no matter what choice you make—in this case, having no idols before God or honoring your father and mother? What does the New Testament say about these two issues? (Answers will vary depending on each student's experience.)

- Does the fact that Suji is a relatively new believer change the situation in any way? What could "bowing down before an idol" mean to Suji's developing faith? (Answers will vary.)

Talking Points for Case Study 3: To Bribe or Not to Bribe? (Hiebert and Hiebert 1987, 136–37; SE pp. 156–57)

- What is the central conflict for Pastor Luke? (Pastor Luke has to decide whether he's going to pay a bribe to ensure the coming of another pastor who will help serve his church.)

- The church elders have given Pastor Luke permission to pay the "gift," or bribe, that will ensure a visa for Reverend John, and they have even encouraged him to do so. What might be the personal consequences for Pastor Luke if he doesn't pay the money to the immigration official? What might happen to Pastor Luke's church? (Answers will vary.)

- Pastor Luke has firm convictions about not participating in bribery. What might be the outcome if he doesn't pay the bribe? Is it possible for God to provide a way for Reverend John's visa to be granted despite the circumstances? What does the Bible say about bribery? about having faith in difficult circumstances? (Answers will vary.)

Objectives

- Students will discuss and evaluate the different facets of several cross-cultural ministry case studies.

- Students will reflect on the complexities of such situations and relate these case studies to their own lives as much as they can.

- Students will consider how they would respond to the scenarios in several challenging vignettes, and they will create an example of a challenging situation that might arise in living out their own faith.

Unpacking

Case Studies (30–45 minutes)

Divide the class into several small groups. Assign each group a specific case study to discuss and evaluate. Give each group the talking points in **BLM 12.1 Case Study Talking Points** that apply to its specific case. Encourage students to discuss the different points and to come to some consensus on what should be done. They should use as much Bible evidence as possible to support their assertions. After groups have had adequate time to discuss and debate their case studies, each group should present to the class a summary of the discussion and the group's ultimate conclusions.

Reflection (10–15 minutes)

Discuss the following questions as a class or assign reflective writing **JE 33 Think About These Things**, which covers them:

- Are there situations in your life that in some way parallel the complexities and uncertainties presented by these case studies? How are you handling them?

- What have you learned about the importance of abiding in Christ and depending on the Holy Spirit to effectively live on mission with God?

- What have you learned about the complexity of cross-cultural relationships from the material in this unit?

What's Next

Journal Entry

Direct students to **JE 34 Imagine This**, which contains several cross-cultural vignettes based on difficult ministry circumstances that pose a choice. Either in class or as a homework assignment, students should respond to each vignette and then provide their own example of similar difficult situations they might face while living out their faith in their own cultural contexts.

Reading

Have students read chapter 13 in preparation for the next lesson.

Looking Ahead

If students are still working on the cross-cultural research project from lesson 22, check on their progress and remind students of the deadline for turning in their project. The next lesson is the final lesson for the Culture Unit.

☙

NOTES

1. Dwight J. Friesen, "Living Incarnationally," *Views from the Edge*, December 2005, http://www.mhgs.edu/Files/Documents/VFE-1-0/Living-Incarnationally (accessed May 12, 2009).
2. Ibid.

Lesson 26 · Review: The Lens of Culture

Teacher's Heart

You've heard the expression "You can't see the forest for the trees"? As you review with your students the concepts introduced in this unit, be aware of the dangers of missing the forest by looking too hard at the trees. In a unit review, the tendency is to focus on the details of key terms and ideas in preparation for a formal assessment but, in the process, miss out on the bigger picture—the heart God has for all people of the world, and our role in joining His mission of relationship with them. As you review the new factual information taught in this unit, don't forget to review the heart lessons God is seeking to instill in your life and in the lives of your students. Since each unit of this course builds on the previous ones, take the time in coming days to remember and discuss the cultural and biblical lenses through which we have learned to view this mission of God. The reminder God gave the Israelites concerning His commands and teachings applies to us as well: "Impress them on your children. Talk about them when you sit at home and when you walk along the road, when you lie down and when you get up" (Deuteronomy 6:7). Similarly, don't leave the wider cultural and biblical lenses behind as you move into the History Unit; continue to talk about these matters and about ways to integrate heart truths from lessons 1 through 25 into your lives.

Teacher's Preparation

Chapter 13 should serve as a guide for discussing the highlights from the chapters in this unit. You should also review lesson plans and any notes you may have taken from teaching the materials in previous lessons to revisit issues that need additional review or clarification before formal end-of-unit assessments. You may wish to compile review facts to use as the basis for an in-class review game to prepare for a written unit exam.

Throughout chapter 13, questions from the material in the other Culture Unit chapters are printed as sidebars titled "What Difference Does It Make?" These questions, which can provide a good review of key application points from each chapter, may also serve as a basis for an alternative assessment. If your class participated in one of the optional cross-cultural learning experiences suggested at the beginning of the unit, that experience might provide the basis for an alternative assessment as well.

Word Play	
Below is a list of the unit's key terms and the chapter in which further discussion of them can be found:	
cultural distance	a term that refers to cultural and worldview factors that may create difficulty in communication between two people groups regardless of other proximity (chap. 10)
culture	"a peoples' way of life, their design for living, their way of coping with their biological, physical, and social environment" (Kraft 1998, 385; chap. 7)
E-Scale	a form of measurement used to describe the varying levels of cultural distance ranging from no cultural distance (E-0) to extreme cultural distance (E-3) (chap. 10)
ethnocentrism	the attitude that stems from the belief that one's own group is superior to other groups, and therefore the worldview and actions of one's own group are also superior to those of others (chap. 8)
Incarnation	the event in which God became man in the person of Jesus of Nazareth (chap. 9)
living incarnationally	living out the example of Christ in any and all situations and contexts; living out the kingdom of God; living missionally, or living as sent on mission and as equipped by the Holy Spirit (chap. 11)
people blindness	the phenomenon of not recognizing different peoples within countries or geographical boundaries (chap. 10)
people group	a group that shares the same ethnicity and language and a common self-identity; a group in which members can communicate well without barriers of understanding or acceptance; a group whose members think of themselves as "us" and those outside their group as "them" (chap. 10)
worldview	"included in culture as the deepest level presuppositions upon which people base their lives" (Kraft 1998, 385; chap. 7)

Objectives

- Students will review through discussion concepts from chapters 7 through 13 in preparation for a unit assessment.

- Students will complete other assessment activities.

- Students will write essays regarding the application of truths from chapters 1 through 13 to their lives.

Unpacking

Review Discussion (15–20 minutes)

Guide a class discussion on chapter 13, using the What Difference Does It Make? questions in chapter 13 as a basis for discussion.

Looking Outside (15 minutes)

Have students share briefly what they learned following the completion of the cross-cultural research project. How did this experience of *looking outside* broaden their understanding of different cultures and people?

Reaction and Response (10–15 minutes)

Invite students to share reactions to any cross-cultural experiences (optional enrichment activities or other assignments designed to broaden their horizons culturally) completed during this unit. Have them consider the following questions:

• What is the most significant concept you learned from this unit of study?

• What is the most difficult for you to understand?

• How do you see your daily life being affected by the lessons you have learned?

Formal Assessment

Formal assessment could be administered by using one or more of the following:

• Unit 2 exam

• Looking Outside: A Cross-Cultural Research Project

• A sampling of What Difference Does it Make? questions (found on SE pp. 160–63 and 165–66) for an essay test

What's Next

Have students read chapter 14 in preparation for the next lesson.

History Unit

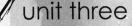

unit three

History Unit Introduction

Student Edition Introduction

In this unit, we will continue to trace the story begun in Genesis 1—the remarkable story of God's mission. Think of this as a travelogue about journeying with God, a travelogue that contains the story of those who have already taken the trip. We will see how God has invited people to participate with Him all along. As we explore the circumstances and people He has used to further His work, we will take a deeper look at how He works and how people are a part of His plans. As you spend time in this travelogue, take note of what it has to offer you: information about points of interest, experiences you don't want to miss, pitfalls you'll want to avoid, and other hints you can glean about how your journey with God can be the best travel possible.

Big Ideas

- God initiates and advances His purpose throughout human history.

- History reveals the challenges, successes, and shortcomings that people throughout history have experienced as they have participated with God in completing His purpose.

- God's redemptive purpose will come to an ultimate completion in human history.

Memory Verses

Ephesians 2:10
For we are God's workmanship, created in Christ Jesus to do good works, which God prepared in advance for us to do.

Psalm 90:1–2
Lord, you have been our dwelling place throughout all generations. Before the mountains were born or you brought forth the earth and the world, from everlasting to everlasting you are God.

Psalm 105:1–8
Give thanks to the Lord, call on his name; make known among the nations what he has done. Sing to him, sing praise to him; tell of all his wonderful acts. Glory in his holy name; let the hearts of those who seek the Lord rejoice. Look to the Lord and his strength; seek his face always. Remember the wonders he has done, his miracles, and the judgments he pronounced, O descendants of Abraham his servant, O sons of Jacob, his chosen ones. He is the Lord our God; his judgments are in all the earth. He remembers his covenant forever, the word he commanded, for a thousand generations.

Acts 1:8
But you will receive power when the Holy Spirit comes on you; and you will be my witnesses in Jerusalem, and in all Judea and Samaria, and to the ends of the earth.

Isaiah 46:9–11

Remember the former things, those of long ago; I am God, and there is no other; I am God, and there is none like me. I make known the end from the beginning, from ancient times, what is still to come. I say: My purpose will stand, and I will do all that I please. From the east I summon a bird of prey; from a far-off land, a man to fulfill my purpose. What I have said, that will I bring about; what I have planned, that will I do.

Web Resources

Link to more resources in our community at www.missiodei-thejourney.com.

God's Purpose Advancing Throughout History

Big Idea

God initiates and advances His purpose throughout human history.

Key Concepts

• Mission is God's. God is at work; we join Him in that work of advancing His purpose.

• The invitation God gives us to join His mission is not limited by time, location, or culture.

• History shows that, even though humankind is fallible in carrying out God's mission, God is sovereign in carrying out His ultimate plan.

Reflective Questions

• Do you believe that God continues to work through people as He did in the Bible to accomplish His plans? If not, then why not? Do you see Him directly initiating and advancing His purpose in the world around you? If so, in what ways? (SE p. 234)

• One extreme that is related to the invitation God gives to join His mission is to ignore the invitation; another extreme is to run ahead of God and "do things for Him" without His leading or equipping. Do you tend toward one of these extremes in your relationship with Him? What are some examples? (SE p. 234)

• What roles do faith and doubt play in your own understanding of how God is at work in your life and in the world around you? Like Abraham, do you ever feel as though you need to "help God out" with His plans? Do you find it difficult to wait on God's timing and leading in your life? (SE p. 234)

Teacher's Heart

Twila Paris sings a song called "God Is in Control" (CD titled *Beyond a Dream*, Sparrow Records, 1994). Some of the lyrics speak of a bottom line that is drawn across the ages of history. But then they say, "Culture can make its plan. Oh, but the line never changes." Wow! The bottom line of history never changes. God's purpose will stand, and God is in control—even today. Sometimes that is hard to see; it is perhaps even harder for your students to believe. The tension between faith and doubt that every Christ-follower experiences at some time or another is one that has existed since the Garden of Eden. But God is in control; the story is ultimately His story. He asks us to participate in His mission. He initiates and advances His purpose. When I was younger, there was a note on my parents' refrigerator that read, "Do not feel personally, irrevocably, totally responsible for everything. That's my job. Love, God" (Stewart 1995). I think of that reminder often. What a relief to know that we don't have to engineer anything for God or guess how best to serve Him. He is working, and He invites us to join Him. Pray for wisdom to understand how best, in the coming unit, to communicate this truth to your students.

Teacher's Preparation

Today's lesson has two general components: to help students (1) identify some general characteristics of the way God directs His work through us, and (2) begin to assess their own perspective on how God works in today's world. We see some of the characteristics of the first component being identified in chapter 14—on SE page 172 through the example of Moses and on SE pages 172–73 through the emphasis on the role of the Holy Spirit. The first activity of this lesson deals with the process God uses to initiate and advance His purpose and with the role our response plays. These topics point to a theme in this lesson—that of the tension between faith and doubt. Students may have questions about the relationship between our obedience to God and His desire to use each of us. The blackline master on Abraham that is part of this lesson shows that God is willing to use us, bless us, and continue fulfilling His promises to us even when we are not fully faithful to Him. As Ephesians 2:3–5 reminds us, though we were objects of God's wrath, God in His mercy made us alive with Christ. His grace toward us even in our failings is beyond measure. And this is the point to which your students should be directed as they seek to understand the relationship between the leading of God and our participation in His mission.

When it doesn't appear that God is leading and working, people are tempted to run ahead of God to bring about the work *for Him* that seems to make sense, just as Abraham did in *helping* bring about the promise of an heir (see SE p. 173). The first activity in this lesson gives students the opportunity to reflect on the difference between following the leading of God to participate in His work and our all-too-human instinct to do something for God and take matters into our own hands. Helping students develop a level of intimacy with God that includes a relationship of trust and faith in His leading is an ultimate objective of this course, an objective that will be developed more fully in the final unit.

The next activity concerns the role of the Holy Spirit in leading and equipping people to participate in the mission of God. This activity is by no means a comprehensive study of the third person of the Trinity, nor is it intended to be. The purpose is to point out that God continues even today to be present and to lead in the lives of His followers through the Spirit. Students may want additional information and discussion on this topic. There are some resources mentioned in the "Extra Mile" section that you might want to recommend to students or consult as you prepare this lesson.

Regarding the second component, which is to help students begin to assess their individual perspective on how God works in today's world, some may find it hard to see that God is still in the business of moving His purpose forward today. It is easy to start thinking that God has ceased to work through His people in the ways we see described in the Bible. But the Big Idea of this chapter is that God initiates and advances His purpose *throughout human history*—right up to the present moment. As you hear students discussing and evaluating their perspective of God's involvement in today's world, you will begin to see what perceptions they have that may be obscuring the truth that God's mission continues to unfold today.

Think of this lesson as one that is building a foundation on which to understand the remainder of this unit on God's mission going forward throughout history. In the student edition chapters, students will take a tour through five different historical eras extending from the resurrection of Christ through the dawn of the twenty-first century. The bottom line of this unit is that God has been and continues to be active, leading His mission of relationship, redemption, and reconciliation to this day; and that His purpose will ultimately be fulfilled. As your students develop a perspective of how God has worked throughout history, help them see themselves as a part of that ongoing story.

Objectives

- Students will compare the results of Abraham's responses to God, responses of both faith and doubt. They will also evaluate their own responses of faith and doubt.
- Students will identify and describe some characteristics of the ways God initiates and advances His purpose.
- Students will reflect on and discuss their attitudes about how God is actively leading His mission in the world today.

Unpacking

How God Initiates and Advances (15–20 minutes)

Direct students to SE page 172 and read together the excerpt about Moses from Henry T. Blackaby and Claude V. King's book *Experiencing God* (1994). Point out the following pattern: God initiates by giving an assignment. He then advances His plan by equipping a person to complete it. We are invited to participate in His work. The more we obey and trust in the leading of God, the more fully we can participate in His purpose.

Next, call attention to the section of chapter 14 that discusses Abraham's experiences of faith and doubt (SE p. 173). Then direct students to complete **BLM 14.1 Abraham: A Man of Faith and Doubt**, which allows them to compare the responses Abraham had to God's different plans for him (see also answer key **BLM 14.1K**).

The Leading of the Holy Spirit (10–15 minutes)

Direct your students' attention to SE pages 172–73 and the work of the Holy Spirit in the believer. Emphasize the role of God the Spirit to equip and work through us to reveal and carry out God's purpose. Help the students see that this type of activity is ongoing, not limited to a specific time in history, that this is how God continues to initiate, advance, and equip His followers today. Then read and discuss each of the following Bible passages as a class, drawing out the points listed in the second column:

Bible Passage	The Holy Spirit's Work
John 14:15–17	The Holy Spirit is our counselor. The Holy Spirit is the Spirit of truth. The Holy Spirit lives in Christ's followers.
John 14:26	The Holy Spirit is a teacher.
John 16:13–15	The Holy Spirit will guide us into all truth.
Luke 12:11–12 (also Mark 13:11)	The Holy Spirit will teach us what to say in different circumstances.

Conclude that God is the one who not only invites us to participate in His work, but also equips us through the Spirit who lives in us. This equipping is the means through which He carries out His purpose through people. Blackaby and King note the way God worked through His people in the Bible: "The Spirit manifested His presence by equipping each individual to function where God had assigned him. The results reflected God's activity" (1994, 75; SE p. 172). God still works through His people in this same manner today.

Reflection and Discussion (10–15 minutes)

Write the following questions on the board and give students time to write answers to them:

- Do you believe that God still works through people today the way He did in the Bible? Support your answer with examples.

- After comparing Abraham's responses to God (involving both faith and doubt) examine areas in your own life in which you have experienced this same tension.

- What difference would it make in your life if you were to recognize that God is at work in the world around you today?

Let students discuss their answers in small groups. As a means of informal evaluation, circulate around the room to listen to their discussions.

If Time Activity

Assign reflective writing **JE 35 Proverbs 19:21** on the following prompt:

- Proverbs 19:21 says, "Many are the plans in a man's heart, but it is the Lord's purpose that prevails." What does this passage mean?

- What does it say about the relationship between our plans and God's plans?

Extra Mile

For a more in-depth study of the ways in which God invites and equips us to participate in His purpose, students may wish to read the following books:

Blackaby, Henry, Richard Blackaby, and Claude King. 2007. *Experiencing God: Knowing and doing the will of God*. Rev. exp. ed. Nashville, TN: LifeWay Christian Resources (a Bible study workbook).
Willard, Dallas. 1999. *Hearing God: Developing a conversational relationship with God*. Downers Grove, IL: InterVarsity Press.

What's Next

Reading

No additional reading of student text is required before you present lesson 28, but you might want to assign the reading of chapter 15 to students now so that they will have it completed by the time you teach lesson 29.

Reflection

If you didn't have time in class for **JE 35**, the reflective writing on Proverbs 19:21, you may wish to assign it as homework.

Looking Ahead

The next lesson introduces a history portfolio project (Looking Back: A Review of History) for the unit. The project will extend through study of the next five chapters of the student textbook. Even though the material provides several resources, you may wish to prepare additional materials to help introduce this project and its parameters to your class.

Introduction to the Era Chapters

Big Idea

History reveals the challenges, successes, and shortcomings that people throughout history have experienced as they have participated with God in completing His purpose.

Key Concepts

- Studying history allows us to see the big picture of how God's story has continued throughout time.
- Reflecting on how God has allowed other people to participate in His mission can help us learn about our own participation in God's purpose.

Reflective Questions

- What do you think the story of others' participation in God's purpose throughout time can teach you about your own journey with God? (SE p. 233)
- Do you perceive God as being a present-day actor in the events of today? Why or why not? (SE p. 233)

Teacher's Heart

I rejoice that God is faithful to give us all that we need to accomplish the tasks He has set before us. Perhaps by this point in the school year you are feeling over-whelmed by the demands of your teaching load, lesson preparation, or students' needs. Take heart! Each of us has been invited by God to participate in His mission in some way, and He always equips generously and completely. Read Paul's encouragement: "I am so pleased that you have continued on in this with us, believing and proclaiming God's Message, from the day you heard it right up to the present. There has never been the slightest doubt in my mind that the God who started this great work in you would keep at it and bring it to a flourishing finish on the very day Christ Jesus appears" (Philippians 1:5–6, The Message). Throughout history, God has been enabling His people to participate in His purpose. And He is still at it today. May you be blessed by that knowledge as you participate with Him.

Teacher's Preparation

Winston Churchill, among several others, is credited with the saying "History is written by the victors." Certainly any recounting of historical events is influenced by the lens of the person doing the telling. The historical survey presented in chapters 15–19 is no exception. The primary goal of the next five chapters in the student text is captured in the Big Idea for this lesson: History reveals the challenges, successes, and shortcomings that people throughout history have experienced as they have participated with God in completing His purpose. These chapters are not written as a comprehensive and detailed account of every aspect of the history of the church or the spread of Christianity. They are, rather, a two-thousand-year overview of history that is meant to focus our attention on the ongoing story of God's mission. These chapters are written in a way that assumes a basic knowledge of world history. To assist you in lesson preparation, a list of events, people, and ideas that are key to each era is included as a sidebar to the "Teacher's Preparation" section in the next five lessons. You may want to consult resources such as encyclopedias, world history textbooks, and online history sites—several of which are listed in the "Further Study" section. Of course, you and your students may wish to pursue additional details about certain periods of time or particular historical events. Feel free to do this, but remember that the main focus of your study should be on God's ongoing activity in history and on the roles that people have been invited to play in fulfilling God's purpose.

The division of information into the particular "eras" found in the coming chapters is to some degree arbitrary. We have followed the lead of scholars such as Hans Kung and David Bosch, who divide Christian history into eras in the manner found in chapters 15–19. Missiologist Stan Nussbaum notes that "each period has a 'general frame of reference' or paradigm which to a large extent molds the 'faith, experiences, and thought processes' of everyone living in that time" (2005, 45). Thus, it is reasonable to speak of those time periods as eras that have some common characteristics. As one era flows into another, events and circumstances influence the way the next generation thinks and acts. And these are the currents we have sought to capture in the coming chapters, since they show how God is at work in different times and through different circumstances.

This lesson is designed to assist you in preparing your students for studying and reflecting on God's story as it has played out since the time of Christ's earthly ministry. Because there is a tremendous amount of information packed into the next five chapters, today's lesson offers strategies and organizational tools that can help your students hook on to Key Concepts presented in this unit. You can pick and choose among these options. Some of these tools you introduce to your students today can be incorporated into the culminating history portfolio project described in the "Unpacking" section. Several themes are present throughout the

story of God's mission over the past two thousand years, and each chapter touches on most, if not all, of them. The theme chart in this "Teacher's Preparation" section offers a summary. The first two columns list and describe the themes. The third column lists the corresponding blackline masters. This information will be helpful for students to have before they read the chapters, especially if they will be using the blackline masters designed for the purpose of completing the portfolio project.

In addition to the major themes listed in the theme chart, there are several subthemes that run through chapters 15–19: the role that experiencing suffering and difficult circumstances plays in the fulfillment of God's mission, the role of the Holy Spirit in leading God's work, and the way in which Christ's incarnational model of mission emerges in different ways in some eras. Of course, something that can be highlighted throughout all the coming chapters is the reality that God allows us to participate with Him despite our imperfections—a theme introduced in the previous lesson.

During the first part of today's lesson, you will be directed to present the above information about themes so that your students can take notes on it as part of their history portfolio project. To enhance your understanding, you may wish to read SE chapter 20, which is an overview of the entire History Unit. Throughout this unit, remind your students that the goal is to keep their eyes on the *big picture*—the story of God at work. Helping your students focus on the larger themes will enhance their understanding of what the past can teach them as they interact with God today. As we continue working toward the culminating unit of this course, look for every opportunity to encourage students to make a personal application of the information they study.

The second portion of this lesson is devoted to introducing students to some reading strategies and an organizational tool that can assist them in studying chapters 15–19. A prereading and postreading tool students can use is described in **BLM 14.2 K-W-L Reading Organizer**. You may also want to instruct students to list any questions they have about each chapter as they read it. Then plan to provide time to discuss their questions in class. Finally, you may want to direct students to any one of the blackline masters that correspond to the different themes listed in the chart. Though the pages are designed to be completed for the history portfolio project, they can also serve as helpful reading guides by directing the students toward specific information.

The third activity in today's lesson allows you to give instructions about completing the history portfolio project, Looking Back: A Review of History, during the course of this unit. A basic outline of suggested portfolio requirements is included in the "Unpacking" section. You may wish to incorporate other elements into your requirements for this project as well.

Theme	Description	Corresponding Blackline Masters
The invitation God gives people to participate in His mission: who and how	In each era, God opened the door for different people to participate with Him. These people, representing every culture, range from laymen to clergy, from slaves to kings. Their means of participation ranges from formal to informal, including a range of "mission strategies."	Era Time Lines BLMs 15.1, 16.1, 17.1, 18.1, 19.1 Who, What, When, Where, How BLMs 15.2, 16.2, 17.2, 18.2, 19.2
Circumstances that provided opportunities for mission	In each era, God worked through the different circumstances of the time to provide a means for His mission to go forward. Often the circumstances were difficult or didn't seem to immediately present themselves as suitable to furthering His mission.	Who, What, When, Where, How BLMs 15.2, 16.2, 17.2, 18.2, 19.2
The spread of Christianity	In each era, God's mission has gone forward into new geographical and cultural territory.	Who, What, When, Where, How BLMs 15.2, 16.2, 17.2, 18.2, 19.2
Decentralization or destabilization of an earthly or institutional locus	Throughout history, God has used various circumstances to disrupt the formation of one central, earthly location for Christianity. Different places in each era served as the main location from which mission sprang.	All Shook Up BLMs 15.3, 16.3, 17.3, 18.3, 19.3
Cultural transcendence of the gospel	As the gospel crosses cultural and geographical frontiers, it maintains unity with the initial message of Christ, and yet it is translatable into every cultural milieu. (You may want to reference the Culture Unit to remind students of this concept.)	All Shook Up BLMs 15.3, 16.3, 17.3, 18.3, 19.3
Challenges, successes, and shortcomings	Every era in history has been filled with challenges to those who would participate with God in His mission. In some cases, these challenges result in success; in others, shortcomings. Though each chapter avoids labeling specific successes or shortcomings in mission history, students are encouraged to discuss and evaluate each era along these lines.	Challenges, Successes, and Shortcomings BLMs 15.4, 16.4, 17.4, 18.4, 19.4

One final note related to the coming chapters is that the student journal contains People in History profiles of different people from each era. We recognize that there are many individuals who could have been profiled; those we've included are merely a sampling. You should assign the profiles as required reading alongside each chapter. Whereas the student text chapters contain a broad overview of each era in mission history, these profiles capture the essence of the era through the lives of ordinary people who lived during that period. These stories, which provide a snapshot of the challenges these people faced and the opportunities they took advantage of, are examples of the different types of people God has worked through to accomplish His mission in each era. In lesson 34, students will be assigned a project in which they will develop their own People in History profiles of someone they know.

Objectives

- Students will record the main ideas of the goals and themes of the historical survey presented in chapters 15–19.

- Students will review several techniques for enhancing and extending their understanding of chapters 15–19.

- Students will explore the various assignments of a portfolio project related to this unit.

Unpacking

Contextualizing the Coming Chapters (10–15 minutes)

Using the material from the "Teacher's Preparation" section, present information to the students on the parameters, limitations, and goals of the mission history survey they will read about in the coming five chapters. Also present information on the different themes they will encounter as they read, and explain the corresponding blackline masters they can complete as they read each chapter. Finally, introduce the People in History profiles they will be reading alongside the chapters. Notes students take during this presentation could be required as part of the history portfolio project.

Ways to Approach the Reading (10–15 minutes)

Use **BLM 14.2** to describe the K-W-L reading technique. Using the K-W-L reading organizer, students will create a K-W-L chart for each chapter as they read it. Discuss other strategies you want your students to use as they read.

Introducing the Unit Portfolio Project, Looking Back: A Review of History (10–15 minutes)

Outline the culminating history portfolio project for students, and give your expectations for what is to be maintained for each chapter and how it is to be prepared for evaluation at the end of the History Unit. Student portfolios should contain any notes taken by the students or given out by the teacher during this unit, completed copies of the blackline masters that accompany each chapter, any assigned reflective writing or research activities from this unit, and any other items you assign. In the student journal is a reflection page for each era of history, and these pages may also be included as part of the portfolio project. This project should represent the learning journey that students have been on throughout this unit. There is also a rubric provided to help you evaluate the project.

The following blackline masters accompany each of the next five chapters:

- **Era Time Line** enables students to track the progression of different events in mission history that are discussed within each chapter.

- **Who, What, When, Where, How** asks students to identify basic information about each era in mission history.

- **All Shook Up** asks students to track cultural themes in each era.

- **Challenges, Successes, and Shortcomings** allows students to evaluate mission work going forward against the backdrop of the circumstances in each era.

If Time Activity

Discuss the following quotation from Stan Nussbaum's *A Reader's Guide to "Transforming Mission"*:

> The way to cope with our cultural limitations is to become aware of them, which is tricky because they are like dirt on the back of our clothing. We cannot see them without a mirror. The mirror we need to look into is history…. If we know who Christians thought they were in other eras, we may understand better who we are today as God's people in mission. (2005, 45)

Have students use **JE 36 Coping with Cultural Limitations** to write a response to Nussbaum's quotation.

What's Next

Have students use whatever reading strategies you assign from today's lesson to read chapter 15. They should also read the People in History profiles **JE 37 James, Son of Zebedee**; **JE 38 Phoebe, Dorcas, and Lydia**; and **JE 39 Paul** in preparation for the next lesson. At the end of each profile is a list of questions for your students to think about in preparation for the next day's lesson.

Looking Ahead

If you want your students to use an organizational tool or other materials for their portfolio projects besides those provided in the course materials, prepare them in advance of when you expect your students to use them.

Further Study

BBC. http://www.bbc.co.uk/history/ (a website that includes general history information).

Best of History Web Sites. http://www.besthistorysites.net/ (a portal to many general history sites).

Bosch, David J. 1991. *Transforming mission: Paradigm shifts in theology of mission.* American Society of Missiology Series, no. 16. Maryknoll, NY: Orbis Books.

Christian Classics Ethereal Library. http://www.ccel.org/ (a searchable database containing a number of public domain documents that can be viewed free; includes the eight-volume comprehensive work *History of the Christian Church*, written in the late nineteenth century by Philip Schaff, as well as primary source documents for many periods in church history).

Coakley, John W., and Andrea Sterk, eds. 2004. *Readings in world Christian history.* Vol. 1, *Earliest Christianity to 1453.* Maryknoll, NY: Orbis Books.

History.com (The History Channel). http://www.history.com/ (a website that includes general history information).

Historyteacher.net. http://www.historyteacher.net/ (a portal to many general history sites).

Irvin, Dale T., and Scott W. Sunquist. 2001. *History of the world Christian movement.* Vol. 1, *Earliest Christianity to 1453.* Maryknoll, NY: Orbis Books.

Neill, Stephen. 1986. *A history of Christian missions.* 2nd ed. Rev. by Owen Chadwick. New York: Penguin Books.

Tickle, Phyllis. 2008. *The great emergence: How Christianity is changing and why.* Grand Rapids, MI: Baker Books.

Era One

Big Idea

History reveals the challenges, successes, and shortcomings that people throughout history have experienced as they have participated with God in completing His purpose.

Key Concepts

- Studying history allows us to see the big picture of how God's story has continued throughout time.

- Reflecting on how God has allowed other people to participate in His mission can help us learn about our own participation in God's purpose.

Reflective Questions

- What do the events of the early Church teach you about how to live on mission with God? Early believers shared their faith wherever they found themselves. Do you see among believers today the same sort of enthusiasm for missional life that the members of the early Church demonstrated? (SE p. 185)

- What characteristics of the earliest believers in Christ would you most like to see in your own life? Why? (SE p. 185)

Teacher's Heart

First Corinthians 1:27 says, "But God chose the foolish things of the world to shame the wise; God chose the weak things of the world to shame the strong." In the first century AD, a small group of men and women devoted to Jesus of Nazareth formed the basis of a fledgling "sect" of Judaism. They were a group that, against the wise and strong of the day, had no real chance of surviving the world, much less transforming it. Of course, the Lord of the universe had other ideas. He used something that appeared small or foolish to some to give birth to a global Christian movement that continues to change the course of history. Is there something "small" in your life that God is wanting to birth into something world-changing? Are there goals or dreams God has given you that seem to be against all the odds? Perhaps you feel weak, small, or insignificant. Ask God to give you His vision for your life. Trust Him to grow even your deepest weaknesses into something strong for His kingdom.

Teacher's Preparation

Students may find many of the events of this first era familiar to them because of any previous study they have had of the New Testament. These earliest years of Christianity offer a great model to us as contemporary believers; it is a time that deserves our attention and reflection. In this era we see believers living out their faith in the truest sense of community and in ways that truly transformed the social order. Sharing the gospel, as this chapter points out, was a lifestyle carried out by all believers in all circumstances—in the marketplace, in interactions with neighbors, even in the face of persecution and disbelief. Mission wasn't simply a part of believers' lives; it formed the core of their identity and influenced all spheres of their lives. This is the missional life—the essence of missio Dei—that this course seeks to inspire students to pursue.

Several contemporary writers look back to that first century to discern a model of missional life for the present day. Among them is Michael Frost, who declares our task to be "not the discovery of a new gospel, or a new Christ, or a new Bible, as some more liberal thinkers have suggested, but the rediscovery of the original genius of the teaching of Jesus and the missional practice of the earliest Christians" (2006, 26). One thing to bring out in this lesson is a comparison of the circumstances for believers in the first century and for believers in the present day, as well as what the methods and practice of the earliest Christians can teach us about living missionally in our own twenty-first-century circumstances.

The lesson plan begins with a reading check of chapter 15, and the majority of today's lesson will be a class discussion of that chapter. You may want to begin that discussion by drawing attention to the context in which the earliest Christians lived and ministered. The "First Era Snapshot" sidebar on SE page 182 can serve as a guide for this. The core of today's discussion should relate to the themes mentioned in the previous lesson. You may also wish to investigate and present some of the topics listed in the "Historical Context" sidebar on this page to round out information about this period in history. A subtheme of this chapter is the roles that persecution and suffering play in propelling mission forward, as exemplified by the events surrounding the stoning of Stephen. You may want to point out this element of the story to your students, who are likely to find additional themes and issues to discuss from this chapter as well. The emphasis of

today's discussion should always point back to the Big Idea and Key Concepts for this lesson.

Since this chapter deals with the era of the early Church, an activity in the "If Time Activity" section in today's lesson directs students to examine specific passages in Acts that help fill in some of the picture of Christian life during the first century AD. You may also want to direct students to maps of Paul's missionary journeys to give them more specific information on cities we know had a Christian witness by the end of the first century. Of course, one of the points the chapter makes is that there were many more people involved in Christian witness than merely the participants in the missionary journeys described in the Bible. Letters of the early Church fathers, such as the First Epistle of Clement to the Corinthians (circa AD 98), testify to ministry by more than just the handful of men and women specifically named in the New Testament. The "Further Study" section lists a source for some of these early letters. Laypeople were critical in the early spread of the gospel, and this era certainly demonstrates the missional idea that every believer is a minister of the gospel. This missional idea is one of the main points the first era can teach us about our own involvement in living missionally.

Finally, students should be directed to focus on the individuals profiled for era one in the student journal. These People in History profiles are designed to help students identify the diverse range of people and circumstances that God uses to accomplish His purpose. Beginning with today's lesson, you should help students draw out common traits and themes that emerge in the profiles of people who have lived on mission with God throughout the centuries. The Focus on People activity in this lesson offers a way to do this.

Historical Context

Familiarity with the following people, places, and events may enhance your presentation of lesson 29:

Jewish Diaspora Prior to Pentecost
The Destruction of Jerusalem in AD 70
Nero's Persecuting of Christians and Ruling of
   the Roman Empire

Objectives

- Students will identify through discussion the themes of chapter 15 and the big picture those themes reveal—God uses people throughout history to accomplish His purpose.

- Students will respond in writing to profiles of specific individuals and classify the characteristics and experiences of these people into categories of common traits and themes.

- Students will evaluate the people and events of era one to determine the challenges, successes, and shortcomings of people on mission with God during this time.

Unpacking

Reading Quiz (5 minutes)

Using the following questions, quiz the students for a check of completion of the assigned reading:

1. During era one, travel was safer and more rapid than at any later time until the nineteenth century. True or false? (**true**)

2. What is the name of the common language spoken across the Roman Empire by those involved in trade? (**Greek, or *koine* Greek**)

3. Which event after Christ's ascension resulted in the scattering of many believers from Jerusalem? (**the persecution of believers that came about alongside and after the stoning of Stephen**)

4. What event occurred in AD 70 that was significant regarding the central location of Christianity? (**the destruction of Jerusalem; specifically, the destruction of the temple in Jerusalem**)

5. Only those set apart by the leadership of the church participated in evangelism and the spread of the gospel during era one. True or false? (**false**)

Class Discussion (20–25 minutes)

Use the resources described in the "Teacher's Preparation" section to guide you in leading a class discussion on the information presented in chapter 15. Encourage students to compare their own experiences as believers and those described for believers in era one. Be sure to allow time to discuss student questions. **BLM 15.4 Challenges, Successes, and Shortcomings** can serve as a means of evaluating students' critical thinking and evaluation of this era.

Have students respond either in small-group discussion or in writing to the Reflective Questions for this chapter.

Focus on People (10–12 minutes)

Draw attention to the People in History profiles that your students read for this lesson (**JE 37 James, Son of Zebedee**; **JE 38 Phoebe, Dorcas, and Lydia**; and **JE 39 Paul**). Give students time to answer the following questions regarding each profile:

• What three adjectives would you use to describe this person?

• What are two characteristics of this person's relationship with God?

• What stands out to you about this person?

• What are some of the talents and abilities this person possesses?

• What are some common traits or themes that emerge from your reading about the individuals in the People in History profiles?

Journal Entry (10 minutes)

Have students write a reflective essay in **JE 40 Reflection on Era One** on the following questions:

• What concepts stand out in your mind from era one?

• What can the events and people of era one teach us about being on mission with God?

If Time Activity

Direct students to read the following verses and to note what they learn about Christianity in the first century:

Acts 2:42–47 and 4:32–35 (the common life of believers in Jerusalem)
Acts 7:54–8:8 (persecution and the scattering of believers)
Acts 10:27–33 and 44–48, 11:19–21 (Gentiles' belief in Christ)
Acts 14:1–7 (the spread of the gospel through persecution)
Acts 16:6–10 (God's leading in the spread of the gospel)

You may wish to assign additional passages from the New Testament.

Extra Mile

The role of written letters in the development of the early Church should not be underestimated. These letters, such as those of the New Testament or those of early Church fathers a generation later, formed the basis of Christian practice for the earliest Christian communities. Students may want to explore some of these primary texts that give a window into the early Church and its organization. In addition to studying the letters of the New Testament, they could explore the *Early Christian Writings* resource listed in the "Further Study" section.

What's Next

Have students read chapter 16 and the People in History profiles **JE 41 Antony**, **JE 42 Perpetua and Felicitas**, **JE 43 Ulfilas**, and **JE 44 Patrick** in preparation for the next lesson. At the end of each profile is a list of questions for your students to think about before the next lesson.

Looking Ahead

If you want your students to use an organizational tool or other materials for their portfolio projects besides those provided in the course materials, prepare them in advance of when you expect your students to use them.

Further Study

Glimpses of Christian History. http://www.christianhistorytimeline.com/ (Christianity Today International's website dedicated to Christian history; provides time lines and contextual information that may be useful in presenting this and other lessons throughout the unit).

Louth, Andrew, ed. 1987. *Early Christian writings: The apostolic fathers.* Rev. trans. Trans. Maxwell Staniforth. London: Penguin Books.

Rose Publishing. 2005. *Rose book of Bible charts, maps, and time lines.* Torrance, CA: Rose Publishing (a great resource that includes Bible maps, biblical and historical time lines, illustrations, and full-color Bible charts).

Era Two

Big Idea

History reveals the challenges, successes, and shortcomings that people throughout history have experienced as they have participated with God in completing His purpose.

Key Concepts

- Studying history allows us to see the big picture of how God's story has continued throughout time.

- Reflecting on how God has allowed other people to participate in His mission can help us learn about our own participation in God's purpose.

Reflective Questions

- Emperor Constantine endorsed Christianity as the state religion of the Roman Empire in the fourth century. What are the benefits of a close relationship between church and state? What are the dangers? How would your life be different if Christianity were banned where you live? (SE p. 195)

- Do you ever experience suffering because of your faith in Christ? How can suffering and persecution be beneficial to the spread of the gospel? What are you willing to experience and endure for the sake of Christ? (SE p. 195)

Teacher's Heart

This morning as I was eating breakfast, an ad on the side of my granola bar box gave me the following instructions: "Claim the life you deserve." It is but one example of the messages of entitlement and self-importance that bombard us in contemporary life. How different is the attitude of those who have surrendered their lives and joined God in His mission throughout the centuries! The lives of godly men and women such as those we are studying in this unit resonate with thankfulness and gratitude for the grace of God—grace that saved them (and that saves us) from the life of wrath and condemnation that is deserved apart from Christ. In the face of breakfast messages and pop-culture images of entitlement, I am reminded of the words of Paul in Colossians 2:8: "See to it that no one takes you captive through hollow and deceptive philosophy, which depends on human tradition and the basic principles of this world rather than on Christ."

Teacher's Preparation

Era two reveals dramatic changes taking place in the practice and spread of Christianity. In the five hundred years between 100 and 600, Christianity "emerged from its first-century identity as a loose network of widely spread small churches to become an organized institution with formal doctrine and leadership hierarchy" (SE p. 187). Throughout these years of transition, the incarnational nature of Christianity was demonstrated again and again as the gospel was shared in new languages, in new geographic regions, and in dramatically variant cultural contexts. As chapter 16 reminds us, during era two the gospel was spreading not only across the Roman Empire, but to the east in places such as Edessa and Armenia, and south to Ethiopia (SE p. 188). By the fifth century it had spread to the northern lands of Ireland and territories ruled by barbaric Germanic tribes (Irvin and Sunquist 2001, 179–80; SE pp. 194–95). During all of that expansion, the truth of the gospel remained constant, yet its message was transcendent enough to powerfully resonate in the many different cultural contexts into which it reached—from the intellectual and political elite ruling classes of Rome to the nomadic and war-mongering Gothic tribes of the north.

Of course, one of the most central transitions for the Christian faith across these five hundred years was its move from a relatively small, grass-roots network of believers to a formally structured church—transforming from a religious practice outlawed by the major political power of the day to the state-sanctioned religion of Rome. A continuing subtheme in this and future chapters is the balance between the benefits and the costs of having the sanction of ruling political powers. In era two, we see how the formal recognition of Christianity in the Roman Empire brings about widespread acceptance of the gospel. In future eras, however, this partnership of church and state, which is often called Christendom, proves to be equally disadvantageous in some respects. In our current day, we are confronted with what some call "the post-Christian West" or "the end of Christendom." This current reality is welcomed by some and feared by others. In either case, your students should find it interesting to note the development of Christendom in the fourth century and to trace its realities and effects throughout the different eras of history.

As Christianity grew and spread in the years between 100 and 600, it became more organized and formalized through such tools as church doctrine and leadership hierarchies. In era two, a number of councils of the church helped formalize orthodox doctrine and settle theological differences. These councils produced the creeds and basic theologies that Christians still adhere to today. Theologically significant among these church councils is the Council of Nicea in 325, which defined

the Trinity and gave us the Nicene Creed, and the Council of Chalcedon in 451, which dealt with understanding the divine and human natures of Christ. From a practical standpoint, the Council of Carthage in 397, which defined the specific books that make up the New Testament, may be the most important regarding all the matters of doctrine and practice that emerged from era two.

Another interesting point from this chapter is the roles that persecution and martyrdom played in spreading the faith. The early Christians generally assumed that they would suffer for their faith—a reality that is perhaps not as resonant with contemporary students. You may want to use some of the resources listed in the "Further Study" section and spend some time discussing with your students the topics of martyrdom, persecution, and suffering for the Christian faith.

As in the previous lesson, today's lesson begins with an optional reading check. The bulk of the lesson plan is a class discussion, which should center on the main themes and ideas from chapter 16. For further contextual information, you may wish to investigate and present some of the topics listed in the "Historical Context" sidebar on this page and to consult the "Second Era Snapshot" sidebar (SE p. 190). Of course, your students are likely to find additional themes and issues to discuss from this chapter as well.

Historical Context

Familiarity with the following people, places, and events may enhance your presentation of lesson 30:

Church History
  The Council of Nicea in 325
  The Council of Carthage in 397
  The Council of Chalcedon in 451
  Benedict of Nursia and His Monastic Order

World/Political History
  The Reign of Roman Emperor Constantine
  The Roman Empire's Ongoing Battle with
    Invading Barbarian Tribes from the North
  The Goths
  The Decline of a United Roman Empire, and
    Its Division into Eastern and Western Empires

Again, to conclude the core of this lesson, students should be directed to focus on the individuals profiled for era two in the student journal. Using the Focus on People activity, help students draw out common traits and themes that emerge in the People in History profiles of people who have lived on mission with God throughout the centuries. As always, the emphasis of today's lesson should point back to the Big Idea and Key Concepts for this lesson.

Objectives

- Students will identify through discussion the themes of chapter 16 and the big picture those themes reveal—God uses people throughout history to accomplish His purpose.

- Students will respond in writing to profiles of specific individuals and classify the characteristics and experiences of these people into categories of common traits and themes.

- Students will evaluate the people and events of era two to determine the challenges, successes, and shortcomings of people on mission with God during this time.

Unpacking

Reading Quiz (5 minutes)

Have students list three facts they learned from reading chapter 16. These should be checked against the chapter for accuracy.

Class Discussion (20–25 minutes)

Use the resources described in the "Teacher's Preparation" section to guide you in leading a class discussion on the information presented in chapter 16. Encourage students to compare their own experiences as believers and those described for believers in era two. Be sure to allow time to discuss student questions. **BLM 16.4 Challenges, Successes, and Shortcomings** can serve as a means of evaluating students' critical thinking and evaluation of this era.

Have students respond either in small-group discussion or in writing to the Reflective Questions for this chapter.

Focus on People (10–12 minutes)

Draw attention to the People in History profiles that your students read for this lesson (**JE 41 Antony**, **JE 42 Perpetua and Felicitas**, **JE 43 Ulfilas**, and **JE 44 Patrick**). Give students time to answer the following questions regarding each person in the profiles:

- What three adjectives would you use to describe this person?
- What are two characteristics of this person's relationship with God?
- What stands out to you about this person?
- What are some of the talents and abilities this person possesses?
- What are some common traits or themes that emerge from your reading about the individuals in the People in History profiles?

Journal Entry (10 minutes)

Have students write a reflective essay, **JE 45 Reflection on Era Two**, on the following questions:

- What concepts stand out in your mind from era two?
- What can the events and the people of era two teach us about being on mission with God?

Extra Mile

Challenge students to research one of the following topics related to chapter 16 and to present a paper or make an in-class presentation on their research:

- An exploration of the origins of monasticism and the role of monasteries in Christian mission
- The great church councils and the process of defining orthodoxy

What's Next

Have students read chapter 17 and the People in History profiles **JE 46 Cyril and Methodius**, **JE 47 Peter Waldo**, and **JE 48 Raymond Lull** in preparation for the next lesson. At the end of each profile is a list of questions for your students to think about before the next lesson.

Looking Ahead

If you want your students to use an organizational tool or other materials for their portfolio projects besides those provided in the course materials, prepare them in advance of when you expect your students to use them.

Further Study

About.com: Ancient/Classical History. http://ancienthistory.about.com/ (a website that provides links to a wide variety of information on this period, including maps and summaries of events).

A Time-Line of the Roman Empire. http://www.scaruffi.com/politics/romans.html (an online resource that provides a time line of rulers and events in the Roman Empire).

DC Talk and the Voice of the Martyrs. 1999. *Jesus freaks: Stories of those who stood for Jesus; The ultimate Jesus freaks.* Tulsa, OK: Albury Publishing.

Foxe, John. *Foxe's book of martyrs.* http://www.ccel.org/f/foxe/martyrs/.

Glimpses of Christian History. http://www.christianhistorytimeline.com/ (Christianity Today International's website dedicated to Christian history; provides time lines and contextual information that may be useful in presenting this and other lessons throughout the unit).

Era Three

Big Idea

History reveals the challenges, successes, and shortcomings that people throughout history have experienced as they have participated with God in completing His purpose.

Key Concepts

- Studying history allows us to see the big picture of how God's story has continued throughout time.
- Reflecting on how God has allowed other people to participate in His mission can help us learn about our own participation in God's purpose.

Reflective Question

Daily life in era three was often filled with violence, oppression, uncertainty, and chaos; yet God continued to bring hope and reconciliation in the midst of such strife. What circumstances of chaos and strife are you struggling with? Do you trust God to be with you through those circumstances? How can you focus your hope on Him and not on your circumstances? (SE p. 206)

Teacher's Heart

The old saying "God moves in mysterious ways" is but one way to describe the fact that His methods are not always what we expect. God is able to redeem any situation; Scripture is full of this truth. Genesis 50:20 records Joseph's attitude toward his brothers and his less-than-ideal life journey: "You intended to harm me, but God intended it for good to accomplish what is now being done, the saving of many lives." Perhaps it is difficult to see how God can be at work in circumstances that seem overwhelming. But nothing is beyond His control. May this truth be real and alive to you as you teach today's lesson.

Teacher's Preparation

Perhaps of all the eras we will study in this unit, era three presents us with some modes of mission that are the most foreign to contemporary Christian thought. Today we can hardly imagine participating in something like the Crusades as a means of Christian evangelism. Yet the image of a religious war is certainly one that rings true in contemporary headlines. Even today, parts of the world are enmeshed in violent conflict that stems from religious conviction. However, since we typically think of these types of conflicts as something that non-Christians rather than Christians participate in, your students may have difficulty viewing the more violent and coercive events and mind-sets of era three with anything but criticism. It is important to remind them that God is still sovereign and at work even during the most difficult (and evil) circumstances.

Political instability and the possibility of invasion by foreign powers was a constant reality throughout the Middle Ages. Indeed, barbarians and Muslims posed threats on many fronts, and many of the geographical gains of Christendom were reversed at the hands of Muslim encroachment during era three (SE p. 198–99). It was from this climate of turmoil that the idea of conversion by force emerged. It is not surprising to find that, in a period of history in which violence was the order of the day, even the church was influenced by methods of violence, perhaps as a result of the deeply entwined relationship between church and state. So closely were these two entities allied at times that "an enemy of the state was easily viewed as an enemy to Christianity and vice versa" (SE p. 198). One lesson we can certainly draw from the history of mission in this period is that God is always at work, bringing forward light in the midst of terrible darkness. The gospel and Christianity did not disappear or die during this period.

As chapter 17 points out, in the midst of so much uncertainty, violence, and chaos, a message of God's love and faithfulness was quietly going forward. One way was in the form of monastic witness. The monastic life described on SE page 200 is an example of the incarnational missional life discussed in the Culture Unit. You may wish to review Michael Frost's aspects of incarnational living (SE p. 146) as a basis of class discussion on the incarnational monastic life described in chapter 17. Monasticism as it was practiced in the Middle Ages is a model of mission that proved to be quite fruitful in a period marked by so much violence and oppression. You may want to draw the attention of the students to the way this method of mission brings hope into the bleakest of circumstances. Also discuss the contrast between the two main paradigms of mission from era three: monasticism and conversion by force.

The first activity of today's lesson invites students to consider the chaotic and turbulent nature of the Middle Ages with an eye toward analogous contemporary examples of turmoil faced by believers.

Discussion and activities should center on the main themes and ideas from chapter 17. For further contextual information, you may wish to investigate and present some of the topics listed in the "Historical Context" sidebar on this page and to consult the "Third Era Snapshot" sidebar on SE page 203. Of course, your students are likely to find additional themes and issues to discuss from this chapter as well.

Again, to conclude the core of this lesson, direct students to focus on the individuals profiled for era three in the student journal. Use the Focus on People activity to help students draw out common traits and themes that emerge in the profiles of people who have lived on mission with God throughout the centuries. As always, the emphasis of today's lesson should point back to the Big Idea and Key Concepts for this lesson.

Historical Context

Familiarity with the following people, places, and events may enhance your presentation of lesson 31:

Church History
   Pope Gregory the Great
   Augustine
   Celtic Monasticism
   Benedictine Monasticism
   Franciscan Monasticism
   Dominican Monasticism
   Boniface
   Cyril and Methodius
   East-West Schism of 1054
   Pope Urban II's Launching of the First
      Crusade in 1095

World/Political History
   The Rise of Islam
   Viking Expansion in Northern Europe
   Feudalism
   The Reign of Charlemagne
   The Crusades
   Everyday Life in the Middle Ages

Objectives

- Students will identify through discussion the themes of chapter 17 and the big picture those themes reveal—God uses people throughout history to accomplish His purpose.

- Students will respond in writing to profiles of specific individuals and classify the characteristics and experiences of these people into categories of common traits and themes.

- Students will evaluate the people and events of era three to determine the challenges, successes, and shortcomings of people on mission with God during this time.

Unpacking

Warm-up Analogies (5–10 minutes)

Read aloud to students the following excerpt from chapter 17 (SE p. 198): "Because of the oppressive facts of life in the Middle Ages, with the constant reality and threat of invasion and domination by a variety of non-Christian influences, it is in some ways astonishing that a vibrant Christianity emerged from this period. God is able to take what is intended for evil and use it for good (Genesis 50:20). What He did for Joseph in the earliest days of Israel, He continued to do through the Middle Ages and continues to do for us today." Have students offer examples of the chaotic and threatening circumstances of contemporary Christian life. Ask them to give examples of how they see God's work going forward even in the midst of chaos today. You can do this as a class or have students work in groups. List their responses on the board.

Class Discussion (20–25 minutes)

Use the resources described in the "Teacher's Preparation" section to guide you in leading a class discussion on the information presented in chapter 17. Encourage students to compare their own experiences as believers and those described for believers in era three. Be sure to allow time to discuss student questions. **BLM 17.4 Challenges, Successes, and Shortcomings** can serve as a means of evaluating students' critical thinking and evaluation of this era.

Have students respond either in small-group discussion or in writing to the Reflective Questions for this chapter.

Focus on People (10–12 minutes)

Draw attention to the People in History profiles that your students read for this lesson (**JE 46 Cyril and Methodius**, **JE 47 Peter Waldo**, and **JE 48 Raymond Lull**). Give students time to answer the following questions regarding each profile:

- What three adjectives would you use to describe this person?

- What are two characteristics of this person's relationship with God?

- What stands out to you about this person?

- What are some of the talents and abilities this person possesses?

- What are some common traits or themes that emerge from your reading about the individuals in the People in History profiles?

Journal Entry (10 minutes)

Have students write a reflective essay, **JE 50 Reflection on Era Three**, on the following questions:

- What concepts stand out in your mind from era three?

- What can the events and the people of era three teach us about being on mission with God?

If Time Activity

Direct students to **JE 49 Monastic Prayers**. Give them an opportunity to read through these prayers and to journal a page of response to them. You may want to play some instrumental praise music in the background during this activity. If you don't have time to do this in class, assign the activity as homework.

Extra Mile

Missiologist David J. Bosch describes the appeal to Luke 23:14 and its "compel them to come in" idea as a dominant theme of the mission methodology of this period (1991, 236). Invite students to research and present four or five specific examples from this period that exemplify the idea of compelling people to become Christians. Have them think about different methods of compelling—such as through force, through personal example, through persuasive argument. They also might want to explore the theological mind-set of this period in which conversion, even by force, was considered to be for the good of the person in question. Bosch notes, "It was to people's own eternal advantage if they could be made to join this body" (237; SE p. 204).

What's Next

Have students read chapter 18 and the People in History profiles **JE 51 Matthew Ricci**, **JE 52 Count Zinzendorf and the Moravians**, and **JE 53 David Brainerd** in preparation for the next lesson. At the end of each profile is a list of questions for your students to think about before the next lesson.

Looking Ahead

If you want your students to use an organizational tool or other materials for their portfolio projects besides those provided in the course materials, prepare them in advance of when you expect your students to use them.

Lesson 32   **Era Four**

Big Idea

History reveals the challenges, successes, and shortcomings that people throughout history have experienced as they have participated with God in completing His purpose.

Key Concepts

- Studying history allows us to see the big picture of how God's story has continued throughout time.

- Reflecting on how God has allowed other people to participate in His mission can help us learn about our own participation in God's purpose.

Reflective Questions

- Ethnocentrism and cultural superiority were often exhibited during era four, even in the realm of Christian mission. Do you have underlying beliefs and attitudes that are counterproductive to effective missional living? Do you find yourself prejudiced against certain cultural practices or groups of people? (SE p. 218)

- The Age of Discovery offered new avenues for sharing the gospel during era four. What are some circumstances in your life that seem to be advantageous for developing new cross-cultural relationships? How could you take advantage of those opportunities? (SE p. 218)

Teacher's Heart

The following prayer, penned in the sixteenth century by Martin Luther, is as vibrant and applicable to the present time as it was to his era. You may want to personalize it for yourself and pray it as you prepare for this lesson.

"Lord God, You have appointed me as a Bishop and Pastor in Your Church, but you see how unsuited I am to meet so great and difficult a task. If I had lacked Your help, I would have ruined everything long ago. Therefore, I call upon You: I wish to devote my mouth and my heart to You; I shall teach the people. I myself will learn and ponder diligently upon Your Word. Use me as Your instrument—but do not forsake me, for if ever I should be on my own, I would easily wreck it all."* Amen.

*"A Sacristy Prayer" by Martin Luther (trans. James Kellerman, Project Wittenberg, 1999)

Teacher's Preparation

In 1500, when era four begins, we see Christianity largely confined geographically to present-day western Europe. But on the horizon were many changes that would set the stage for Christianity to become more diverse and geographically widespread than ever before. Of course, one of the major features shaping the Christian world in era four was the Protestant Reformation. Even though the events of the Reformation dramatically altered the structure and practice of Christianity, the movement didn't initially place much focus on mission. Chapter 18 discusses several reasons for this lack of mission participation during this time period (SE pp. 211–12). Theology regarding how God operates played a key role. According to Bosch, a major theme of Reformation theology at the time was that "all initiative [for] salvation lay with God alone. The attitude was that no human being could undertake any mission work; God would, in his sovereignty, see to this" (1991, 250; SE p. 212). In today's discussion of chapter 18, spend some time contrasting this theology of era four with both the Big Idea for this lesson and the Big Idea for chapter 3 (God invites us to participate in His purpose; He blesses us so that we can bless others).

Chapter 18 does show, however, that there were at least three movements within Protestantism that were involved in formally following God across cultural boundaries to share the gospel with those who had never heard it before. In the Anabaptist, Puritan, and Pietist movements, we can see the foundations of Protestant mission for the centuries to come. Call attention to these movements in today's discussion, and identify them as a precursor of what students will read about in chapter 19. It might also be interesting to have your students identify different features of these early Protestant mission movements and discuss how those features are either still present or absent in the type of mission emphasis they have seen in today's world. Particularly resonant with the perspective of this course are the Pietists, who "simply went when and where Christ was sending them" (Nussbaum 2005, 67; SE p. 213).

One facet of the Reformation, an aspect we may take for granted today, is the role of individual relationship with God. The student text explores some of the issues of unity and diversity related to individual versus corporate faith practice (SE pp. 210–11). These issues could be a fascinating point of discussion for your students. Help them focus on the dynamics of a Christian faith that is to be practiced within a community and yet to be based on individual intimacy with God. Challenge your students to think through the issues related to emphasis on the individual and how that individualism relates to unity within the Body of Christ.

Ask them to consider the balance between individualism and community life in their own practice of Christian faith.

The advent of the Age of Discovery brought about another example of the double-edged sword that resulted from a deeply entwined relationship between church and state—particularly in the lands that were naval powers during era four. Even though exploration during this time period allowed the gospel to go forward to previously unknown lands and peoples, the text on SE pages 214–16 offers some detail regarding the expansionist, colonizing mind-set that today is the subject of much critique. Noteworthy in terms of cultural sensitivity and Christian mission in this period was Francis Xavier's insights regarding the widely held belief that Christian mission should seek to eradicate all traces of previous customs in the quest to build "correct" Christian life and practice in a new culture (Neil 1986, 133; SE p. 216). If you have been discussing the enmeshing of church and state affairs in previous chapters, era four events will provide an extension of that discussion.

The first activity of today's lesson is a reading quiz. Discussion and activities should center on the main themes and ideas from chapter 18. For further contextual information, you may wish to investigate and present some of the topics listed in the "Historical Context" sidebar on this page. Of course,

Historical Context

Familiarity with the following people, places, and events may enhance your presentation of lesson 32:

Church History
  The Protestant Reformation
  The Council of Trent
  The Diet of Worms
  The Peace of Augsburg in 1555
  The Peace of Westphalia in 1648
  The Wesleyan/Evangelical Revival
  The First Great Awakening

World/Political History
  The Renaissance
  Exploration and Colonization
  Religious Wars in Europe

your students are likely to find additional themes and issues to discuss from this chapter as well.

Again, to conclude this lesson, direct students to focus on the individuals profiled for era four in the student journal. Use the Focus on People activity to help students draw out common traits and themes that emerge in the profiles of people who have lived on mission with God throughout the centuries. As always, the emphasis of today's lesson should point back to the Big Idea and Key Concepts for this lesson.

Objectives

- Students will identify through discussion the themes of chapter 18 and the big picture those themes reveal—God uses people throughout history to accomplish His purpose.

- Students will respond in writing to profiles of specific individuals and classify the characteristics and experiences of these people into categories of common traits and themes.

- Students will evaluate the people and events of era four to determine the challenges, successes, and shortcomings of people on mission with God during this time.

Unpacking

Reading Quiz (5 minutes)

Using the following questions, quiz the students for a check of completion of the assigned reading:

1. Name three Protestant mission movements of era four.
   (**Anabaptist, Puritan, and Pietist**)

2. Which group from this era is known for a 100-year, 24-hour-a-day prayer watch?
   (**the Moravians**)

3. What "age" provided the means for men and women to take the gospel to lands and people that were previously unknown to the Europeans of era four?
   (**the Age of Discovery**)

4. Name one of the dominant sea powers of era four. (**any of the following: Spain, Portugal, later England, Holland, and Denmark**)

Class Discussion (20–25 minutes)

Use the resources described in the "Teacher's Preparation" section to guide you in leading a class discussion on the information presented in chapter 18. Encourage students to compare their own experiences as believers and those described for believers in era four. Be sure to allow time to discuss student questions. **BLM 18.4 Challenges, Successes, and Shortcomings** can serve as a means of evaluating students' critical thinking and evaluation of this era.

Have students respond either in small-group discussion or in writing to the Reflective Questions for this chapter.

Focus on People (10–12 minutes)

Draw attention to the People in History profiles that your students read for this lesson (**JE 51 Matthew Ricci**, **JE 52 Count Zinzendorf and the Moravians**, and **JE 53 David Brainerd**). Give students time to answer the following questions regarding each profile:

- What three adjectives would you use to describe this person?
- What are two characteristics of this person's relationship with God?
- What stands out to you about this person?
- What are some of the talents and abilities this person possesses?
- What are some common traits or themes that emerge from your reading about the individuals in the People in History profiles?

Journal Entry (10 minutes)

Have students write a reflective essay, **JE 54 Reflection on Era Four**, on the following questions:

- What concepts stand out in your mind from era four?
- What can the events and the people of era four teach us about being on mission with God?

If Time Activity

For extra contextual information about the Reformation, view the 2003 movie *Luther* with your students. (See the "Further Study" section for DVD details.)

Extra Mile

Students who are interested in learning more about this era's mission methods—particularly methods used in North America—might be interested in reading the writings of David Brainerd and John Eliot listed in the "Further Study" section.

What's Next

Have students read chapter 19 and the People in History profiles **JE 55 Ann and Adoniram Judson**, **JE 56 Lott Carey**, **JE 57 Mary Slessor**, **JE 58 Semisi Nau**, **JE 59 Cameron Townsend**, **JE 60 William Wade Harris**, and **JE 61 Mother Teresa** in preparation for the next lesson. At the end of each profile is a list of questions for your students to think about before the next lesson.

Looking Ahead

Remind your students of any upcoming due dates for their portfolio project, and review with them your requirements and expectations before the project is to be turned in.

Further Study

Edwards, Jonathan, ed. 2006. *The life and diary of David Brainerd.* Peabody, MA: Hendrickson.

Eliot, John. 1670. *John Eliot's brief narrative.* http://www.bartleby.com/43/12.html (a narrative that describes mission to the North American Indians by Eliot, a Puritan mentioned in chap. 18).

Neill, Stephen. 1986. *A history of Christian missions.* 2nd ed. Rev. by Owen Chadwick. New York: Penguin Books (a book that provides a detailed look at the specific mission endeavors of this era).

Thomasson, Camille. 2003. *Luther.* DVD. Directed by Eric Till. Century City, CA: MGM.

Era Five: Part 1

Big Idea

History reveals the challenges, successes, and shortcomings that people throughout history have experienced as they have participated with God in completing His purpose.

Key Concepts

- Studying history allows us to see the big picture of how God's story has continued throughout time.

- Reflecting on how God has allowed other people to participate in His mission can help us learn about our own participation in God's purpose.

Reflective Question

In what ways can you see the influence of Enlightenment ideas in your own thinking about the world? How does this affect your concept of Christian life? of truth? of God? (SE p. 231)

Teacher's Heart

Your students are probably familiar with the movie *End of the Spear* (Ewing and Gavigan 2006; DVD details in the "Further Study" section). This movie chronicles the events leading up to the 1956 martyrdom in Ecuador of five men who set out to share the gospel to an unreached tribe of Aucas Indians (now called Waorani). One of these five men was Jim Elliot, who in his journals describes his attitude toward a life of service to God: "He is no fool who gives what he cannot keep to gain that which he cannot lose." Elliot wrote this in 1949, seven years before his death in Ecuador.[1] He was a man who understood the nature of being yielded to God. We, too, must understand that the things we sometimes want to hold on to in this life often have no eternal significance at all. Ask God to help you submit all areas of your life to Him, even the ones you desperately want to try to control yourself.

Lord, please teach me how to be yielded to You. Help my students and me grow into an ever-deeper commitment and communion with You. Amen.

Teacher's Preparation

Chapter 19 contains more than enough material to do several lessons. We have divided the material into two lesson plans, but you should feel free to extend your time on this material as your situation permits. The first lesson is designed to help you lead a general discussion of the chapter in the same manner as done in previous lessons. The second lesson will explore transitioning from era five to the realities of our own day. Some new material for students is presented in **JE 64 Present Era Mission Snapshot** and **JE 65 Back to Jerusalem**. You will want to assign these as reading that should be done before the next lesson.

Note that in chapter 19 we are focusing almost exclusively on Western mission. That is not to say that mission was not going forward from other parts of the world; however, the world during the period of colonization was influenced primarily by Western ideals that were exported globally. Ralph Winter notes that "by 1945, Europeans had achieved virtual control over 99.5% of the non-Western world.... Twenty-five years later, the Western nations had lost control over all but 5% of the non-Western population of the world" (1999b, 210; SE p. 227). Not only do these statistics show the domination of Western ideals on mission thinking during much of era five, but they show the foundation for the rise of what we are currently experiencing in world mission—what's known today as the "global South." Lesson 34 will focus more on the implications of these changes that Winter points out.

If you and your students have been discussing the thread in these chapters regarding the relationship between church and state, you may wish to discuss the following quotation from R. Pierce Beaver regarding the colonial-era mind-set the students

read about: "Even in countries with a high culture, such as India and China, European missionaries stressed the 'civilizing' objective as much as their brethren in primitive regions because they regarded the local culture as degenerate and superstitious—a barrier to Christianization" (1999, 247; SE p. 226). Students could consider how this mind-set has changed since the nineteenth century and where they still see vestiges of it. Ask them to consider how God worked through the circumstances of colonialism to bring His purpose forward and how He is working in today's postcolonial world to do the same.

There are, of course, many different directions to turn for further in-depth study related to the material in chapter 19. Two possible topics for research, listed in the "Extra Mile" section, are the role of women in mission in era five and the history of the student volunteer movement, each of which is profiled briefly in sidebars of chapter 19. The advent of widespread voluntary mission societies in the nineteenth century afforded women an unprecedented opportunity to play a formal and large-scale role in world mission. That same volunteerism was a circumstance God worked through to fuel much global mission. The story of the development of the student volunteer movement represents a good example of the "unity within diversity" principle we have been examining in this unit. As mission began to spring from collaborations that crossed denominational lines, a picture of unity and cooperation within the Body of Christ was drawn that reminds us of the first century when there was no such thing as a "denomination." The "Further Study" section lists resources to supplement a study of these topics.

The first activity in today's lesson invites students to make comparisons between life in the year 1900 and life today. You should develop a chart on the board that looks like the following:

Category	1900	Today
Communication		
Transportation		
World political power		
Other		

Direct students to the information found on SE page 227 to complete the chart. Feel free to add additional details and categories to the chart. The objective is to show the difference between these two points in history and yet note that God is still at work even through the transitions.

Discussion and activities should center on the main themes and ideas from chapter 19. For further contextual information, you may wish to investigate some of the topics listed in the "Historical Context" sidebar in this "Teacher's Preparation" section. Of course, your students are likely to find additional themes and issues to discuss from this chapter as well. The lesson concludes with a focus on the individuals profiled for era five in the student journal. Use the Focus on People activity to help students draw out common traits and themes that emerge in the profiles of people who have lived on mission with God throughout the centuries. In the next lesson, students will begin their own profiles of contemporary people who are serving on mission with God.

Finally, be sure that the emphasis of today's activities points back to the Big Idea and Key Concepts for this lesson.

Objectives

- Students will identify through discussion the themes of chapter 19 and the big picture those themes reveal—God uses people throughout history to accomplish His purpose.

- Students will respond in writing to profiles of specific individuals and classify the characteristics and experiences of these people into categories of common traits and themes.

- Students will evaluate the people and events of era five to determine the challenges, successes, and shortcomings of people on mission with God during this time.

Unpacking

Opening Context (7–10 minutes)

Using the information and chart presented in the "Teacher's Preparation" section, guide students to compare some of the circumstances of the year 1900 with those of the present day. Ask them to consider the ways in which they know that God was able to use the circumstances in 1900 to further His mission. Then ask them to do the same with the circumstances of today. Conclude that regardless of technology, communication, or politics, God does work in every phase of history.

Class Discussion (20–25 minutes)

Use the resources described in the "Teacher's Preparation" section to guide you in leading a class discussion on the information presented in chapter 19. Encourage students to compare their own experiences as believers and those described for believers in era five. Especially note the ways in which era five has informed our present-day outlook and practice. Be sure to allow time to discuss student questions. **BLM 19.4 Challenges, Successes, and Shortcomings** can serve as a means of evaluating students' critical thinking and evaluation of this era.

Have students respond either in small-group discussion or in writing to the Reflective Questions for this chapter.

Focus on People (10–12 minutes)

Draw attention to the People in History profiles that your students read for this lesson (**JE 55 Ann and Adoniram Judson**, **JE 56 Lott Carey**, **JE 57 Mary Slessor**, **JE 58 Semisi Nau**, **JE 59 Cameron Townsend**, **JE 60 William Wade Harris**, and **JE 61 Mother Teresa**). Give students time to answer the following questions regarding each profile:

- What three adjectives would you use to describe this person?

- What are two characteristics of this person's relationship with God?

- What stands out to you about this person?

- What are some of the talents and abilities this person possesses?

- What are some common traits or themes that emerge from your reading about the individuals in the People in History profiles?

Journal Entry (10 minutes)

Have students write a reflective essay, **JE 62 Reflection on Era Five**, on the following questions:

- What concepts stand out in your mind from era five?

- What can the events and the people of era five teach us about being on mission with God?

If Time Activity

View the movie *End of the Spear* with your students (see DVD details in the "Further Study" section).

Extra Mile

- Students may be interested in pursuing in-depth research on either women in mission or the student volunteer movement. Some resources they could begin with are listed in the "Further Study" section.

- Have students read and report on primary source documents from era five. Several are anthologized in *Perspectives on the Worldwide Christian Movement*, including several by people mentioned in chapter 19 (William Carey, J. Hudson Taylor, John R. Mott, and others).

What's Next

Have students read **JE 64 Present Era Mission Snapshot** and **JE 65 Back to Jerusalem** in preparation for the next lesson.

Looking Ahead

- In the next lesson, students will be asked to write profiles similar to the ones they have been reading throughout this unit except that theirs will be of contemporary people. You may wish to look ahead at this assignment to determine due dates and to decide whether it will be an in-class experience or a homework assignment.

- Remind your students of any upcoming due dates for their portfolio project, and review with them your requirements and expectations before the project is to be turned in.

Further Study

Ewing, Bill, and Bart Gavigan. 2006. *End of the spear*. DVD. Directed by Jim Hanon. Century City, CA: 20th Century Fox.

Kraft, Marguerite, and Meg Crossman. 1999. Women in mission. In *Perspectives on the world Christian movement: A reader*, ed. Ralph D. Winter and Steven C. Hawthorne, 269–73. 3rd ed. Pasadena, CA: William Carey Library.

U.S. Center for World Mission. *Mission Frontier*. http://www.missionfrontiers.org/ (a good resource for contemporary issues in mission).

Walls, Andrew F. 1996. *The missionary movement in Christian history: Studies in the transmission of faith*. Maryknoll, NY: Orbis Books (several chapters include information on the student volunteer movement).

❧

NOTE

1. Wheaton College, Jim Elliot quotation, Billy Graham Center Archives, http://www.wheaton.edu/bgc/archives/faq/20.htm (accessed July 17, 2008).

Era Five: Part 2

Big Idea

History reveals the challenges, successes, and shortcomings that people throughout history have experienced as they have participated with God in completing His purpose.

Key Concepts

- Studying history allows us to see the big picture of how God's story has continued throughout time.

- Reflecting on how God has allowed other people to participate in His mission can help us learn about our own participation in God's purpose.

Reflective Questions

- How would you describe the attitude of the culture around you toward the message of the gospel? What means of communicating the love of Christ are most powerful in influencing those around you? (SE p. 243)

- Where do you see yourself in the ongoing, unfolding story of God's mission in the coming years? (SE p. 243)

Teacher's Heart

During this unit, we have spent a lot of time "in the past," exploring what it has to teach us about God and His mission. But the past is not where we live. We live face forward, looking to where God wants us to go with Him. Of course, that can be daunting because so much about the future is unknown. But as we are reminded by the 1971 Bill Gaither tune "Because He Lives," knowing *who* holds the future makes all the difference. We can face tomorrow without fear, the future is in God's hands, "and life is worth the living, just because He lives!" Meditate on these words as you prepare to teach today's future-facing lesson.

Teacher's Preparation

The previous lesson served as a general introduction to the material covered in chapter 19. Today we will be focusing specifically on the present moment in mission history as an outgrowth of the events of era five. There are three specific elements that we will explore in today's lesson: the realities of our present "post-Christendom West," the similarities between circumstances of the early Church and those of today, and the changing nature of world mission. A major subtext of this lesson is that God is at work regardless of whether Christians are at the center of earthly society or on its fringes. In any sort of circumstance, we can participate with God in the mission He brings forward. Each activity in today's lesson sheds a different slant of light on that truth. Let's begin with a look at what is meant by post-Christendom.

A number of writers and thinkers recently have been describing the dynamics of the age in which we live—an age that is increasingly described as the post-Christian West, or post-Christendom. You will begin the lesson today by clarifying for students the terms *Christendom* and *post-Christendom*. Your students will probably recognize the contours of post-Christendom as the reality they live in here in Western culture. Writer Michael Frost describes Christendom this way: " 'Christendom' is the name given to the religious culture that has dominated Western society since the fourth century. Awakened by the Roman emperor Constantine, it was the cultural phenomenon that resulted when Christianity was established as the official imperial religion, moving it from being a marginalized, subversive, and persecuted movement to being the only official religion in the empire" (2006, 4). The enmeshed relationship between church and state that we have noted throughout much of this unit is at the heart of Christendom. Under Christendom, "church is perceived as central to society and [the] surrounding culture," notes author Alan Hirsch in *The Forgotten Ways* (2006, 64). It isn't difficult to see that, in our time, the dominance of the church and its ideals in Western culture is on the wane—at least in North American and European culture. But this doesn't mean that God has stopped working; it simply means that the circumstances through which He will work are different from what they were even two or three decades ago.

The simplest definition of *post-Christendom* is that we are living "after Christendom." In other words, the language and values of Christ are increasingly foreign to the sociopolitical culture of much of the Western world. British church-planting consultant Stuart Murray Williams describes it this way: "We experience this as a period of decline and discouragement as the church in western societies (but not in many other parts of the world) loses ground in terms of numbers and influence."[1] You will recall from chapter 10 the concept of cultural distance that is measured by E-Scale. Increasingly in contemporary Western life, Christians experience everwidening gulfs in cultural distance from the society around them. This increase in distance is an effect of our post-Christendom environment. As noted on SE page 231, "at the dawn of the twenty-first century, the Christian cultural context has shifted, much as it had in the closing years of the first century, when crossing cultural boundaries ensured the very survival of the Christian faith."

Post-Christendom has several things in common with the believers of the first and second centuries. Most notably, the commonality is that the Christian church is on the fringes of Western society and culture for the first time since the fourth century. The early Church's method of mission was clearly organic, grounded in Christ, and focused outward—to a world that didn't know Christ yet. Mission was incarnational. As an introduction to the second activity in today's lesson, you may want to review with your students the distinctives of incarnational living in chapter 11 (SE p. 146). We should focus on modeling our lives after the life of Christ, as the earliest believers did in earnest. The distinctives of era one described in chapter 15 remind us that the primary means of communicating the gospel in the early Church was through the regular activities of daily life—in the marketplace, in the streets and public spaces, in homes over a shared meal. **JE 63 Looking Back—Going Forward** has some food for thought on this topic. Use the quotations and questions found there as the basis of small-group discussions in your classroom.

Despite the fact that the West is experiencing a decline in the prominence of Christianity, there are many places in the world where the opposite is true. Andrew F. Walls says that there has been a "massive movement towards Christian faith in all the southern continents—sub-Saharan Africa, Latin America, certain parts of Asia, the Pacific Islands—which means that Christian profession in the southern continents now outnumbers that in the northern" (1996, 68; SE p. 230). Not only are there more Christians in these locations than in the West, but the Christians in these locations are serious about being on mission with God. **JE 64 Present Era Mission Snapshot** portrays the state of Christian mission in the world today, and the realities demonstrate a theme we have been tracking throughout this unit: decentralization. As we have noted before, throughout history God has used various circumstances to disrupt the formation of one central, earthly location for Christianity. There may be post-Christendom in the West, but God works through any circumstance, as the story of the past two thousand years surely tells us. And there is much to rejoice about globally. Historian Philip Jenkins points out the following in *The Next Christendom*: "Whatever Europeans or North Americans may believe, Christianity is doing very well indeed in the global South—not just surviving but expanding" (2002, 2).

A more specific example of what God is doing in the world today is found in **JE 65 Back to Jerusalem** in the description of the Back to Jerusalem movement of the Christian church in China. There are several noteworthy features in the information about this movement. First, you might want to discuss with your students the nature of the underground church in China and the similarities between its circumstances and those of the early Church. Second, look at the geographical spread of Christianity as traced through the History Unit to contextualize the Chinese plan to "complete the circuit" by going from east to west on "silk road" trading routes that were in use during the first century. Additional resources on this movement are found listed in the "Further Study" section.

For the final activity, which uses the People in History profiles, be sure to point out the variety of people, who are but a small sampling of those that God has used to complete His purpose over the past two thousand years. The people in these profiles are from a variety of cultures, professions, and seasons in life. Having differing talents, they were used to complete different portions of God's mission. Though there are common themes that will emerge—such as being yielded to God, having a willingness to go where God leads, being faithful in the face of suffering—be sure that students are not looking to create a one-size-fits-all template for "those fit to serve God," but rather that they begin to see that God calls us all to participate with Him.

Objectives

- Students will explore the concepts of Christendom and post-Christendom.

- Students will analyze the characteristics of the present day and compare them with the characteristics of Jesus' circumstances and those of the early Church.

- Students will discuss some of the dynamics of contemporary mission and its global nature.

- Students will create profiles of contemporary individuals who exhibit core characteristics of being on mission with God.

Unpacking

Coming to Terms (5 minutes)

Using the material from the "Teacher's Preparation" section, define the terms *Christendom* and *post-Christendom* for your students.

Going Back to Go Forward (10–15 minutes)

Divide the class into several small discussion groups. Direct students to **JE 63 Looking Back—Going Forward** and use the material in the "Teacher's Preparation" section to introduce this activity. Students should then read and discuss the passages and questions together. You may wish to have each group report to the whole class a summary of its discussion. You may also have students respond either in writing or in small-group discussion to the Reflective Questions for this chapter.

Twenty-First-Century Mission (10–15 minutes)

Discuss with your students the information presented in **JE 64 Present Era Mission Snapshot** and **JE 65 Back to Jerusalem**, which each offer some perspectives on contemporary global mission.

Focus on People (10–15 minutes)

Have students look through their journals at the People in History profiles (JEs 37–39, 41–44, 46–48, 51–53, 55–61) and the responses they wrote regarding the reflective questions they answered for each profile. Either on a sheet of paper individually or on the board as a class, they should create a list of adjectives, characteristics, talents and abilities, and outstanding features that they have identified in the People in History profiles. Once some common themes have emerged, ask students to brainstorm about living people (peers or otherwise) whose lives exhibit these same sorts of characteristics. Then have the students use **BLM 19.5 People in History Profile Template** to guide them as they research and write one or more contemporary profiles. Students might want to conduct a short interview with the individual, or individuals, they decide to write their profile about. Students should be prepared to share these profiles with the class as part of the unit review activities on the due date you assign.

Extra Mile

Students may wish to further explore either the role of the global South in world mission or the Back to Jerusalem movement and the church in China. Resources are listed in the "Further Study" section.

What's Next

Have students read chapter 20 in preparation for the next lesson.

Further Study

Armstrong, Chris. 2008. The future lies in the past. *Christianity Today* 2:22–29 (an article that offers a brief look at ancient-future evangelicals who look to the earliest church for inspiration).

Back to Jerusalem: God's Call to the Chinese Church to Complete the Great Commission. http://www.backtojerusalem.com/.

Escobar, Samuel. 2003. *The new global mission: The gospel from everywhere to everyone.* Christian Doctrine in Global Perspective series. Downers Grove, IL: InterVarsity Press (a book that provides in-depth information about the locus of Christianity and global mission).

Hattaway, Paul. 2003. *Back to Jerusalem: Three Chinese house church leaders share their vision to complete the Great Commission.* Waynesboro, GA: Authentic Media.

Jenkins, Philip. 2002. *The next Christendom: The coming of global Christianity.* New York: Oxford University Press (a book that provides in-depth information about the locus of Christianity and global mission).

Post Christendom. http://www.postchristendom.com/node/4/ (a website that includes a listing of a number of links to historical time lines; also includes a downloadable study guide on the dynamics of post-Christendom and mission).

Note

1. Stuart Murray Williams, *After Christendom: A Study Guide*, http://www.postchristendom.com/node/4/ (accessed June 22, 2008).

Review: The Ultimate Completion of God's Purpose

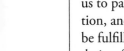

Big Idea

God's redemptive purpose will come to an ultimate completion in human history.

Key Concepts

- Even the frailty of humankind does not jeopardize God's mission. God's purpose will be completed.

- God's mission transcends circumstances and boundaries of culture, geography, and even methodology. God is sovereign to complete His purpose in the ways that He chooses.

Reflective Questions

- What difference does it make to you personally to know that God's purpose will be fulfilled? Are you willing to commit yourself to God's purpose even if you won't see it completed in your lifetime? (SE p. 235)

- What does the past have to teach us about the future in terms of the mission of God? What does it have to say to us about His faithfulness? (SE p. 235)

Teacher's Heart

In Acts 13:36, David is described as having fulfilled the purpose of God in his generation. God did this through David despite David's failures. The sins David committed did not go without consequences, but they didn't render him unusable either. He continued to experience intimacy and favor with God. You don't have to be a king, or even a leader for that matter, to be used of God. God invites every one of us to participate in His purpose, to join Him on a mission of relationship, redemption, and reconciliation to this world. And He will accomplish His purpose; it will be fulfilled in human history. As you prepare for this lesson, reflect on what God desires for you and your students—the opportunity to join Him on the adventure of a lifetime. He gives us the opportunity, the privilege, the blessing of participating in missio Dei to bring about His purpose in the world.

Teacher's Preparation

Chapter 20 has three goals: (1) to convey the Big Idea for this segment of the History Unit (that God's redemptive purpose will come to an ultimate completion in human history); (2) to serve as a general review of the entire History Unit; and (3) to serve as a formal transition into this course's final unit, which is designed to challenge students to focus on their personal participation in God's mission. The activities in this lesson will explicitly center on the first two goals. As you lead these activities, you will be adding to the foundations laid in the rest of the course and helping students transition into the final unit of material. Depending on which activities you plan to use with your students and how much of a chapter review you wish to have, the activities in this lesson could be spread out over two or more class periods.

The chapter begins with a reminder of the sovereign agency of God in the completion of His mission. As we have seen throughout thousands of years of history, God's interest has always been in the command Jesus spoke of in Matthew 22:37–40: love God, love others. As Richard Mouw reminds us on SE pages 235–36, God's redemptive purpose is to all people in all nations, and it will be completed. The first activity of today's lesson uses the simplicity of two familiar children's songs to invite students to reflect on the sovereignty of God and the scope of His love. Before the lesson, you should secure the music for the songs "Jesus Loves the Little Children" and "He's Got the Whole World in His Hands" so that you can play them for your students. You will also need to have crayons or markers on hand.

The second activity listed in this lesson will lead students to study several passages of Scripture that relate to the Big Idea of chapter 20: that God's redemptive purpose will come to an ultimate completion in human history. Students may simply read these passages and discuss how they relate to the Big Idea, or you may want to provide study aids for your students and invite them to dig a little deeper into these passages either in class or as a homework assignment. The Blue Letter Bible website, www.blueletterbible.org, is an excellent resource for in-depth Bible study. Study Light's website, www.studylight.org, has links to many useful study tools as well.

The unit review presented in chapter 20 stands in contrast to the unit review chapters for this course's two previous units, which focused on each individual chapter of those units. Chapter 20 is set up as a general review, summarizing the contents of the History Unit by using some of the themes presented in the unit. The unit themes highlighted by this chapter include the following: God invites people to participate (SE pp. 236–37); God shapes history regardless of circumstances (SE pp. 237–39); Christ is the center of Christianity rather than Christianity having one geographical locus (SE pp. 239–40); and the gospel is culturally transcendent, and there is unity within diversity in Christianity (SE pp. 240–42). Though not specified by today's lesson plan, you may wish to discuss in class each of these particular sections of chapter 20 as part of your unit review activities. One of the overarching themes of this unit (and of this course) is the cross-cultural nature of God's mission, which should resonate clearly from all the eras presented in our five-chapter tour of mission history. **JE 67 Thoughts on the Nature of Mission** presents several passages and questions on this topic, and it serves as the basis for the third activity in this lesson.

The final activity of the lesson is the conclusion of the unit-long examination of the People In History profiles. This activity can also serve as a form of unit review. Whether students make a formal presentation of the profiles they have written or just turn in the profiles, take some time in discussion to draw out the fact that no one particular type of person is better suited to participate with God—we are all invited and gifted by Him to be used in His mission. This idea is foundational to the personal application focus of the next unit.

Additionally, you may opt to have students formally present portions of the portfolios they have been compiling throughout this unit, if you chose to do that ongoing assignment. You should also conduct whatever additional unit review activities you deem appropriate before administering a unit test or an alternate assessment.

Objectives

- Students will reflect on and respond to the nature and scope of God's purpose of relationship, redemption, and reconciliation.

- Students will explore and analyze passages of Scripture related to the ultimate fulfillment of God's purpose.

- Students will evaluate and analyze statements summarizing mission history, and they will identify some characteristics of God's mission throughout history.

- Students will present the profiles they have written of people who are on mission with God in the present day.

Unpacking

The Scope of God's Plan (5–10 minutes)

Provide students with crayons and paper, and invite them to draw responses as they listen to the songs "Jesus Loves the Little Children" and "He's Got the Whole World in His Hands." Afterward, talk about how these songs reflect the heart of God. Lead in prayer, asking God to give each of them His heart for all the people of the world.

God's Lasting Purpose (10–15 minutes)

To enhance student understanding of biblical teaching on the certainty that God's purpose will stand, read aloud to your students two of the passages referenced in chapter 20: Isaiah 46:9–11 and Psalm 33:11. Then direct students to read the following passages and to note, in **JE 66 God's Purpose Will Stand**, any additional insights or questions: Isaiah 14:24, 27; Proverbs 19:21; Hebrews 6:17–20; and Daniel 4:35. Provide any reference or study material you would like students to use. Discuss student conclusions as a class.

The Nature of Mission (10–15 minutes)

Ask students to work with a partner or in groups of three to read and discuss answers to the questions in **JE 67 Thoughts on the Nature of Mission**. If there is time, let them journal individual responses to this activity.

Focus on People (activity time to vary)

Students should either turn in or present to the class the People in History Profile project (their completed profiles of contemporary people on mission with God). Discuss as a class the varieties of people and circumstances through which God is at work in the world today. Challenge students to consider their own role in participating in God's mission to the world.

If Time Activity

Place the following quotation from Stephen Neill (1986, 379) on the board: "No reader of the New Testament need be surprised to learn that the work of God in the world goes forward in spite of the imperfections as well as because of the virtues of Christian believers." Ask students to respond to the following questions either in writing on **BLM 20.1 Stephen Neill on God's Work Going Forward** or as part of a class discussion:

- What examples from the New Testament demonstrate the principle that Neill articulates?

- What examples from our study of the past two thousand years of history demonstrate it?

- What examples do you see in your own life and in the lives of those around you that bear out this truth?

Formal Assessment

- Unit 3 exam

- Looking Back: A Review of History portfolio project

- People in History Profile project

- Student essay in response to the following:

  ○ What is the difference between the "mission of God" and "mission for God"?

  ○ Which represents a biblically sound understanding of the relationship between people, God, and mission? Give examples to support your answer.

What's Next

Chapter Reading

Have students read chapter 21 in preparation for the next lesson.

Introduction to Getting to Know a People Group: An Ethnographic Study

In the next and final unit, your students will be challenged to participate in a long-term research project that culminates in class presentations alongside the study of the final chapter of the course. The project can be tailored to your individual classroom needs, and you can set your own pace and timeline for the different elements of the project that are listed in **BLM 20.2 Getting to Know a People Group: An Ethnographic Stud**y and **BLM 20.3 People Group Profile Template**. Feel free to be creative in extending the project and adapting it for your particular needs. The goal of the project is for students to begin extending their focus outward and to think about applying some of the concepts from the book.

Two central components make up the project. In the first component, students individually conduct a basic ethnographic study of a specific people group whom they select and study. In the second component of the project, students are directed to assess what their own unique gifts, talents, and interests are and to determine how those are related to their participation in God's mission. Suggested research focus and reflections are designed to help students become more aware of the unique ways in which God has formed them to participate in His purpose.

You will want to pace your students' work on this project so that they can complete it before the Celebration activity that is the core of lesson 47. There are three separate research phases suggested for this ethnographic study: choosing a group, getting to know your group, and exploring incarnational ministry to your group. A fourth phase of the project is both a portfolio presentation and an in-class presentation. In the outline of these phases in **BLM 20.2** are suggested time frames (that can certainly be adapted to your needs) and some resources for undertaking this type of study.

Practices Unit

unit four

Practices Unit Introduction

Student Edition Introduction

So, what does it look like to be on mission with God? Where do we pick up now that we understand more about God's story in the Bible, God's love of unity within diversity, and people's ways of participating in the mission of God during previous times? That is the heart of this final unit—practices. What are some ways in which we accept our personal invitations to live missionally with God?

Being on mission with God looks different for different people. In this unit, you won't find a one-size-fits-all label. There aren't any cookie cutters here. Instead, you'll find some general principles and some stories about what being on mission with God can look like and what it has looked like for others. Just as no two people pack exactly the same items in the same way in their backpacks as they prepare for a hike, your life with God will take on additional shades of depth and personal meaning that make it uniquely your own. Think of these chapters as a bundle of basics that you should take along on any journey, basics that are the essential items for the backpack—including highlights you won't want to miss as you journey on your adventure with God. The topics in this chapter are essential components of participating in missio Dei—the stuff you want to have along in your backpack as you go. Happy travels!

Big Ideas

• Participating in missio Dei requires a personal intimacy with God.

• Participating in missio Dei requires spiritual passion.

• Participating in missio Dei is lived out in the context of community.

• Missio Dei culminates in the gathering of every tribe, tongue, language, and nation around the throne of God.

Memory Verses

John 10:2–4

> The man who enters by the gate is the shepherd of his sheep. The watchman opens the gate for him, and the sheep listen to his voice. He calls his own sheep by name and leads them out. When he has brought out all his own, he goes on ahead of them, and his sheep follow him because they know his voice.

Matthew 22:37–40, The Message

> Jesus said, " 'Love the Lord your God with all your passion and prayer and intelligence.' This is the most important, the first on any list. But there is a second to set alongside it: 'Love others as well as you love yourself.' These two commands are pegs; everything in God's Law and the Prophets hangs from them."

Revelation 5:9–10

> And they sang a new song: "You are worthy to take the scroll and to open its seals, because you were slain, and with your blood you purchased men for God from every tribe and language and people and nation. You have made them to be a kingdom and priests to serve our God, and they will reign on the earth."

John 13:34–35

A new command I give you: Love one another. As I have loved you, so you must love one another. By this all men will know that you are my disciples, if you love one another.

Matthew 7:24–27

Therefore everyone who hears these words of mine and puts them into practice is like a wise man who built his house on the rock. The rain came down, the streams rose, and the winds blew and beat against that house; yet it did not fall, because it had its foundation on the rock. But everyone who hears these words of mine and does not put them into practice is like a foolish man who built his house on sand. The rain came down, the streams rose, and the winds blew and beat against that house, and it fell with a great crash.

Revelation 7:9–10

After this I looked and there before me was a great multitude that no one could count, from every nation, tribe, people and language, standing before the throne and in front of the Lamb. They were wearing white robes and were holding palm branches in their hands. And they cried out in a loud voice: "Salvation belongs to our God, who sits on the throne, and to the Lamb."

1 Corinthians 12:12–27

The body is a unit, though it is made up of many parts; and though all its parts are many, they form one body. So it is with Christ. For we were all baptized by one Spirit into one body— whether Jews or Greeks, slave or free—and we were all given the one Spirit to drink.

Now the body is not made up of one part but of many. If the foot should say, "Because I am not a hand, I do not belong to the body," it would not for that reason cease to be part of the body. And if the ear should say, "Because I am not an eye, I do not belong to the body," it would not for that reason cease to be part of the body. If the whole body were an eye, where would the sense of hearing be? If the whole body were an ear, where would the sense of smell be? But in fact God has arranged the parts in the body, every one of them, just as he wanted them to be. If they were all one part, where would the body be? As it is, there are many parts, but one body.

The eye cannot say to the hand, "I don't need you!" And the head cannot say to the feet, "I don't need you!" On the contrary, those parts of the body that seem to be weaker are indispensable, and the parts that we think are less honorable we treat with special honor. And the parts that are unpresentable are treated with special modesty, while our presentable parts need no special treatment. But God has combined the members of the body and has given greater honor to the parts that lacked it, so that there should be no division in the body, but that its parts should have equal concern for each other. If one part suffers, every part suffers with it; if one part is honored, every part rejoices with it.

Now you are the body of Christ, and each one of you is a part of it.

Revelation 21:1–4, 23–26

Then I saw a new heaven and a new earth, for the first heaven and the first earth had passed away, and there was no longer any sea. I saw the Holy City, the new Jerusalem, coming down out of heaven from God, prepared as a bride beautifully dressed for her husband. And I heard a loud voice from the throne saying, "Now the dwelling of God is with men, and he will live with them. They will be his people, and God himself will be with them and be their God. He will wipe every tear from their eyes. There will be no more death or mourning or crying or pain, for the old order of things has passed away."

The city does not need the sun or the moon to shine on it, for the glory of God gives it light, and the Lamb is its lamp. The nations will walk by its light, and the kings of the earth will bring their splendor into it. On no day will its gates ever be shut, for there will be no night there. The glory and honor of the nations will be brought into it.

Web Resources

Link to more resources in our community at www.missiodei-thejourney.com.

Intimacy with God

Big Idea

Participating in missio Dei requires a personal intimacy with God.

Key Concepts

- God desires to have an intimate, conversational relationship with us as a normal part of everyday life.

- God speaks to us today as faithfully and regularly as He has to His children in the past.

- Developing an intimate relationship with God requires practice in learning to recognize His voice.

Reflective Questions

- Do you believe that God is really concerned and interested in the day-to-day decisions and events of your life? Why or why not? (SE p. 250)

- If you could hear God's perspective on your circumstances, feelings, and decisions, how would that change the way you make decisions? Would you want that kind of relationship? Why or why not? (SE p. 250)

- How would a conversational relationship with God affect your participation with Him in the work He is doing to fulfill His purpose? (SE p. 250)

Teacher's Heart

A friend who has been journeying toward a relationship with God for almost two decades once said to me, "God doesn't talk to me like He talks to you." She was implying that God didn't speak to her at all, but, of course, that is not the case. He speaks to all of us, though we are all in different places in learning to hear Him and in recognizing His specific way of speaking to each one of us. Another friend told me that she gets really suspicious of people who say "God told me ..." or who make other such statements. Since she doesn't discern the voice of God clearly in her own life, she's not sure other people can hear Him either.

Perhaps you find that you have similar thoughts. It isn't unusual at all for believers to have walked in proximity with God for many years without walking intimately with Him or feeling as though they have a clear sense of His communicating with them personally. Your students may have hesitations in believing in or wanting an intimate, conversational relationship with God. But this level of intimacy is at the heart of our life with Him. Jesus says, "And I will ask the Father, and he will give you another Counselor to be with you forever—the Spirit of truth. The world cannot accept him, because it neither sees him nor knows him. But you know him, for he lives with you and will be in you" (John 14:16–17).

Teacher's Preparation

The following quotation is in the last paragraph of chapter 21: "Intimacy with God is what fuels the spiritual passion that drives our participation in His mission, our involvement in the kingdom of God now, our living incarnationally, and so many other things we have talked about in this course" (SE p. 260). The crux of the whole matter of our participating with God in His mission rests on the relationship we have with Him. We are often planning and strategizing about how to live out our Christian lives, but at the heart of it, relationship with God *is* the strategy. Relationship with God is the place from which all other action must spring in order to have any value or staying power. It is the foundational element of living out missio Dei.

This unit is titled Practices Unit because the issues we discuss here are "where the rubber meets the road"—the essentials of day-in, day-out walking with God. Your students will be challenged to consider their own practices and participation in God's mission. Here, they will be filling their backpacks with essential tools for the journey. As in the previous unit, we include people profiles, which expose students to a variety of ways people participate in missio Dei. We encourage you to incorporate these profiles into your conversations in class and to use the activities involving them, since they offer additional glimpses of how to practice the disciplines we focus on in this unit. The lessons in this final unit are application-oriented in content and designed to give students multiple opportunities and means for practicing the concepts discussed in each chapter. For example, the three lessons for chapter 21 offer a range of activities designed to both provoke a desire for intimacy with God and offer ways to practice developing deeper intimacy with Him. Resist the temptation to rush through these activities; instead, think of these lessons as an intensive retreat or workshop time in which your students will have lots of different experiences for practicing the disciplines discussed in this unit.

This final unit is also a point in the course at which you can really begin tying the content of the chapters into *where your students are* in life. Many are in the throes of planning for post–high school life,

beginning to discern the different gifts, interests, and callings in their individual lives. Some have already begun hearing God's invitation to specific "next" places, but others are just beginning to discern their direction in life. As often as possible, tie the previous content of the course and especially this final unit into the reality of *where* they are living right now and the choices and decisions they are praying through and making. There is very little prescribed in the lessons in this regard, but you know the needs of your students and should strive to make the connections as often as possible between the material they are studying and the decisions they are making as they look toward the end of their high school experience.

Intimacy with God couldn't be more foundational and essential to participating in God's mission. Your students may not recognize that there is something living, personal, and intimate to having a relationship with God. Many may not have a positive image of a relationship with God because they don't realize that it is possible to have conversational intimacy with Him or that it can be as real and as conversational as any other relationship. Some may have become disillusioned or may have even stopped trusting God because of something that has happened in their lives. Or, they may view the "relationship" as some sort of contractual "get out of hell free" exchange that took place once in their lives. Beyond that they may think they are on their own to try to figure out the best life they can. Chapter 21 seeks to point out the reality and the importance of having an intimate relationship with God. This lesson and the two following it offer some ways to begin exploring and practicing that relationship.

You will want to begin today's lesson by discussing chapter 21 and the students' reaction to it. At this point in the course, your students may be encountering new possibilities in their walk with God, and they will need ample time to continue processing information. You may wish to linger an extra day to discuss and explore the material presented in these lessons.

After a general discussion of the chapter, your students will evaluate whether they even want to have a relationship with God that is intimate and conversational. They may assume it to be impossible, too intrusive, or too much work. Or they may be very excited by the prospect of a deeper intimacy with God. Today's first activity is designed to help assess their assumptions and attitudes. You should stress to the students that this activity is "for their eyes only." Set a mood for some reflective time in your classroom, and let them respond to the statements in **JE 68 Assessing My Assumptions**. Following that time, you will guide them in looking at those attitudes in a different way that involves the sources and the outcomes of our assumptions.

Our assumptions and attitudes toward God and a relationship with Him very much affect the practice of intimate conversation with God in our lives. For example, if we assume that God doesn't speak to us today, the outcome will be that we won't pursue an intimate relationship with Him. A key to understanding attitudes and assumptions that might block a relationship with God is to look back at their sources. Sometimes our negative assumptions spring from ignorance, fear, lies we have believed or agreed with, or sinful choices we've made. In the second activity you will walk students through the process of looking at and considering the sources of some of their attitudes and assumptions, particularly those that might stand in the way of intimacy with God. Direct them to consider how their assumptions and attitudes can influence an intimate relationship with God. To facilitate this train of thought, you might want to put the following diagram on the board:

Once students have used **JE 68** to identify their assumptions, have them look both forward to the logical outcomes of those assumptions and backward at the possible sources of their attitudes. We have provided some verses in the following chart to help you affirm truth to your students about who God is and how He desires to be in relationship with each of us. Depending on your students' willingness to share, you may want to read together through the truths from the chart and leave it at that. Or this may be a time when you again present the gospel to your students or discuss some of the barricades, such as unconfessed sin, that the Bible says can stand in the way of an intimate relationship with God. For some students, this exercise and discussion will be the starting point of working through barricades that have kept them from having a real relationship with God. Ask God for sensitivity as you walk alongside students who are working through deeper layers of issues. You may want to be prepared to offer suggestions for additional help in praying through and working through some of the issues this exercise uncovers for them.

The next portion of this lesson deals with raising the "want to" quotient for your students. They will first examine some statements from the chapter that affirm why God would want to speak to us individually today, and then students will work through **JE 69 Intimacy Versus No Intimacy**, a chart that contrasts a life characterized by intimacy with God with a life characterized by no intimacy with God. If you run out of time, you can assign this portion of the lesson as homework.

Event/Decision/Agreement

↓

Assumptions/Attitudes

↓

Behavior/Outcome

Circumstances and Lies We Might Agree with That Keep Us from Intimacy with God	The Truth Is …
A lack of faith can keep us from hearing God's voice. The lie is that God doesn't speak.	Hebrews 3:7–8 says, "So, as the Holy Spirit says: 'Today, if you hear his voice, do not harden your hearts as you did in the rebellion, during the time of testing in the desert.' " Hebrews 3:12 says, "See to it, brothers, that none of you has a sinful, unbelieving heart that turns away from the living God."
A sense of guilt or condemnation can keep us from hearing God's voice. The lie is that God doesn't waste His time with losers or that He wouldn't like you very much if He really knew you.	Romans 8:1 says, "Therefore, there is now no condemnation for those who are in Christ Jesus." Romans 8:38–39 says, "For I am convinced that neither death nor life, neither angels nor demons, neither the present nor the future, nor any powers, neither height nor depth, nor anything else in all creation, will be able to separate us from the love of God that is in Christ Jesus our Lord." Psalm 139 celebrates the fact that God knows us intimately. He knows us better than we know ourselves.
Thinking we have to "be good enough" can keep us from hearing God's voice. The lie is that you have to earn God's love and attention.	Romans 5:8 says, "But God demonstrates his own love for us in this: While we were still sinners, Christ died for us."
Failing to seek God can keep us from hearing His voice. So can unconfessed sin. The lie is that sin and ignoring God don't matter to Him.	James 4:8 says, "Come near to God and he will come near to you. Wash your hands, you sinners, and purify your hearts, you double-minded."
Being busy or being consumed with other priorities keeps us from hearing God's voice. The lie is that we are in charge of providing for ourselves, and we deserve to live comfortably.	Matthew 6:20–21 says, "But store up for yourselves treasures in heaven, where moth and rust do not destroy, and where thieves do not break in and steal. For where your treasure is, there your heart will be also."
Being discontent with our circumstances can keep us from hearing God's voice, either because we blame God for them, or because we are so consumed with them that we cannot lift our eyes to see Him. The lie is that God's plan for our lives should match up to our expectations.	Hebrews 13:5 says, "Keep your lives free from the love of money and be content with what you have, because God has said, 'Never will I leave you; never will I forsake you.' " In 1 Timothy 6:6, we read, "But godliness with contentment is great gain."
Believing that God doesn't care about us can keep us from hearing God's voice. The lie is that God is disinterested in the world, its people, and its events.	Deuteronomy 31:8 says, "The Lord himself goes before you and will be with you; he will never leave you nor forsake you. Do not be afraid; do not be discouraged." In Matthew 28:20, Jesus says, "And surely I am with you always, to the very end of the age."

Objectives

- Students will discuss their reaction to material presented in chapter 21.

- Students will assess their own feelings about having an intimate, conversational relationship with God.

- Students will evaluate and respond to statements about the fact that God speaks to us today and about the purpose of an intimate relationship with Him.

- Students will begin to record in their journals the different incidents of God's speaking to them.

Unpacking

Reaction to Chapter Discussion (10–15 minutes)

Give students an opportunity to react to the material in chapter 21 through class discussion. Answer questions or clarify any misunderstandings from their reading of the chapter.

Assessing Your Assumptions (15–20 minutes)

Direct students to **JE 68 Assessing My Assumptions** and give them some time to reflect on the statements and to identify those that match their own assumptions and beliefs. Then, using the "Teacher's Preparation" material, help students see the possible outcome of their assumptions and encourage them to reflect on the source of those. Guide them through considering the truth of Scripture in the face of the assumptions they hold about intimacy with God.

Raising the "Want To" Quotient (10–15 minutes or as homework)

Discuss the following passage in their textbooks: "Stanley notes four reasons God speaks today. First, '*[God] loves us just as much as He loved the people of the Old and New Testament*.' Second, '*we need His definite and deliberate direction for our lives*' as much as they did. Third, '*we need [His] comfort and assurance*' just as much as they did. Finally, '*the most important reason God is still talking today is that He wants us to know Him*' (1985, 3). Remember, it is not what you *know about* God but rather, do you *know* God?" (SE pp. 252, 254).

Next, draw attention to **JE 69 Intimacy Versus No Intimacy**. Ask the students to read through the comparisons either in class or as homework and to write a reflection on what they would like in their own lives. You may choose to collect these reflections as an assessment.

A Second Look (5 minutes and as ongoing assignment)

Draw attention to the following quotation by Susan D. Hill in **JE 70 A Second Look**: "There is no trick to hearing God's voice. It has nothing to do with the number of years someone's been a Christian. Nor is it about being more spiritual than another. Once the barriers are cleared away, it comes down to noticing things, taking a second look, and pausing to reflect" (2008, 77; SE p. 256). Challenge students to recognize the need to "clear the barriers away," and remind them to consider some barriers that may have been revealed through the previous activities in class. Assign this journal entry as a place where students will record different messages that God is speaking to them. This can be assigned for a period of days or weeks, whichever works best for your situation. If you can, allow time in the coming days or weeks for students to discuss as a class what they are noticing.

What's Next

In preparation for the next lesson, have students read **JE 71 Listening Is Key** along with the people profiles **JE 72 Conversation with God** and **JE 73 Hearing from God**. Also have the students answer the questions that follow each profile.

Looking Ahead

If you have not already done so, assign the people group project (Getting to Know a People Group: An Ethnographic Study), using the resources referred to in lesson 35.

Practicing Intimacy with God

Big Idea

Participating in missio Dei requires a personal intimacy with God.

Key Concepts

- God desires to have an intimate, conversational relationship with us as a normal part of everyday life.

- God speaks to us today as faithfully and regularly as He has to His children in the past.

- Developing an intimate relationship with God requires practice in learning to recognize His voice.

Reflective Questions

- Do you believe that God is really concerned and interested in the day-to-day decisions and events of your life? Why or why not? (SE p. 250)

- If you could hear God's perspective on your circumstances, feelings, and decisions, how would that change the way you make decisions? Would you want that kind of relationship? Why or why not? (SE p. 250)

- How would a conversational relationship with God affect your participation with Him in the work He is doing to fulfill His purpose? (SE p. 250)

Teacher's Heart

What if God says something you don't want to hear? What if He asks you to do something you really don't want to do? These are the situations in which we are most likely to turn away from intimate relationship with God. We sometimes just shut Him out when He doesn't meet our expectations of how we think He should operate. And yet, God is far wiser and more loving than we can ever imagine. Why is it so hard for us to trust Him? Perhaps your students (or even you) are struggling with this very issue—intimacy with God. Be open with your students about areas in your own life in which you have struggled or are struggling in your intimacy with God. It is important for them to see your transparency. Even in the hard places God is walking beside us, perhaps waiting for us in our brokenness to invite Him in. Even if our conversation turns to ranting and raving, God is there—He can handle it. The key is to keep the lines of communication open, to continue the dialogue. It is OK to just sit in His presence and recognize that we may never fully understand our circumstances. And our gracious Lord has thought of everything. He can and will equip us with the trust and the faith we need to walk with Him—even over difficult terrain. "His divine power has given us everything we need for life and godliness through our knowledge of him who called us by his own glory and goodness" (2 Peter 1:3). Ask God to strengthen your understanding of His provision. And celebrate His goodness today both in your heart and with your students.

Teacher's Preparation

This lesson and the next are designed to give students some different ways to practice developing intimacy with God. The first activity is an object lesson to demonstrate our role and the role God plays in developing an intimate relationship with Him. It relates to the portion of chapter 21 that talks about "plugging in" to God rather than trying to "make" a relationship with Him happen (SE p. 255). You may want to spend some time discussing the toaster analogy from the chapter before presenting the sponge object lesson to your students.

Just as the chapter describes a toaster being plugged in to a power source as an analogy for our role and God's role in an intimate relationship, the sponge object lesson demonstrates the same concepts: we set aside the time to show up, and God meets with us. In today's object lesson, the sponge represents each of us, and water represents God as living water (see John 7:37–38 and Isaiah 55:1–2). A sponge is a dried-up, useless object until it is wet. When wet, it grows, becomes flexible, can fit into various spaces, and can be very useful. All these things can be discussed as analogies to our own "soaking" in an intimate relationship with God. The sponge gets wet when an intentional choice is made to move the sponge into contact with the water. To carry out the object lesson, give students each a small piece of dry sponge (a one-inch piece will be large enough). Explain to them that the dry sponge is

like a person who isn't in an intimate relationship with God—dried-up—or like a toaster that isn't plugged in—useless. Next, read John 7:37–38 and Isaiah 55:1–2, and talk about the metaphor of God as living water.

The next activities are concerned with setting the stage for and actually engaging in practicing intimacy with God (a topic dealt with in **JE 71 Listening Is Key**). The first is a short discussion about the fear of failure or "doing it wrong." Next, students will answer some questions about what they have done in the past that helps them hear from God. Depending on the climate in your classroom, you can have students answer these privately as a journaling experience or have them discuss the questions either in small groups or as a class.

Then ask students to look at **JE 72 Conversation with God** and **JE 73 Hearing from God**, the profiles that go along with chapter 21. These profiles are anecdotal pictures of how God intimately communicates with two different people. As is true of the profiles in the History Unit, these profiles can reveal inspiring characteristics and traits in others who have journeyed, or are journeying, with God. Students should note anything that strikes them as significant about each profile. You can assign the listening exercise in the "If Time Activity" section as an in-class activity or as homework.

Objectives

- Students will participate in an object lesson that demonstrates their role and the role God plays in developing an intimate relationship with Him.

- Students will evaluate their concerns related to their mistakes, or failures, in developing intimacy with God.

- Students will discuss and devise ways that they might practice conversation with God.

Unpacking

Object Lesson (10–15 minutes)

Spend some time discussing the toaster analogy on SE page 255. Then introduce a companion analogy through the sponge object lesson discussed in the "Teacher's Preparation" section. To carry out the object lesson, you will need a sponge and some water. It is more dramatic if the sponge you have is shriveled up or very flat when dry. The object lesson will be even more personal if you can provide a small piece of sponge for each of your students and a common source of water to which they bring their sponges. Depending on how elaborately you set up this activity, this time in your classroom could become very worshipful. You could have a central fountain of water, or a bowl of water, set up as a place of response during the object lesson, or you could simply demonstrate the concept of soaking in the living water of God's presence. To demonstrate that passing a sponge through a small trickle or stream of water won't really change it much, pour out a small cup of water over the bowl, and pass the sponge through the stream of water. Explain that this represents a casual relationship with God. Some but not all of the sponge is wet, and the few wet spots on it don't particularly change it or make it useful. Now immerse your sponge in a bowl or tub of water and show students that it is filled up by this act. Talk about the analogy of spending significant and intimate time with God, immersed in the living waters. You may then invite them to bring their sponges to the tub of water as a sign of commitment to pursuing deeper intimacy with God through spending more time with Him. If you do this, point out that they are taking action to get to the water—just as they must make a choice to spend time with God, listening for His voice and learning to "connect the dots" (see SE p. 258). Tell the students to take their sponge home as a visual reminder of the difference between intimacy with God and a casual or nonexistent relationship with Him. You may also want to leave a sample sponge or two sitting on your desk or on a shelf as a reminder of what happens over time when the sponge dries up (when our intimacy with God wanes over time).

Addressing Failure (8–10 minutes)

Write on the board the following quotation that is most commonly attributed to hockey great Wayne Gretzky[1]: "You miss 100% of the shots you don't take." Discuss the quotation with students. Then read the paragraph from SE page 259 that begins "At this point some of you may be very skeptical." Discuss with students the value of learning to have conversational intimacy with God in terms of taking baby steps and being willing to give it a try, even if it is slow going at first.

Intentionally Pursuing God (10–12 minutes)

Either as a journaling assignment, a small-group discussion, or a class discussion, ask students to respond to the following questions in **JE 74 Intentionally Pursuing God**:

• Where do you feel closest to God? Any particular locations?

• In what places or circumstances have you heard Him in the past?

- Is there anything you have to leave behind as you pursue intimacy with God? Do you have attitudes or habits that will need to be changed to make time for talking with God regularly?

- What are some specific ways you can "soak in the fountain of life"—in other words, how can you engage in intimacy with God?

Challenge students to choose some specific ways they might experiment with conversation with God.

Focus on People (8–10 minutes)

Direct your students to the profiles **JE 72 Conversation with God** and **JE 73 Hearing from God**. Give students the opportunity to discuss their answers to the questions that follow each profile.

If Time Activity

This listening activity should take about 10–20 minutes. First, discuss **JE 71 Listening Is Key**. Keeping in mind the ideas from that discussion, direct students to the "Conversation Starters" sidebar (SE p. 259) as a way to begin a time of simply listening for God's voice in answer to a question. Change the lighting in your room and maybe play some soft instrumental praise music in the background. Or if you can, take students outside for this activity. Have them capture on **JE 70 A Second Look** anything they hear. If class time is limited, assign this activity as homework.

What's Next

If there was not time in class to do the listening activity just described in the section above, assign it as homework. Also, have students read **JE 75 A Beautiful Mind and Life** in preparation for the next lesson.

☙

NOTE

1. Kyle Weaver, "Osceola's Sharpshooter," *Osceola (WI) Sun*, January 13, 2009, http://www.osceola sun.com/ (accessed January 28, 2009).

More Practicing Intimacy with God

Lesson 38

Big Idea

Participating in missio Dei requires a personal intimacy with God.

Key Concepts

- God desires to have an intimate, conversational relationship with us as a normal part of everyday life.
- God speaks to us today as faithfully and regularly as He has to His children in the past.
- Developing an intimate relationship with God requires practice in learning to recognize His voice.

Reflective Questions

- Do you believe that God is really concerned and interested in the day-to-day decisions and events of your life? Why or why not? (SE p. 250)
- If you could hear God's perspective on your circumstances, feelings, and decisions, how would that change the way you make decisions? Would you want that kind of relationship? Why or why not? (SE p. 250)
- How would a conversational relationship with God affect your participation with Him in the work He is doing to fulfill His purpose? (SE p. 250)

Teacher's Heart

I have a little cube of sponge like the ones needed for the sponge analogy in the previous lesson. I got it during a worship service at my church, and it has lived in different places in my home ever since. I sometimes pull out a little bowl of water for it when I am having a quiet time and then leave the wet sponge on the counter to see how long it takes for it to dry out. It is amazing what a reminder it can be of my spiritual condition if I am not continually returning to the source of life in an intimate relationship with God. Maybe you have some sort of similar means of "taking your spiritual temperature." I find that I do much better when I have little reminders of my need to constantly seek the Lord; otherwise I am likely to think I can make it on my own. Here's a favorite prayer of mine from Saint Philip Neri, who lived in the sixteenth century: "O Jesus, watch over me always, especially today, or I shall betray you like Judas" (Saint Benedict 1993, 117). Intimacy with God is an everyday matter. Ask Him to help you understand this afresh today.

Teacher's Preparation

This lesson is a continuation of our lessons on practicing intimacy with God. The focus today is on three things: interacting with God through His Word, using our senses of sight and hearing to experience intimacy with God, and exploring the ways that movement and speech can affect our conversations with God.

The first activity involves **JE 75 A Beautiful Mind and Life**, text from John Ortberg regarding meditating on Psalm 16:8. Begin by discussing Ortberg's example of how to meditate on a verse from the Bible. You may also want to share your own experiences of meditating on passages from the Bible. Primarily you want to communicate to students that there is no "wrong" way to meditate on God's Word. The practice basically involves spending time thinking about what God's Word says from a lot of different angles, or as Ortberg calls it, "positive worry" (2005, 99). Do let students know, however, that there is a difference between meditating on a verse and studying it. Rather than focusing on other resources to gain a better understanding of a verse, the practice of meditating on passages from the Bible focuses on hearing what God brings to your mind. If students find themselves with wandering minds, remind them to simply refocus their thoughts either by slowly repeating the verse (or a portion of it) or by slowly reading it to themselves. Once you have discussed the idea of meditation, let students practice. A list of possible verses is found in the "Unpacking" section.

A related practice of interacting with the Bible comes in the form of praying the "divine hours," or fixed-hour prayer, described in the "Further Study" section. Also there are many resources available regarding using the Bible for praying. You and your students may be interested in learning more about these practices. There is additional information in the "Further Study" section. Research into these ancient practices forms the basis of an activity in the "Extra Mile" section.

The second activity in this lesson focuses on using the senses to help discern God's voice. By taking a nature walk with your class, you can invite students to include the senses of sight and sound as they learn to recognize the presence of God and His reaching out to them. To prepare students for this activity, ask them to think about the different ways they communicate with their friends (this is discussed on SE page 258). Remind them that God often uses different ways to speak with us, and one of them can be through His creation. Read Psalm

19:1–6 and discuss it briefly as a class before you go outside together. Instruct students to refrain from talking to one another during your walk outside, and remind them to pay attention to the particular sights and sounds that they notice. You may want to have your students pick a special spot where they can then spend some time alone with God. You can reconvene at a designated time. As they will discover through a postwalk discussion, that which God prompts them each to notice will often vary from what He prompts their classmates to notice. You could also ask the students to capture their response to this activity through writing in their journal (**JE 70 A Second Look**) or in a stand-alone reflection to be turned in.

After the nature walk, there are three more ways of practicing that you could have students try once in class and then continue as ongoing homework. Each involves another way of developing and practicing intimacy with God. If you don't have time to try them in class, you could still encourage the students to practice them on their own.

Finally, in the "What's Next" section, you'll be assigning homework that each student should complete privately. You will ask the students to explore responding to God in different ways. Ask them to take some time to experiment with different postures as they talk with God. Some suggestions include walking, sitting still, kneeling, or lying facedown on the floor. They could try lifting their eyes or hands toward the sky or bowing their heads or their bodies as they listen or speak. Some students may even feel comfortable dancing or singing to God. These are all biblical acts of worship. Tell students that if they normally journal their prayers, they should try speaking them aloud. Or if they normally speak their prayers aloud, have them try praying silently or writing their prayers. Remind them to try to concentrate on God and not on how odd they might feel. Instruct them to reflect on what works for them and what is just plain uncomfortable. Give them your instructions about whether you want a written response or an in-class discussion about the homework.

Objectives

- Students will meditate on a Bible verse and describe their experience in writing.

- Students will participate in a nature walk and outline the different things that they heard or saw from God as they walked or as they spent time alone with Him.

- Students will practice developing intimacy with God through activities that help them experiment with different movement, voice, and reflection.

Unpacking

Hearing God's Voice by Focusing on the Bible (15–20 minutes)

Discuss **JE 75 A Beautiful Mind and Life**. Then let students choose a verse from the following list to meditate on during class, and have them note their experiences in their journal (**JE 70 A Second Look**). Some verses to suggest are Psalm 23:1, Philippians 4:19, 2 Thessalonians 3:5, Hebrews 13:8, 1 John 4:7, or any other verses you would like to emphasize.

Seeing and Hearing: Take a Nature Walk (15–20 minutes)

Using the guidelines in the "Teacher's Preparation" section, prepare your students for a walk outside around your campus. After their walk, discuss as a class the different sights or sounds they noticed. Draw attention to the variety of items God focused their attention on, and ask them to record in **JE 70** any specific messages or affirmations they heard from God.

More Ways to Practice (as time allows and as ongoing homework)

- John Ortberg describes the practice of "reviewing the dailies" (a filmmaking technique of reviewing the film shot during the previous day) as a way to develop an ear for God's voice. Read this description to students and then ask them to try this activity:

    You can do this right now by walking through yesterday in your mind with God and asking where he was present and at work in each scene. Start with the moment when you woke up in the morning. God was present, waking you up, giving you a mini-resurrection. What were your first thoughts? What do you think God wanted to say to you in that moment?

    Then go on from one scene to the next through your day. As I review what happened when I greeted my family, ate breakfast, and went through meetings at work, I see patterns emerging—the ongoing presence of anxiety or anger—that I miss when I don't take time to review the dailies.… The more often I review, the better I get at recognizing [God] in "real time." (2005, 39)

- Direct students to **JE 76 Foundational Truths**, in which they will find a list of foundational truths for living close to God. Ask them to read these and then to continue to review them once a day for two weeks as they begin to cultivate a more intimate relationship with God.

- Assign **JE 77 I Am Thankful** as a way for students to start a conversation with God. Remind them that we are good at asking for "stuff" from God, but we don't always talk to Him about what we are thankful for. Over the next ten days, have students list three things they are thankful for, and then have them journal a response to God about what they have written.

Extra Mile

- Students could research the different postures and forms of expression people in the Bible used during conversations with God. Another possible study is to look at the different places where conversations between men and God took place in the Bible. The students' findings could be the basis of a class presentation on different settings for intimacy with God, or the students could work to incorporate one new finding into their own practice of intimacy with God.

- Students could research and participate in either fixed-hour prayer (praying the divine hours) or praying with the Bible. Some resources for learning more about these practices are listed in the "Further Study" section.

What's Next

Students should complete the homework assignment involving different movement and speech described in the "Teacher's Preparation" section. Also, have students read chapter 22 in preparation for the next lesson.

Further Study

Fixed-hour prayer, or praying the divine hours, is the practice of praying through psalms, hymns, and other written prayers at set times of the day. It is an ancient practice that immerses one particularly in the psalms. For more information, see the websites www.explorefaith.org/prayer/fixed/ or www.phyllistickle.com/fixedhour prayer.html, and Phyllis Tickle's book *The Divine Hours* (New York: Oxford University Press, pocket edition, 2007).

Other general resources that cultivate conversational intimacy with God are as follows:

Blackaby, Henry, and Richard Blackaby. 2002. *Hearing God's voice*. Nashville, TN: B&H Publishing.
Brother Andrew. 2007. *The practice of the presence of God*. Amberson, PA: Scroll Publishing. (Also available for downloading at http://books.google.com/.)
Eldredge, John. 2008. *Walking with God*. Nashville, TN: Thomas Nelson.
Hill, Susan D. 2008. *Closer than your skin: Unwrapping the mystery of intimacy with God*. Colorado Springs, CO: WaterBrook Press.
Laubach, Frank C. 2007. *Letters by a modern mystic: Excerpts from letters written to his father*. Colorado Springs, CO: Purposeful Design Publications.
Ogilvie, Lloyd John. 2007. *Conversation with God*. Eugene, OR: Harvest House.
Ortberg, Nancy. 2008. *Looking for God: An unexpected journey through tattoos, tofu, and pronouns*. Carol Stream, IL: Tyndale House.
Stanley, Charles. 1985. *How to listen to God*. Nashville, TN: Thomas Nelson.
Willard, Dallas. 1999. *Hearing God: Developing a conversational relationship with God*. Downers Grove, IL: InterVarsity Press.

Lesson 39

Passion: Part 1

Big Idea

Participating in missio Dei requires spiritual passion.

Key Concepts

- Spiritual passion is controlled by the Spirit of God and characterized by the fruit of the Spirit.

- Spiritual passion is birthed through an intimacy with God that transforms our desires so that we can move in harmony with His purpose and mission.

- Spiritual passion is more than enthusiasm or religious duty. It is God-seeking rather than self-seeking.

Reflective Questions

- What are you passionate about? Are your passions characterized by the fruit of the Spirit or by something else? Where does your passion come from? The world? Your own pleasure? God's desires for you? (SE p. 262)

- What are you willing to suffer for? What are you willing to sacrifice comfort, time, money, or other things for? (SE p. 262)

- What is the difference between being a believer and being an experiencer (see SE p. 276)? Which are you in your relationship with God? Which do you have more of: information about God or intimacy with God? (SE p. 262)

- Do you fall prey to engaging in facsimiles of spiritual passion? Do you ever find yourself trying to fake spiritual passion? What can you do to stay focused on the true source of spiritual passion when you feel dry or feel as though you're on the wrong track? (SE p. 262)

Teacher's Heart

One of the points mentioned in chapter 22 is that word usage tends to change over time. Because of this, we often lose some of the richness and intent of a word or a phrase; some words we use have lost their original flavor and depth. For example, the words *awesome* and *love* are examples of words that are so casually used today that they have in some ways ceased to convey the grandeur of the ideas they represent. As this chapter describes, *passion* is another such word. We have perhaps lost sight of its original intensity, and the Christian zeal and focus with which the term was originally steeped. Ask God to reveal to your students and to you the passion with which He pursues us, and ask Him to enable all of you to experience a lifetime of ever-deepening passion for Him.

Teacher's Preparation

Chapter 22 introduces the idea of spiritual passion, and it challenges students to pursue God with an intensity and zeal that the original meaning of *passion* conveyed. The chapter begins with the observation that we as human beings are driven by a core desire for what John Eldredge calls "*life as it was meant to be*" (2007, 1, emphasis added; SE p. 261). The chapter then unfolds some aspects of spiritual passion that you should discuss with your students in today's lesson: defining the parameters of what spiritual passion is and isn't, and exploring the process of being transformed into spiritually passionate people through intimacy with God.

You may want to begin your discussion by brainstorming a list of characteristics of "life as it was meant to be," to help students focus on the need for the redemptive work of God in the world around us. When we recognize that God alone can restore life as He intended it to be, we have the beginning of a life of passion for the things of God. Discuss next the history and meaning of the term *passion*, using the etymological information on SE pages 262–63. Highlight the term's aspects that deal with intensity and suffering, particularly as they relate to the sufferings of Christ during His crucifixion. This intensity springs from deep love, and to emphasize this you might want to read and discuss 1 John 4:19 and Revelation 2:4 mentioned on SE page 263. Next, draw student attention to the following definition from the chapter: "*Spiritual passion*—a desire for God and His purpose that is so consuming that we are willing to sacrifice and even suffer for it" (SE p. 264). Let the students discuss their reactions to this definition.

Ask students to consider the source of spiritual passion. As noted on SE page 264, "Spiritual passion is a passion that is 'Spirit of God controlled.' " It is cultivated and ignited through an intimate relationship with God. To further explore this idea, discuss things that stand in contrast with true spiritual passion. Chapter 22 distinguishes between passion and enthusiasm, and between spiritual passion and religious duty. It also notes that self-preservation is not a hallmark of true spiritual passion. Because we are often tempted to "perform" for God out of a sense of duty rather than a true passion, you may want to take some time contrasting these two ideas using a chart similar to the one below.

Your students may have additional thoughts to add. Teenagers are often very attuned to authenticity, and the contrast between religious duty and spiritual passion is something they will probably be very able to identify with. You may want to conclude your discussion of defining spiritual passion by considering that the fruit of the Spirit mark true spiritual passion. A separate activity focusing on Galatians 5:22–23 (**BLM 22.1 A Tree Shall Be Known by Its Fruit**) will extend teaching on this part of chapter 22.

Next, discuss with students the development of spiritual passion. It starts with an intimate and honest relationship with God. Emphasize that, just as cultivating intimacy with God is a lifelong process, the development of spiritual passion is also. Intimacy with God and passion for Him are deeply entwined. In fact, you cannot have true spiritual passion that is not grounded in an intimate

Religious Duty ...	Spiritual Passion ...
is performed externally (behavior), reflecting the belief that outside behavior will create goodness on the inside (heart).	comes from the inside (heart) and informs the outside (behavior).
is controlled by the person "performing" for approval, resulting in self-centeredness and a tendency toward self-preservation.	is controlled by the Spirit of God within the believer, resulting in God-centeredness and a willingness to take risks for God's sake.
is performed by one who is concerned with appearance and who can often be just "going through the motions."	is filled with substance and meaning, and is found in one who is concerned with the heart of God.

relationship with God. Draw attention to the following: "True spiritual passion cannot be manufactured, no matter how hard you try to muster it in your own strength. It flows from the heart of God through faith into your life. It transforms you. It makes over your character and your heart" (SE p. 268). Discussion of this statement might also provide an opportunity for students to share what they have been learning through exercises of practicing intimacy with God from previous lessons.

Finally, discuss the role that spiritual passion plays in participating in God's purpose. As noted on SE page 269, "True spiritual passion will lead us into the story God is telling." Guide students to consider the relationship between intimacy with God, spiritual passion, and participation in His mission. The concept of spiritual passion will be explored further in the next lesson.

Once your discussion of the chapter is concluded, direct students to **BLM 22.1**, an activity that gives students the opportunity to examine their lives in terms of the fruit of the Spirit found in Galatians 5:22–23. Students will also read passages in 1 Corinthians 13:4–8, Philippians 4:8, and Colossians 3:12–16 to identify more of what true spiritual passion is marked by.

Objectives

- Students will discuss the definition and source of spiritual passion.

- Students will contrast spiritual passion with counterfeits of it, such as enthusiasm, religious duty, self-preservation, and other facsimiles and substitutes.

- Students will examine and discuss the characteristics of the Spirit of God and the hallmarks of true spiritual passion.

Unpacking

Class Discussion (25–35 minutes)

Using the notes in the "Teacher's Preparation" section, discuss the definition of *spiritual passion*, where it comes from, and what characterizes it. Draw attention to what the chapter has to say about the difference between spiritual passion and enthusiasm or religious duty. Conclude your discussion with a focus on the relationship between having intimacy with God, developing spiritual passion, and participating in God's mission. Conclude by asking for student questions regarding the material in chapter 22.

Fruit of the Spirit (10–15 minutes)

In small groups or as a class, students should read and discuss these passages that reveal some of the characteristics of a Spirit-controlled life: 1 Corinthians 13:4–8, Philippians 4:8, and Colossians 3:12–16. These, along with the classic listing in Galatians 5:22–23, paint a picture of the characteristics of true spiritual passion. After reading these passages, direct students to complete **BLM 22.1 A Tree Shall Be Known by Its Fruit**.

Extra Mile

- Watch Mel Gibson's movie *The Passion of the Christ* (released in 2004 by 20th Century Fox) and then discuss or record descriptions of the intensity and suffering present in Jesus' passion. Assign a creative response activity afterward in which students can create music, poetry, or a visual representation as a response to Christ's passion.

- Students could identify and research different words they encounter in language about God or their faith journeys to see whether the words have changed over time or whether current usage dilutes or distorts their original meanings (words such as *love* and *awesome*). Have the students catalog the frequency with which those words are used (or misused), and ask them to draw conclusions about their own choice of words and when to use them.

What's Next

Students should complete **JE 78 Check Your Focus**, which will be the basis for some of the activities in the next lesson. Students should also read the people profiles **JE 81 The Passion of William Wilberforce** and **JE 82 Be the Change**, and they should answer the questions that follow each profile in preparation for the next lesson.

Lesson 40

Passion: Part 2

Big Idea

Participating in missio Dei requires spiritual passion.

Key Concepts

- Spiritual passion is controlled by the Spirit of God and characterized by the fruit of the Spirit.

- Spiritual passion is birthed through an intimacy with God that transforms our desires so that we can move in harmony with His purpose and mission.

- Spiritual passion is more than enthusiasm or religious duty. It is God-seeking rather than self-seeking.

Reflective Questions

- What are you passionate about? Are your passions characterized by the fruit of the Spirit or by something else? Where does your passion come from? The world? Your own pleasure? God's desires for you? (SE p. 262)

- What are you willing to suffer for? What are you willing to sacrifice comfort, time, money, or other things for? (SE p. 262)

- What is the difference between being a believer and being an experiencer (see SE p. 276)? Which are you in your relationship with God? Which do you have more of: information about God or intimacy with God? (SE p. 262)

- Do you fall prey to engaging in facsimiles of spiritual passion? Do you ever find yourself trying to fake spiritual passion? What can you do to stay focused on the true source of spiritual passion when you feel dry or feel as though you're on the wrong track? (SE p. 262)

Teacher's Heart

Even as a young person, I knew I wanted passion to be a part of my life. I can remember telling a friend in college, "I don't want to do something that I am not passionate about." Sometimes we want something so much, we are tempted to try to create for ourselves things that only God can give to us. Spiritual passion is one such thing. We often overlook the obvious need we have to turn to God our Provider, and we create and settle for a "reasonable substitute" rather than seeking His transformation in our lives. Only He can ignite the fires of our spiritual passion. Make this your prayer today for both you and your students.

Teacher's Preparation

Today's lesson focuses on the latter portion of chapter 22, specifically on the relationship between spiritual passion and participation in the mission of God. But we begin with a focus on the relationship between adoration and passion. Chapter 22 describes the relationship between having intimacy with God and developing true spiritual passion. One facet of developing spiritual passion is a focus on why God is worthy of our passion. Spend a few minutes presenting that concept to your students. You may want to read to them the John 4:23–24 quotation from The Message (SE p. 263). Then give them time in today's first activity to practice focusing on spiritual passion through adoration and worship. You may want to provide a worshipful atmosphere in your classroom for this activity by lighting candles or by playing softly in the background some praise songs or instrumental music.

The activity **JE 79 Isn't He Good?** focuses on God's blessings and attributes. Then the second activity (Into the Story He's Telling) centers on discussing how allowing God to develop spiritual passion in our lives will propel us into moving "in harmony with God's kingdom" (Sandras 2004, 35; see SE p. 269). This activity lists several quotations from chapter 22 that focus on this topic. Spend some time in discussion, drawing your students to conclude that one must have spiritual passion in order to participate in God's mission and purpose.

Today's third activity, Focus on People, directs students to two profiles of people with spiritual passion: two teenagers, one living in the late 1700s, William Wilberforce, who gave his life to the cause of abolishing slavery; and another living today, Zach Hunter, who was inspired by Wilberforce's life. Finally, today's lesson concludes with a time of personal reflection for students. Direct them to **JE 78 Check Your Focus**, which they completed for homework. Ask them to spend some time evaluating their answers to each of the questions and to journal their responses in **JE 80 Transformed Desires**. Finally, make any reminders needed about the people group project.

Objectives

- Students will make a list of God's blessings and attributes, and they will use that list to respond to God.

- Students will discuss the relationship between spiritual passion and participation in a life on mission with God.

- Students will respond to profiles of spiritually passionate people.

- Students will evaluate their own level of spiritual passion and identify areas they would like to see God strengthen in their lives.

Unpacking

Isn't He Good? (10–12 minutes)

Assign students the following activity from **JE 79 Isn't He Good?**:

- Make a list of all that God has done for you.

- After that, make a list of God's attributes (He is loving, kind, full of grace and mercy …).

- Then, look over your lists and use them as a basis for writing, praying silently, or speaking aloud praises to Him.

Into the Story He's Telling (10–12 minutes)

Read the following to your students and discuss each point:

- "We are challenged in a missional life to share our blessings with others, to live incarnationally, and to pursue, with abandon, intimacy with God" (SE p. 262). How does this kind of life get fueled? What role does spiritual passion play in each of these challenges? (**Answers will vary but should include concepts from the chapter.**)

- "True spiritual passion will lead us into the story God is telling" (SE p. 269). How does this happen? (**Spiritual passion focuses on God; when we have it, we are drawn into His plan.**)

- "This is a walk 'by faith, not by sight' (2 Corinthians 5:7)" (SE p. 269). What is the role of faith both in developing intimacy with God and in developing spiritual passion? What are some things that strengthen your faith in God? (**The deeper and more intimate our relationship with God grows, the more a desire to live like Jesus did is fueled; as we learn to trust God more and more, our faith builds.**)

Focus on People (8–10 minutes)

Direct your students to the people profiles **JE 81 The Passion of William Wilberforce** and **JE 82 Be the Change**. Give students the opportunity to discuss their answers to the questions following each profile. If you have time, you may want to discuss in class the role of passion in the lives of the two individuals in these profiles.

Transformed Desires (10–12 minutes)

Direct students to look through their responses to **JE 78 Check Your Focus**. Instruct them to use their responses to identify some areas in which they would like to ask God for transformation. They may need to spend some time in confession and repentance before God. Remind students that they should prayerfully focus on only one or two areas at a time, trusting God's timing and plan for developing spiritual passion in their lives. Have them journal their responses in **JE 80 Transformed Desires**.

Extra Mile

- Watch *Amazing Grace* (Knight 2007) with your students, and discuss the life and faith journey of William Wilberforce. Discuss how his spiritual passion helped him weather the many hurdles in his work toward abolishing slavery. Discuss how God used Wilberforce's circumstances and passion to help Wilberforce find a unique way to participate in God's mission.

- Students with an interest in science or electronics could investigate the properties of the conduction of electricity as a deeper understanding of the "toaster analogy." Encourage them to seek out further analogies between electric circuitry and the development of spiritual passion and intimacy with God.

What's Next

Have students read chapter 23 in preparation for the next lesson.

Loving God, Loving People

Big Idea

Participating in missio Dei requires spiritual passion.

Key Concepts

- Jesus demonstrates that spiritual passion is based in the "greatest commandment": love God, love people.

- We can express our love to God through our willingness to follow Him and participate in His work regardless of personal cost.

- Jesus is our model for how to live out spiritual passion by loving God and loving people. Spiritual passion must be infused with love for God and people.

Reflective Questions

- Do you love God? How do you demonstrate that love to Him? Are obedience and openness to His leading characteristics of your life? Why or why not? (SE p. 277)

- What kinds of people do you find the most difficult to love? Why? What fears are involved? Do you want to grow in this area? How can you grow in this area? (SE p. 277)

- Do you think God intends for us to live out the literal example of Jesus that we see in the New Testament? Are we truly supposed to love our enemies, go the extra mile, and give to those who can't or won't return the favor? (SE p. 277)

Teacher's Heart

Most of my life I have struggled with a fear of rejection. I would put up walls with people so that they wouldn't get a chance to hurt me. Because I was fearful of being betrayed, rejected, and hurt, I was not the kind of person to reach out to those around me. I found that it was awfully hard to love people as long as I was self-protective and afraid. This is an area in which God has been working His transforming power in my life. I am beginning to reject the lie that "I am not a people person," and I have begun to focus more on loving people rather than fearing them. Perhaps you have a similar story, or you have another issue that keeps you from freely loving others. As the Bible demonstrates, our model for living, Jesus Christ, held nothing back in His love for either God or people. Ask God to begin revealing to you what might be holding you back from more love for Him and the people He created. Challenge your students to do the same.

Teacher's Preparation

Today's lesson focuses on spiritual passion demonstrated by Jesus. Specifically, chapter 23 focuses on the call of the "greatest commandment": to love God and love people with our whole beings (see Matthew 22:36–40 and Mark 12:28–31). We see in Christ a demonstration of true spiritual passion, and the bottom line of His passion is His love for God and His love for people.

Unless you and your students acknowledge that God knows how difficult it is for humans to obey the greatest commandment, this lesson could easily be a discouragement to each of you. We are absolutely called to be about the business of pursuing intimacy with God and passion for Him, aspiring to the standard set by Jesus. But we should be fully aware that we will make mistakes and fall short. Otherwise we would not be in need of a Savior, His mercy, or His grace. Eric Sandras puts it this way: "It is the *pursuit* of the kind of relationship with the Father that Jesus had, and not the expectation of attainment in this lifetime, that we've needed all along" (2004, 21). This is the essence of journeying with God. There is no magic wand to wave that will instantly create in you deep intimacy with God or boundless spiritual passion. There is just pressing into Him, journeying alongside Him, following the Lord, and crying out for His Spirit to continually draw us into deeper and deeper fellowship, obedience, and participation with Him. You may want to begin this lesson with a word of encouragement and grace to your students. Also, the Closing Encouragement activity is designed to be a short time of encouragement for your students after they complete some of the self-reflective activities of this lesson.

The first activity in today's lesson centers on the first half of the greatest commandment—love God. As both chapters 22 and 23 emphasize, an intimate love relationship with God is at the heart of spiritual passion. Your students will have some time today to discuss what loving God looks like and to suggest some specific ways we are to do it. First, review the section of chapter 23 that talks about loving God (SE pp. 272–74). Discuss the idea of loving God and brainstorm specific ways to demonstrate one's love for God. This conversation should be centered on the ideas found in the chapter, ideas about giving Him your heart and your devotion.

Next, spend some time in discussion with your students regarding Jesus' model of how to love people. Review the material on SE pages 274–78 with students and give them an opportunity to ask questions and to discuss the main point—that the spiritual passion of Jesus was exhibited in His love toward others and that we are called to do the same. Then take time for them to either individually or as a class read and react to the list by pastor Rudy Rasmus on **BLM 23.1 Are You Walking like Jesus?** (also on SE pages 275–76). To close this activity, give students individual time to reflect and journal on the questions included in this activity.

Next, read the passages of encouragement and grace listed in the Closing Encouragement activity. Discuss the nature of pursuing spiritual passion as a lifelong process of journeying with God. Help students identify steps they can be taking right now to pursue God and to develop more passion for Him. At the end of today's class, introduce **JE 83 The One Thing Challenge**, which offers an opportunity to journey with God through carrying out acts of love. The students will carry out an act of love to God and an act of love to another person daily for a week. You can extend this challenge over several weeks or over the remainder of the course if you so choose.

Objectives

- Students will analyze and discuss some of the ways Jesus demonstrated His love for God and for people, and they will evaluate, in writing, their own response to and obedience regarding the command to love people.

- Students will carry out demonstrations of their love for God and for another person each day for a specified time, and they will record their thoughts regarding those demonstrations.

Unpacking

Love God (8–10 minutes)

As a class, discuss the material on SE pages 272–73 about loving God. Next, brainstorm some ways to demonstrate your love for God. As part of your discussion, consider how Jesus demonstrated His love for God.

Love People (20–25 minutes)

Review SE pages 274–78 with your students, and then focus specifically on Pastor Rudy Rasmus' list of the fingerprints of Jesus, reprinted on **BLM 23.1 Are You Walking like Jesus?** and on SE pages 275–76. Have students, either individually or as a class, read and react to each item on the list. As needed, help students evaluate their responses to each item, asking them to consider why they respond in the way they do. Finally, give them some individual time to reflect and journal on the following questions:

- Can you think of anything else about Jesus that you would add to the list?

- How much are you really walking as Jesus walked?

- Which of these areas on the list do you find most difficult? Why do you think that is?

- Which are the easiest for you?

Remind your students that they need to pay attention to whatever God might be nudging them to participate in.

Closing Encouragement (7–10 minutes)

Spend some time reading and discussing some or all of these passages related to the tremendous grace and patience of God with His children:

> Ephesians 2:4–9 (God loved us even when we were His enemies)
> Philippians 3:12–14 (even Paul had to keep pressing forward in his relationship with God)
> Philippians 4:6–7 and 1 Peter 5:7 (God will meet us in our anxiety and fear)
> Philippians 1:6 (God will continue good work in us)

Encourage your students by reminding them that, even though God is holy and desires our obedience, He is also rich in mercy and grace toward our faults.

Extra Mile

Take some time to really explore the Sermon on the Mount. Divide the class into several small discussion groups. Instruct them to spend some time reading through the Sermon on the Mount in Matthew 5–7 (you may want to do this a chapter at a time over the course of several days). As the students read, they should list the commands found there about how we are to live our lives, paying particular attention to those that involve how to treat and love other people. Challenge students to try to rephrase each one in contemporary language and using contemporary circumstances.

What's Next

The One Thing Challenge

Assign **JE 83 The One Thing Challenge** as a weeklong homework assignment for students. Be sure to remind them about it each day. Challenge them to carry out one act of love to God and one act of love to another person daily for one week, or longer if you so choose. They should journal their activities each day, including how successful they were in finding ways to show these acts of love and what other thoughts they may have about this intentional focus.

Focus on People

In preparation for the next lesson, have students read the people profiles **JE 84 Ryan and the Empty Bowls** and **JE 85 Serving God by Saving the Planet**, and have them answer the questions that follow each profile.

Taking the Opportunity

Big Idea

Participating in missio Dei requires spiritual passion.

Key Concepts

- Jesus demonstrates that spiritual passion is based in the "greatest commandment": love God, love people.

- We can express our love to God through our willingness to follow Him and participate in His work regardless of personal cost.

- Jesus is our model for how to live out spiritual passion by loving God and loving people. Spiritual passion must be infused with love for God and people.

Reflective Questions

- Do you love God? How do you demonstrate that love to Him? Are obedience and openness to His leading characteristics of your life? Why or why not? (SE p. 277)

- What kinds of people do you find the most difficult to love? Why? What fears are involved? Do you want to grow in this area? How can you grow in this area? (SE p. 277)

- Do you think God intends for us to live out the literal example of Jesus that we see in the New Testament? Are we truly supposed to love our enemies, go the extra mile, and give to those who can't or won't return the favor? (SE p. 277)

Teacher's Heart

To participate in God's mission, we must almost always step out in faith, seeing less than the full picture and often having only pieces of information. We have to trust that God will unfold what He is doing as we follow Him. This was certainly the case for Joshua and the Israelites as they prepared to cross the Jordan River into the Promised Land. The priests had to actually step into the flood-stage river before God would create a dry way for them to cross (see Joshua 3); this was literally a step of faith. I often think of this passage when I am called to do something for God that doesn't seem to make sense or that seems impossible. In the adventure of participating in God's mission, we must have not only ears to hear God's voice and eyes to see where God is at work, but also feet to step out in faith as did the Israelite priests of long ago. Ask God to develop your eyes, ears, and feet in such a way that you are able and willing to join Him where He is at work.

Teacher's Preparation

Today's lesson focuses on the aspect of loving God and loving people that involves noticing where God is at work around you and joining in what He is doing. Think of a time when you sensed a nudge from the Lord to participate in something He was doing around you. You may want to begin today's lesson by sharing this type of experience with your students to help them consider ways that they can recognize God at work all around them.

The first activity in this lesson allows students to report back on the first day of The One Thing Challenge from the previous lesson. Give them the opportunity to share their experiences of trying once a day to participate in one act of love toward God and one act of love toward another person. Be encouraging if some of your students found it difficult to even remember to do this or found it hard to complete their tasks. Encourage them to help each other find ways to join in what God is doing around them.

In today's second activity, you are asked to draw attention to the Brennan Manning quotation on SE page 278, "Authentic, evangelical faith cannot be separated from a readiness to act on the Word of God according to present opportunities" (2005, 45). Ask students to discuss what this quotation is saying (**that true faith acts; that it engages in one's circumstances in a biblically consistent way**). Remind them of the concept of living incarnationally that we studied in chapter 9. Living incarnationally means paying attention to your surroundings, the people around you, the needs around you, and the way that God might be inviting you to connect with those people and help meet those needs. It means viewing yourself as one sent into your present context (whatever it may be) as God's

ambassador of reconciliation (see 2 Corinthians 5:11–21). As students consider ways to love the people around them, you may want to share the following suggestions from Rudy Rasmus (2007, 124) as possible starter ideas:

- Ask God to open your eyes to see people the way He sees them—people in your family, at work, or in the neighborhood, and who cross your path each day.

- If people are annoying you, ask yourself, "What's going on in this person's life that might be causing him or her to need some attention?"

- Identify people who can't repay you for any acts of kindness you show.

If you have time for additional study, you may want to lead your students through the 2 Corinthians 5:11–21 passage.

Next, direct students' attention to the profile of a group of students from New York and to a young author, Emma Sleeth. These are people who have demonstrated a spiritual passion that is manifested in love for God through loving others and caring for His creation. Point out the ways in which these profiles demonstrate sensitivity to different opportunities God places around us. Finally, make any reminders needed about the people group project.

Objectives

- Students will report on their first day of purposefully showing one act of love toward God and one act of love toward other people.

- Students will discuss and synthesize the concepts of living incarnationally and responding biblically to present opportunities.

- Students will discuss and develop ways of noticing people around them and of responding to their needs.

- Students will respond, in writing and in discussion, to profiles of people who, fueled by spiritual passion, have lived on mission with God.

Unpacking

The One Thing Challenge (10–12 minutes)

Ask students to report back on their experiences from the first day of doing **JE 83 The One Thing Challenge**. Discuss their experiences. Ask them to describe how they found opportunities to love God and other people. How and where did they see God's leading? Where do they see God at work around them? Focus their attention on developing a sense of recognizing where He is at work around them.

Christ's Ambassadors (15–25 minutes)

Using the notes in the "Teacher's Preparation" section as a guide, discuss the Manning quotation on SE page 278 and the idea of living incarnationally that we studied in chapter 9. Consider the examples in chapter 23 of how to walk out this type of spiritual passion. Students should respond either by journaling in **JE 86 Incarnational Living** or by participating in a class discussion:

- What people around you need to experience the love of Christ through you? Brainstorm some ways to demonstrate your love for these people.

- How do you expand your focus to include those around you?

Focus on People (8–10 minutes)

Direct students' attention to the people profiles **JE 84 Ryan and the Empty Bowls** and **JE 85 Serving God by Saving the Planet**. Give students the opportunity to discuss answers to the questions following each profile.

Extra Mile

Challenge students to "get outside their comfort zones." Instruct them to brainstorm a list of ten situations that would cause them to be in places that are culturally different from their own or that aren't normally a part of their daily routine (for example, attending worship in a very different type of church, having a meal in a different ethnic area of town or just hanging out there, or seeking to befriend someone from a significantly different background). Perhaps they could plan to minister to the homeless, the mentally challenged, or the terminally ill. Challenge students to prayerfully select one or two activities to participate in during a week's time. Ask them to record their choices of activities, a narrative of their experiences, and a reflective essay explaining what they learned through the experience. Have them focus on how they were able to express love to God and His people in ways they might not normally have expressed it.

What's Next

Have students read chapter 24 and **JE 87 Where Do I Belong?** in preparation for the next lesson.

Community

Big Idea

Participating in missio Dei is lived out in the context of community.

Key Concepts

- Community is at the heart of God.

- There is unparalleled inclusiveness in the kingdom of God. You will never meet someone that God wasn't willing to die for.

- Community life isn't always easy, but it is vital for followers of Christ. Not only do we grow and practice loving others while in community, but through community we can demonstrate His love to the world.

- Community is a reality that we are invited to participate in, not something we are asked to create.

Reflective Questions

- Are you willing to pray the prayer "Help me not to be okay just because everything is okay with me"? Why or why not? (SE p. 280)

- Who do you naturally include in your life? Who are you inclined to overlook? Are you willing to ask God to show you things through His eyes, even if it means you have to adjust your thinking? (SE p. 280)

- Do you grasp that you are precious in His sight? Do you believe that others are equally precious in His sight? (SE p. 280)

Teacher's Heart

I am a "word nerd" by nature and by training, so I was delighted with the excerpt from Nancy Ortberg on pronouns and community in chapter 24, particularly one of the quotations: "The kind of sacrificial, others-focused love that Jesus puts within our reach is reflected in the big word *we*" (2008, 37; SE p. 284). For the last several years, God has placed me in a wonderful Christian community that has shown me so much more than I have ever known about what this aspect of God's kingdom is all about. I am so thankful for "we" and so grateful that God has designed it so that we are to be a part of community in order to participate in life with Him. Spend some time praising God for the opportunity and blessing of community. Ask Him to fill you and your students with an awareness of the riches of life as part of "we."

Teacher's Preparation

Begin today's lesson with a class discussion of the chapter. Because you know your students and their particular needs, you may want to vary the focus of the discussion from class to class. Here are some possible talking points for a more in-depth probe of students' thoughts and understandings:

- How do we know that community is at the heart of God (SE pp. 280–81)?

- What is the cultural attitude toward community where you live? Are you encouraged to be a lone ranger or a part of a group? How is Christian community encouraged? Or is it encouraged (SE pp. 281, 283)?

- Discuss Nancy Ortberg's excerpt on community and pronouns (SE pp. 283–85). What stands out to you from this Luke 14 passage?

- What does the Bible show us about the inclusiveness that is to be a part of Christian community (the "Some One Anothers" sidebar and SE pp. 285–87)? Discuss what Dietrich Bonhoeffer says about possibly excluding Christ when we exclude people from community (1954, 23–24; SE p. 287). How can we make sure that this doesn't happen?

- Discuss the difference between trying to "create" community and "stepping into" community that God has already created (SE pp. 287–88). What are the dangers of trying to create community rather than letting God lead? What are the dangers of expecting your community life to take the place of intimacy with God?

Choose some of the above points for discussion now, and save some for an ongoing class discussion that uses a class blog or a bulletin board. You can use the textbook website (www.missiodei-thejourney.com) as a place to blog or to post a forum, or you can set up a blog for your class using a free blog publishing tool such as Blogger or Blogspot. Or, if you don't have the technology available for all students to participate in a class blog, create a public in-class discussion board by posting a discussion prompt on a bulletin board or wall in your classroom and by providing large sticky notes or slips of paper for students to write and post their responses. Encourage students to participate in reading all the responses and adding to the discussion. This activity, which can be ongoing throughout the remainder of the course, could be a way for you to do an informal assessment. You can, of course, create more prompts of your own or encourage students to post their own new threads of discussion.

The activity **JE 87 Where Do I Belong?** guides your students to think about the types of community they are involved in, and it gives them a chance to think about how those places of community interaction might be points at which God is calling them to join Him in His work. Lead your students to consider the characteristics of the different communities in which they spend time in light of the biblical characteristics of community. This activity leads directly into the next activities, which are two journal entries for individual reflection (**JE 88 Getting In** and **JE 89 Your Misery, Your Ministry**). These entries can be done in class or as homework, but you should create a means for verifying that students are working through these reflective questions, whether that be a quick journal check for a grade or an in-class discussion. You may wish to assign these journal entries as homework so that you can use class time for the role playing and discussion in the "If Time Activity" section, which gives students an opportunity to practice some elements of community. Also, remind your students to continue doing **JE 83 The One Thing Challenge**, which will be reviewed in lesson 44 (or at a later date specified by you).

Objectives

- Students will discuss in class, and in an ongoing discussion, some elements of community.

- Students will list and assess the different communities to which they belong.

- Students will reflect in writing on what it is like to be on the outside of a community or group, as well as what they can do from the inside to help new people feel a part of a community.

- Students will practice becoming more comfortable greeting new people and learning to spend time getting to know a person.

Unpacking

Class Discussion (10–15 minutes)

Using the suggestions in the "Teacher's Preparation" section or using the students' questions as a starting point, discuss the material presented in chapter 24.

Ongoing Blog Discussion (5 minutes)

Explain to students the blog system or the bulletin board system you will have set up for them to use as a means of continuing class discussion on community and on practicing some elements of community.

Community Ties (10–15 minutes)

Discuss **JE 87 Where Do I Belong?** with your students. Get their reaction to the article by Erwin Raphael McManus regarding the concepts that "we are a world of joiners" who have the need to belong to something and "we are created by a relational God for relationship" (2006, Intimacy entry 15). Discuss the different ways we define *community* (for example, the place we live, the church we attend, the school we attend, groups we hang out with). Then ask the students to each list the various communities they belong to. Next, direct them to think about the characteristics of each of the communities they participate in. Ask them to consider whether the characteristics are in line with a biblical picture of community.

Getting In (5–10 minutes)

Direct students to **JE 88 Getting In**, and give them time to complete the reflections there.

Your Misery, Your Ministry (5–10 minutes)

Direct students to **JE 89 Your Misery, Your Ministry**, and give them time to complete the reflections there.

If Time Activity

Give your students the opportunity to "practice" one or two elements of community life through role-playing opportunities. One aspect of community life people often feel uncomfortable with is that initial encounter with a new group of people. Divide the class into several small groups and let students role-play welcoming new people to their community group. Have one or two people in each group be the "new people" and the other students be the "welcomers." Let all the groups simultaneously act out welcoming new people into their group. Repeat this several times so that everyone gets a turn being "new" and being "welcoming." Encourage students as they discuss authentic ways to welcome someone and as they prepare some potential discussion topics or questions to have in mind when needed to keep a conversation going. Some people are naturally gifted at this, and others are very fearful of this type of interaction. Let students discuss their experiences briefly.

Students can also practice some relational skills for community life by spending some time chatting with those people in class whom they may not know very well. Even though it is late in the semester, there may be students who aren't well acquainted with one another. Give students time to seek out a classmate whom they don't know as well as others and to spend at least five minutes discovering two or three new things about that person. Encourage them to discover whether they have common interests or experiences. Then give time for students to introduce that classmate to the class and to share one or two interesting facts they learned about that person.

What's Next

In preparation for the next lesson, have students read chapter 25. Also assign the reading of the people profiles **JE 93 Four Souls**, **JE 94 Breaking Ground**, and **JE 95 Waterskiing Community**, and have the students answer the questions that follow each profile.

The Purpose of Community

Big Idea

Participating in missio Dei is lived out in the context of community.

Key Concepts

- Community is at the heart of God.

- One of the purposes of Christian community is the proclamation of God and His purpose to the world.

- Another purpose of Christian community is the nurture and spiritual growth of its members.

- Authentic Christian community is more than just hanging out with other Christians, or "life in a crowd."

Reflective Questions

- Are you a "lone ranger" Christian, interested in individual pursuits and skeptical of community life? What contributes to those feelings if you have them? (SE p. 290)

- How has community played a role in your spiritual growth and development? Has it been a positive influence or a negative one? How have you been able to love others and minister to them through community? Or does that even play an important role in your life? Why or why not? (SE p. 290)

- How might God be calling you to proclaim Him to the world through participating in community? What difference does it make for the world to see authentic Christian fellowship? (SE p. 290)

Teacher's Heart

When I was first learning to live on my own as a young adult, I was mentored in my Christian faith by a dear friend who offered me a great deal of wise counsel, spent hours in prayer with me, taught me to study the Word of God, and lived out many of the events of my daily life with me. She invested in me and brought me into deeper levels of Christian community than I had ever experienced before that time. In the years since, God has called me to many different forms of Christian community, and not only have I sought to have a mentor in my life, but I have also been blessed to serve in that capacity for a number of teenagers (many of whom are now adult friends) and young adults. You play a critical role in fostering and nurturing Christian community in your classroom each year. May God strengthen you for this holy task and guide you to inspire others to offer that same service to God's kingdom. The Body of Christ needs all of us!

Teacher's Preparation

This is the first of two lessons on chapter 25, which describes the purpose of community life as two sides of a coin: one inwardly focused and the other outwardly focused. Today's lesson will be directed toward the inward-focused purpose of community, and the next lesson will address the larger, outward-focused purpose of missional community. As chapter 25 makes clear, one role of community is to benefit its participants. Authentic Christian community gives its participants the opportunity to be nurtured and encouraged in their spiritual growth, it offers them accountability in Christian life, and it provides its members a place to practice walking out the Christian life and exercising spiritual gifts. In this way, Christian community is different from other communities we may participate in. The most central difference, of course, is that authentic and missional Christian community has Christ as its center and exists for Him and through Him.

Today's first activity gives you an opportunity to discuss these distinctives with your students. In some ways it is a follow-up discussion to the previous lesson's Community Ties activity, which included a time for students to discuss communities that they are a part of. Today, you should push the discussion to a deeper level, offering the chance to really compare the distinctives of Christian community and those of other types of community students may be involved in. Begin this time by asking students to react to the information on SE pages 289–93. They will probably have much to say in reaction to the section of the chapter that deals with "online community" (SE pp. 291–92). As the discussion progresses, be sure to point out and discuss the following distinctives:

After you have discussed as a class these larger themes, divide students into small groups of three or four and instruct them to discuss the questions listed for this purpose in the "Unpacking" section.

Next, look at the people profiles **JE 93 Four Souls**, **JE 94 Breaking Ground**, and **JE 95 Waterskiing Community**. Discuss how they present different "snapshots" of what community looks like and ways that community is expressed. As part of this discussion, allow students to report back on The One Thing Challenge activity assigned in lesson 41. Give them the opportunity to share their experiences of trying once a day to participate in one act of love toward God and one act of love toward another person. Encourage those who struggled during this assignment, and instruct them to pay close attention to the next activity, which describes a community that is intentional about loving God and blessing others. Direct students' attention to **JE 90 BELLS**. The acronym BELLS describes the way one Christian community in New Zealand seeks to be intentional about community life with both an inward and outward focus. You may wish to discuss BELLS as a class, or let students work on the journal entry alone. Allow time for students to reflect on the questions presented, and encourage them to experiment in the coming days with this type of intentional community focus.

Finally, direct students' attention to **JE 91 Crowd or Community?** and **JE 92 Your Community**. Have students use the information on SE page 293 to discuss in class the difference between life in a crowd and life in a community. Then instruct them to work on the questions presented in both journal

Distinctives of Christian Community	
Exhibits selflessness and servanthood	SE pp. 289–90
Makes Christ the center	SE pp. 290–91
Exhibits the type of love described in 1 Corinthians 13	SE pp. 293–94
Demonstrates mutual responsibility, belonging, and caring	SE pp. 293–94
Is marked by submission and sacrifice	SE p. 294
Walks and lives in the hard places of getting along	SE p. 294
Is knitted together with widely diverse people	SE pp. 294–95

entries. These may need to be completed as homework if there isn't time in class. Also, remind students to continue participating in your community topics blog or bulletin board activity, and make any announcements you need to about their ongoing people group project.

Objectives

- Students will discuss and analyze the Christian community distinctives described in chapter 25.

- Students will read about some intentional ways of fostering deeper community proposed by the acronym BELLS, and they will express their own plan for intentional community life.

- Students will reflect on the difference between life in a crowd and life in community, and they will assess their personal patterns of participation.

- Students will appraise their own participation in community and what God may be leading them to do further.

Unpacking

Small-Group and In-Class Discussion (15–20 minutes)

Using the information in the "Teacher's Preparation" section as a guide, lead a discussion of the material in chapter 25 that deals with the inward-focused purpose of community. After the main points are covered as a class, allow for five to eight minutes of small-group discussion of these questions:

- Where are you involved in community?

- What are the distinctives of that community?

- Does that community demonstrate some of the characteristics we just discussed as a class?

- How much of your time is spent in community that doesn't have these distinctives?

- What influence does where you spend your time have on your life and particularly on your relationship with God and on your spiritual passion?

Focus on People (8–10 minutes)

Direct students to the people profiles **JE 93 Four Souls**, **JE 94 Breaking Ground**, and **JE 95 Waterskiing Community**. Give students the opportunity to discuss answers to the questions following each profile. Explore with your students the different ways that community is expressed.

The One Thing Challenge (8–10 minutes)

Ask students to report back on their experiences from doing **JE 83 The One Thing Challenge**. Discuss their experiences and ask them to describe how they found opportunities to love God and other people. How and where did they see God's leading? Where do they see God at work around them? Focus their attention on developing a sense of recognizing where God is at work around them and how He wants to use them in that work.

BELLS (8–10 minutes)

Direct students to **JE 90 BELLS**. Let students, either as a class or alone, work through the information and questions presented there. They may need to finish the questions as homework.

Crowds and Community (8–10 minutes)

Direct students to **JE 91 Crowd or Community?** and **JE 92 Your Community**. Lead a brief discussion as indicated above. Give students time to complete these journal entries or assign the questions as homework.

If Time Activity

Discuss the "one anothers" as a distinctive of community (see the "Some One Anothers" sidebar from chapter 24 on SE p. 282). Ask students how much these practices are a part of their daily lives. How do they see these practices developing and playing out in the future? Challenge them to prayerfully consider the Bible's "one another" verses and to select one or two to focus on in the coming week.

Extra Mile

In chapter 25, Eric Sandras notes, "[Jesus] knows what his community should look like in your city and mine" (2004, 60; SE p. 291). Have students research different types of Christian community, which can range from "new monastic" communities (like The Simple Way, www.thesimpleway.org) to very traditional worship communities, to urban outreach communities (like Mosaic, http://mosaic.org), to international ministries on college campuses, to mission communities, and more. Even within your classroom, students are likely to come from a variety of different Christian community backgrounds. Emphasize to your students that Christian community doesn't necessarily have to be a church. There are all kinds of other ways Christian community is expressed.

What's Next

Students should read **JE 96 God and Basketball** in preparation for a discussion in the next lesson.

Christian Community as Witness

Big Idea

Participating in missio Dei is lived out in the context of community.

Key Concepts

- Community is at the heart of God.

- One of the purposes of Christian community is the proclamation of God and His purpose to the world.

- Another purpose of Christian community is the nurture and spiritual growth of its members.

- Authentic Christian community is more than just hanging out with other Christians, or "life in a crowd."

Reflective Questions

- Are you a "lone ranger" Christian, interested in individual pursuits and skeptical of community life? What contributes to those feelings if you have them? (SE p. 290)

- How has community played a role in your spiritual growth and development? Has it been a positive influence or a negative one? How have you been able to love others and minister to them through community? Or does that even play an important role in your life? Why or why not? (SE p. 290)

- How might God be calling you to proclaim Him to the world through participating in community? What difference does it make for the world to see authentic Christian fellowship? (SE p. 290)

Teacher's Heart

I got a letter this afternoon from a dear sister in the Lord with whom I have served in our community for several years. Every now and then she sends me a note of encouragement just affirming me for what she sees God doing in my life. I cannot tell you what a blessing it is to hear God's voice of love and encouragement through another believer. God often can speak to our deepest places of self-doubt and brokenness through loving words from someone with whom we spend time in community. It is a tremendous blessing, too, to be able to speak those types of encouraging words to others. Ask God to lead you specifically to someone you can encourage through words of blessing this week. May Christian community richly encourage you! Praise God for the wonderful blessing of His Body.

Teacher's Preparation

As a continuation of studying chapter 25, today's lesson centers on the outward-focused side of the "coin" of Christian community. The majority of this information is found in the second part of the chapter, beginning on SE page 293. As we live our lives in open and inclusive community that is centered in Christ and empowered by His Spirit, we are proclaiming to the world the character and nature of God.

Unfortunately, we are not always accurate representatives of His character. It is for this reason alone that we should take very seriously our participation in Christian community, seeking to live out with others the love, forgiveness, and grace we receive from God. In an explication of passages from Ephesians, Dr. Charles Davis, pastor emeritus of Grace Church in Tuscaloosa, Alabama, said, "We are called to recommend as worthy the qualities and attributes of God" (2008). Therefore, the question for us is, As we participate in Christian community, how well are we serving as a recommendation for God's being worthy of trust and praise? This is the focus of today's lesson.

You should begin today's discussion by pointing out the following sentence from SE page 293: "The community is a means by which we join God in His mission in the world." Ask students to describe ways they have seen this to be true. Ask them to consider the reactions of people in the world to what they see of Christian community (both positive and negative). One area in particular that your students may pick up on is hypocrisy. Using **JE 96 God and Basketball**, which students read as homework, lead a discussion addressing the issue of authentic community. What does this journal entry say to us about the importance of living in harmony with others as a demonstration of Christ to the world? Leading directly into the next activity, read Romans 15:5–7 and discuss the truths found there about community life proclaiming God. Ask students whether they have ever considered the significance of their life in Christian community as a form of participating in God's mission. Nancy Ortberg noted the following in chapter 24: "[Community] is the way of life out of which evangelism and discipleship emerge" (2008, 36–37; SE p. 283). Discuss how this is true. (**Evangelism is the outward focus; discipleship is the inward focus.**)

After a brief full-class discussion of the points listed in the "Teacher's Preparation" section, the third activity calls for small-group discussion and sharing. Divide the class into five groups. Give each group one of the metaphorical images of community found in the verses listed on SE page 295. Ask each group to read its specific verse and, for context, the surrounding verses. Ask them to discuss the questions listed in the "Unpacking" section, and then each group should present its conclusions to the class. The objective of this assignment is to help students begin to think of the different ways in which Christian community can speak truth about God to the world.

Because of the importance of Christian community to God and to the completion of His mission, it is impossible to rationalize a way to "opt out" of community life. We see no biblical support for a "lone ranger" Christian life. As chapter 25 points out, it may be tempting to think that we are not needed or that we would not be missed in the Body of Christ. But we are each designed with a specific and unique role to play in God's story. The fourth activity gives students the opportunity to acknowledge the contributions of others in the Body of Christ. To accompany this activity, you may want to prepare a specific word of encouragement to give to each of your students. For this Encouraging Words activity, attach a piece of paper to the back of each student (tape or safety pins will work). Instruct students to write one genuine compliment about the student on that student's piece of paper. Each student in the class should write something on all other students' papers. Monitor to make sure everyone participates and that no hurtful words are exchanged. You might want to remind students of words they've probably heard countless times from their parents: "If you can't say something nice, don't say anything at all." Consider your classroom dynamics, and use your discretion in handling any potential negative outcome. At the end of the activity, students will have a reminder of what they contribute to the community of your classroom or school. A less chaotic (but not as much fun) version of this is to have each student label a piece of paper with his or her name and pass the papers around the class until everyone has had a chance to add a compliment to each of them. This Encouraging Words activity can be very valuable, so you may want to make time to do this on another day if you can't get to it in this lesson.

Note that there are three journal entries (**JE 96 God and Basketball**, **JE 97 Every Part Matters**, and **JE 98 Missional Community**) that have activities and reflections tied to this lesson. **JE 97** is an extension of the Encouraging Words activity; you may want to point out the connection. The entries **JE 97** and **JE 98** should be assigned as homework (or begin them in class if you have time). Also, remind students about participating in the ongoing blog or bulletin board discussions. Encourage them to share their thoughts about the in-class activities and reading on community. Finally, make any reminders needed about the people group project.

Objectives

- Students will identify ways in which community life is a witness to the world around us, and they will discuss the importance of their participation in community as a means of participating with God in His mission and purpose.

- Students will discuss metaphors from the Bible and will infer principles about community from those metaphors.

- Students will express encouragement to their classmates about their classmates' contributions to community life.

- Students will compile and evaluate feedback about the gifts they bring to community.

- Students will assess the ways in which God is inviting them to participate in missional community.

Unpacking

Journal Entry Discussion (5–7 minutes)

Your students should have already read **JE 96 God and Basketball** before coming to class. Highlight as points of discussion some key phrases by Erwin Raphael McManus in his book *Soul Cravings* (2006, Intimacy entry 16; bullets added):

- Love can never be simply between you and God.

- When we belong to God, we belong to each other.

- A healthy community is not a place of perfect people.

- The problem, of course, is that we are all hypocrites in transition.

- I am not who I want to be, but I am on the journey there, and thankfully I am not whom I used to be.

Witness to the World (5–8 minutes)

Using the points outlined in the "Teacher's Preparation" section, lead students in a discussion of the importance of the Christian community as a witness to the world regarding who God is.

Pictures We Can Paint (10–15 minutes)

Divide the class into five groups. Give each group one of the passages found at the top of SE page 295. Give the groups time to read the passage (and surrounding verses where needed) and answer the following questions. Afterward, each group should share its thoughts with the whole class.

- What metaphor does your passage contain? (the Christian community as ____)

- In your word picture, how do the different parts relate to one another? (For example, How do sheep interact? How is a flock led? What has to happen for the parts to work well together?) How does an observer see the success or failure of this interaction?

- What connections can you make between your metaphor, the Christian community, and the expression of truths about God to a watching world?

Encouraging Words (15–20 minutes)

Using one of the options found in the "Teacher's Preparation" section, facilitate this activity with your students. Remind students that every person has an important role to play in God's kingdom community; this activity is designed to highlight those gifts and talents. Pray with students before the activity, and ask God to speak through each of them to each other. Remind students to be sensitive to God's leading as they write words of encouragement to one another.

If Time Activities

Journal Entry

Draw the students' attention to **JE 97 Every Part Matters**, an entry that will help students collect more insight into how God has gifted them for participation in His Body. If possible, give students several days to complete this activity.

Journal Entry

Have students work on **JE 98 Missional Community**. This journal entry contains guidelines for reflecting on some material from chapter 25.

What's Next

If you didn't have time to begin **JE 97** and **JE 98**, assign them as homework. Have students read chapter 26 in preparation for the next lesson. Also, have students read the remaining people profiles for the unit, **JE 101 Sacrifice—the Soil of True Life** and **JE 102 Being Missional**, and have them answer the questions that follow each profile. You may want to look ahead to lesson 47, which has a culminating celebration, and begin to think about how you want that experience to be for your students so that it is as unique and individual as they are.

Further Study

Barrett, Lois Y., ed. 2004. *Treasure in clay jars: Patterns in missional faithfulness.* The Gospel and Our Culture Series. Grand Rapids, MI: Wm. B. Eerdmans.

Lesson 46 · # The Rest of the Story

Big Idea

Missio Dei culminates in the gathering of every tribe, tongue, language, and nation around the throne of God.

Key Concepts

- God's mission of relationship, redemption, and reconciliation to all nations will ultimately be fulfilled in the kingdom of God—a glorious multiethnic community united in worship of Jesus.

- Our participation in the mission of God here and now will be enhanced and completed as a part of His future kingdom. Each of our lives can play a role in the larger story of God's plan to reach all nations.

Reflective Questions

- How would your day-to-day interactions and choices be different if you lived in constant awareness that in God's kingdom only Jesus matters? that His blood creates equality and forgiveness for all who will receive Him? Is it possible to live a kingdom-of-God life *now*, even though some of it is *not yet*? (SE p. 301)

- What difference does it make to you that your participation in the mission of God here and now will accomplish its purpose, whether or not you see it at the present time? Does that inspire you to seek and serve God more? Why or why not? (SE p. 304)

- Do you view all moments of your life as opportunities to worship God, or do you think of worship as something that happens at certain times of the week in certain corporate settings? Why or why not? How do your views on worship affect your daily life? your enthusiasm for God and His mission? (SE p. 304)

Teacher's Heart

"For while we are in this tent, we groan and are burdened, because we do not wish to be unclothed but to be clothed with our heavenly dwelling, so that what is mortal may be swallowed up by life. Now it is God who has made us for this very purpose and has given us the Spirit as a deposit, guaranteeing what is to come" (2 Corinthians 5:4–5). There are some days that I spend a lot of time groaning and feeling burdened. Praise God that His Spirit reminds me that what I see around me is not all that there is. I receive comfort and hope in knowing that God is at work and that He is constantly revealing more of His kingdom. It is a blessing to know that His purpose and mission are accomplished in the heavenlies. Spend some time praising God for the fact that we are not left to wonder whether everything will work out. Through faith and through His Spirit we can express our gratitude to Him for the truth of His kingdom that will be fully revealed in due time.

Teacher's Preparation

Welcome to chapter 26, the last chapter of this course. Appropriately, it is a chapter concerned with the final word in God's mission. Here we read about the fully revealed future kingdom of God. Though we have the witness of the Bible to reveal some of the future to us, there are certainly many things we can speak of only in fragments. There is no way for our finite minds to fully comprehend the details of the wonders our infinite God has prepared for us in His perfect kingdom! As a result, any discussions of the future kingdom of God are necessarily incomplete and naturally a place in which differing theologies may come into play. Your classroom will probably be no exception as you discuss chapter 26. But as the N. T. Wright quotation in chapter 26 points out, Christian language about the future is like "signposts pointing into a mist." These signposts tell "the particular sort of truth that can be told about the future" (2008, 132; SE p. 299 sidebar). In other words, you can say truthfully that there will be weather tomorrow, but the more-difficult task from today's vantage point is to describe tomorrow's weather in accurate, precise detail. Perhaps the wisest thing for today's discussion is to steer clear of too much emphasis on details that we cannot know definitively until the future. Instead, use today's lesson to focus student attention on the multiethnic, Christ-centered worship that will occur at the completion of God's mission. This we can be sure of!

You may encounter questions in today's discussion related to the *now* and *not yet* aspects of God's kingdom and the realities of present spiritual warfare that we talked about in chapters 4 and 5. You might want to refresh your memory and reread those chapters or do whatever is necessary to be able to reference them as needed. Some students will immediately make the link between material from those earlier chapters and what is presented in chapter 26. Of course, there are many connections between a number of earlier chapters in this course, since chapter 26 is not only the picture of the culmination of God's mission throughout history, but also a review of concepts we have been discussing all along the way. You might want to flip back through the table of contents to be prepared to direct student attention to sections in which some of these concepts were originally discussed in the course.

Today's lesson basically has two parts: discussion and reflection. You should obviously let student questions and interests play a major part in shaping class discussion, but try to always draw the focus back to the completion and fulfillment of God's mission to all peoples. The "fulfillment of the one story of the Bible" theme is the heart of both chapter 26 and the entire book of *Missio Dei*. In the next several paragraphs you will find some key points from chapter 26 along with some class discussion topics.

In general, chapter 26 presents the culmination of each unit in this course. The Bible Unit focused on the one story of the Bible: the mission of God to redeem people from all nations and to reconcile them to relationship with Himself. In chapter 26, we see a picture of the one story of the Bible fulfilled. In Revelation we see the completion of the Genesis 12 Abrahamic call. Draw attention to the quotation by David Joel Hamilton: "The pages of Scripture reveal a God who wants *every* individual, *every* family, *every* community, *every* town and village, *every* sphere of society, *every* people group and nation to experience the transforming redemption of the gospel" (2008, 49; SE p. 300). Ask students to discuss how Revelation 7:9–10 is an outcome of God's promise to bless all nations through Abraham. Discuss the beginning, middle, and end of the one story of the Bible.

The Culture Unit further illuminated God's heart for people of all nations. It also introduced students to the concept of unity within diversity (first introduced in chapter 7). A recapitulation of these themes begins on SE page 301. In God's fully revealed kingdom, only the blood of Jesus matters. No longer do bloodlines, political affiliations, or other dividing lines carry any weight or power. Jesus is the unifying point amid all the diversity of the nations around His throne. What we see in Revelation 7:9–10 is still diverse; diversity is not erased in heaven. What is pictured is a display of God's creativity and glory. Spend some time discussing these ideas with students. The first of this lesson's Reflective Questions might be an interesting starting point on this topic.

We learned in the History Unit that throughout time God's purpose has been marching forward, and people have been participating in it all along. In chapter 26, we see that these activities have not been in vain. God will transform, complete, redeem, and incorporate our participation in His mission into the reality of His future, perfect kingdom. Quotations by Lesslie Newbigin on SE page 302, N. T. Wright in the "Cathedral" sidebar on SE page 303, and Bob Sjogren on SE page 304 contain affirmations of the purposefulness of our participation in God's mission. You may want to point out these quotations and discuss them further with your class. You can also tie this truth back to what we have just studied in chapters 24 and 25 about community life and how each part of the Body of Christ has a specific and important role to play. Try to direct students' thoughts to how the students are being called to proclaim God to the nations through each student's specific gifts, talents, and interests. The second Reflective Question ties to this theme. You may also want to share the 2 Corinthians 5:4–5 passage from the "Teacher's Heart" section as an encouragement to students. Similar passages are found in Ephesians 1:13–14 and 2 Corinthians 1:21–22.

In our fourth unit, the Practices Unit, we highlighted several key practices that strengthen us for the journey of missio Dei. In chapter 26, we discuss the continuation of the practices of worship and adoration that spring forth even here and now in lives that are intimate with God and spiritually passionate. "[Worship] is, quite simply, living our lives in participation with God on His mission, and constantly recognizing and responding to the fact that God is worthy of praise, obedience, and loyalty" (SE p. 305). Discuss this concept with students, along with the third Reflective Question.

Ask students to consider how important worship is as a focus of our lives now since it is one thing we are sure will continue to be a part of our lives in the future kingdom of God. Guide them to expand their concept of worship beyond a specific set-aside time of corporate singing of praise songs to a lifestyle that declares the worth of God to be praised, honored, and served. **JE 100 What Is Worship?** guides students to think more deeply about what worship is.

The final people profiles for this unit focus on two couples: Ryan and Heather Murphy, who serve at an international Christian school in Kenya; and Floyd and Sally McClung, who have ministered in Afghanistan and Amsterdam and who currently live in South Africa. Through the experiences of these couples, students will get a glimpse of what missional living is all about.

Spend about half to two-thirds of your class time today in discussion, and then give students time for reflection, processing, and journaling. Their student journals have at least one reflective prompt (see **JE 99 What Are You Waiting For?**); you may want to suggest others. As you may have done in the past, you could play some soft praise music in the background or perhaps even take your students outdoors for this time of reflection and journaling.

You may also want to discuss with your students your requirements for their presentations of Getting to Know a People Group: An Ethnographic Study. These presentations may take a few days of in-class time to complete. You will want to complete these presentations before starting the next lesson. Inform students regarding when individual presentations will be due.

Objectives

- Students will integrate various themes presented throughout the course into specific ideas presented in chapter 26.

- Students will read about the definite completion of God's mission, and they will assess how that reality should affect their daily lives.

- Students will reflect on specific actions that they might take in response to the story of the Bible, the mission of God, and His invitation for them to participate with Him.

Unpacking

Class Discussion (20–25 minutes)

Using the above paragraphs as a guide to chapter 26, discuss its contents with students.

Focus on People (8–10 minutes)

Direct your students to the people profiles **JE 101 Sacrifice—the Soil of True Life** and **JE 102 Being Missional**. Give students the opportunity to discuss answers to the questions following each profile. Examine some of the insights about missional life that are described in these profiles.

Reflection (10–15 minutes)

Direct students to **JE 99 What Are You Waiting For?** and give them time to reflect on the questions in it and to journal about other thoughts from today's discussion. Provide a worshipful atmosphere for this quiet, reflective activity.

If Time Activity

Direct students to **JE 100 What Is Worship?** and ask them reflect on and respond to the material there.

What's Next

If you didn't have time to direct students to **JE 100**, assign it as homework. Before you begin the next lesson, students should make their presentations of Getting to Know a People Group: An Ethnographic Study. Review the schedule with your students. You will also want to help students begin preparing whatever elements you want them to bring for the celebration outlined in the next lesson.

Further Study

Mouw, Richard J. 2002. *When the kings come marching in: Isaiah and the new Jerusalem.* Rev. ed. Grand Rapids, MI: Wm. B. Eerdmans.

Wright, N. T. 2008. *Surprised by hope: Rethinking heaven, the resurrection, and the mission of the church.* New York: HarperOne.

A Celebration!

Big Idea

Missio Dei culminates in the gathering of every tribe, tongue, language, and nation around the throne of God.

Key Concepts

- God's mission of relationship, redemption, and reconciliation to all nations will ultimately be fulfilled in the kingdom of God—a glorious multiethnic community united in worship of Jesus.

- Our participation in the mission of God here and now will be enhanced and completed as a part of His future kingdom. Each of our lives can play a role in the larger story of God's plan to reach all nations.

Reflective Questions

- How would your day-to-day interactions and choices be different if you lived in constant awareness that in God's kingdom only Jesus matters? that His blood creates equality and forgiveness for all who will receive Him? Is it possible to live a kingdom-of-God life *now*, even though some of it is *not yet*? (SE p. 301)

- What difference does it make to you that your participation in the mission of God here and now will accomplish its purpose, whether or not you see it at the present time? Does that inspire you to seek and serve God more? Why or why not? (SE p. 304)

- Do you view all moments of your life as opportunities to worship God, or do you think of worship as something that happens at certain times of the week in certain corporate settings? Why or why not? How do your views on worship affect your daily life? your enthusiasm for God and His mission? (SE p. 304)

Teacher's Heart

A new song our church praise team has been learning is Mark Altrogge's "Glorious" (CD titled *Come Weary Saints*, Sovereign Grace Music, 2008). Here are some of the lyrics: "How great You are, Your greatness none can fathom, upholding all by Your almighty Word. The universe fulfills Your every purpose, and all You've made will bring You praise, O God." What cause for celebration! The universe fulfills God's every purpose. And we will lift our voices to praise God both now and forever. We truly will *always* be in awe of Him. Ask God to keep you mindful of His worthiness. Though it is easy for us to get distracted, nothing is as awe-inspiring or as worthy of our praise as Almighty Abba Father.

Teacher's Preparation

By now, your students should have presented their people group projects, thus giving them a greater awareness of the exquisite creativity of God that will be present around His throne as pictured in Revelation 7:9–10. Today's lesson should be a celebration of this reality. Our God reigns, and He receives glory from all people. You may choose any number of ways to carry off your celebration, but your main objective should be to celebrate the picture of God's ultimately fulfilled kingdom and to embrace with your students a renewed sense of commitment to the purpose of God and our individual roles within His mission. The ideas presented here are arranged according to several suggested components for today's celebration: setting, praise and celebration, diversity, and commitment. We present ideas in each category. Draw from them, add to them, or ignore them as you create an experience that should be as unique and individual as are each of your classes.

Setting. Your celebration can take place within your classroom or in some other venue that you choose (outdoors, the school auditorium or cafeteria, a local restaurant outside of class, or anyplace else that is festive). If you choose the outdoors as a setting, you might want to be near a stream to represent the River of Life (Christ). You should strive for the atmosphere to be festive, different from the everyday, and representative of a sense of jubilee and celebration. You may want to use fabrics, flower petals, fruits and vegetables (to echo a "harvest" theme), a large cross, a chair for a throne, a crown representing Jesus, or some other visual elements to create an atmosphere of worship and celebration. Together with your students, let your imaginations, your creative juices, and images from the Bible guide you during your preparations for this celebration.

Praise and celebration. The possibilities here are almost limitless. There are countless praise songs, many based on Bible passages, that you can choose from to accompany your time of celebration. You may want to set aside a specific portion of your celebration time to sing praise songs with your students. If your class includes students who have special musical abilities, let them present a song or two; or you could bring in other people who could provide live music. For a festive, upbeat celebration with music, provide tambourines or other instruments for your students to play. You may want to incorporate a quiet, worshipful atmosphere of praise and celebration for at least part of your time, so choose musical selections to match the tone of the different portions of celebration.

You may have students who are talented at creative movement or dance, so you may want to incorporate that type of movement into your celebration. Think of ways to use your students' different talents as a part of your celebration and praise. If you want to add a visual element to your praise time, you can either give students palm branches to wave, or have students construct colorful ribbon banners by tying ribbons to the end of two-foot-long dowel rods.

You might want to spend part of your celebration time declaring truths about God from the Bible. Verses could be written out on poster board or displayed another way, or you could assign each student the task of picking out some verses to read aloud during the celebration. There could be a time of sharing during which students talk about ways that God has particularly spoken to them about His heart for the nations, about their joining His purpose, or about other themes that have been studied in this course or that go along with celebrating the fulfillment of His purpose. Let God guide you in how to express praise and worship and celebration of Him during your time.

Diversity. One of the most prominent features of Revelation 7:9–10 and the themes we have been studying in this course is God's heart for people of all tribes, tongues, languages, and nations. Therefore, you will want to incorporate as much representation of cultural and ethnic diversity into your celebration as possible. You may have asked students to research ethnic food, costume, flags, or phrases in another language as a part of their people group project. These elements could certainly be incorporated into your worship time. If students contribute some visual representation of their people groups to the celebration, your celebration will have a little flavor of the multiethnic throng described in Revelation 7. If you live in a culturally diverse area, you might want to invite people from different ethnicities to participate in your celebration through attending, bringing greetings or statements of praise in different languages, or adding various musical styles of praise or different musical instruments to any music you have planned. One element highlighting the ethnic diversity of God's kingdom is the music video *Carrier* (song written by Jared Anderson, Integrity Music, 2009) provided for your time of celebration. A portion of your celebration time should include the presentation of the video (4:50 minutes in length), which you will find on the DVD of this teacher edition. The video will give students a visual glimpse of Revelation 5:9 and 7:9, and it will provide an opportunity for students to reflect on the message of this course—that all of us are "carriers" of missio Dei (a concept from Isaiah 61).

Commitment. You may want to include in your celebration a time for student commitment, particularly if God has been stirring in your students and pushing them to a new or deeper relationship with Him or to new levels of participating in His mission. There are, of course, a number of ways to facilitate this. You could have a traditional "altar call" time when students could step forward for prayer or for sharing specific commitments they have made to God during this course. You could have a time of silent, reflective meditation that culminates with a symbolic activity such as nailing written commitments to a wooden cross display

or having a public space (whiteboard or bulletin board) for students to write out their commitments. If you are outdoors, you could have students put a stake into the ground as a visual representation of staking a claim to a particular promise of God or to a commitment they have made to the Lord. If you have students who are preparing for specific acts of service, you may want to have a formal commissioning service of prayer to celebrate what God is calling them to do. Or you could pray over the whole class as your students move forward in participating in missio Dei. You might invite your school chaplain or a local pastor to participate in such a time of commitment or commissioning. Invite parents too! This time of celebration can be an exciting time for families to experience as well.

There are also other elements you might want to consider for your celebration time. For example, you might have several students present an overview of God's story in the Bible, culminating with the Revelation picture you are celebrating in this lesson. You could reread portions from Lesslie Newbigin's *A Walk Through the Bible* that is reprinted in chapter 1. You might have your students present information summarizing different themes that have particularly resonated with them throughout the course. There are many possibilities and no single "right way" to carry out this celebration. Let God guide you into a special time of celebrating Him and His kingdom in all its fullness and glory so that you and your students will leave this experience with an even-deeper passion for God and His heart for all nations.

Objective

Students will celebrate and worship God for His purpose and its ultimate fulfillment.

Unpacking

Celebration (entire class time)

Use the material in the "Teacher's Preparation" section as a guide, and spend the entire class time celebrating and worshipping God with your students. You may also want to extend your celebration time over several days (if time allows).

What's Next

Students should use **JE 103 Celebrate God!** as space to journal the various aspects they celebrate about God in light of today's celebration.

Reflecting and Looking Forward

Big Idea

Missio Dei culminates in the gathering of every tribe, tongue, language, and nation around the throne of God.

Key Concepts

- God's mission of relationship, redemption, and reconciliation to all nations will ultimately be fulfilled in the kingdom of God—a glorious multiethnic community united in worship of Jesus.

- Our participation in the mission of God here and now will be enhanced and completed as a part of His future kingdom. Each of our lives can play a role in the larger story of God's plan to reach all nations.

Reflective Questions

- How would your day-to-day interactions and choices be different if you lived in constant awareness that in God's kingdom only Jesus matters? that His blood creates equality and forgiveness for all who will receive Him? Is it possible to live a kingdom-of-God life *now*, even though some of it is *not yet*? (SE p. 301)

- What difference does it make to you that your participation in the mission of God here and now will accomplish its purpose, whether or not you see it at the present time? Does that inspire you to seek and serve God more? Why or why not? (SE p. 304)

- Do you view all moments of your life as opportunities to worship God, or do you think of worship as something that happens at certain times of the week in certain corporate settings? Why or why not? How do your views on worship affect your daily life? your enthusiasm for God and His mission? (SE p. 304)

Teacher's Heart

The wind in the trees is one of the ways that God speaks to me. It is His little love language to me. During the writing of this book, my thoughts have been drawn to trees: the one at the beginning of the Bible, found in the Garden of Eden (Genesis 1–3); and the one at the end of the Bible, found in the new Jerusalem (Revelation 22). We live, as author and Mars Hill pastor Rob Bell observes, in a time between these two trees (2005). Our privilege is to join God's mission. It has been a joy to participate with God in the creation of this book. May you and your students be blessed by it as you seek to find your path "between the trees."

Teacher's Preparation

There are a number of ways you may want to wrap up your time with students as you complete this course. Any way that you choose, however, should focus students' attention on what the students have learned along the way and on preparing them for participation with God both now and in the future. We have offered a few suggestions for today's lesson and have provided some journal entries for ongoing reflection, but you may have other thoughts in mind regarding the final direction of the course. Feel free to adapt what is here or to add to it according to the needs of your class.

The first activity listed in the "Unpacking" section is designed to give students some time to complete a journal entry on what they've learned overall throughout this course. **JE 104 A Time of Reflection** can be used for this purpose. Then direct them back to the beginning of their journal, **JE 1 Reflection on Missio Dei**. Have them review what they wrote as they started this course. Spend some time in a discussion comparing and contrasting the two entries.

The second activity suggested is a reflection on "life between the trees." Call attention to the following portion of the quotation from Christopher J. H. Wright: "And the river and tree of life, from which humanity had been barred in the earliest chapters of the Bible's grand narrative, will, in its final chapter, provide the healing of the nations … (Rev. 22:2)" (2006, 530; SE p. 305). Then read to students this passage from chapter 3: "The Bible begins with a beautiful setting and a very significant tree—the Garden of Eden and the tree of the knowledge of good and evil described in Genesis 1–3. The Bible concludes with another beautiful setting and another significant tree—the new Jerusalem of

heaven and the tree of life whose leaves 'are for the healing of the nations' (Revelation 22:2)—nations that have been cursed by inheriting Adam's sin nature. What happens in the time between these two beautiful settings is the story of God's purpose being carried out to completion. As author and pastor Rob Bell says, 'We live between the trees' [2005]" (SE p. 50). Next, draw their attention to the two trees pictured on the cover of their textbooks. Spend some time discussing the idea of "life between the trees" and the journey of missio Dei. Get them to share and discuss what they have learned throughout the course. You might also ask them to flip back through their journal entries to discern the ways God has been leading them to new understanding this semester. If you have time, watch the video *Nooma: Trees 003* with your students.

A third activity for reviewing some themes of the course is to reread to your students the "parable" found in chapter 3 of the student edition, "The Parable of the Race" by Brian D. McLaren and Tony Campolo (2003, 26–27; SE pp. 56–58). Give students a few minutes to respond to hearing this parable again. What are their reactions? Where do they see themselves in this parable now? Then, direct students to look at their responses from their original encounter with this parable (**JE 11 "The Parable of the Race"**). Ask them to compare their understanding of the parable and how that understanding may have changed since they first heard the parable. Discuss how the race parable relates to their own callings related to joining God's mission (to participating in the race).

Finally, listed in the fourth activity are journal entries for reflection that you may want to use with your students.

Objectives

- Students will compare and contrast their thoughts on missio Dei today with their responses at the start of this course.

- Students will discuss various themes presented in this course, and they will reflect on what God has taught them throughout the course.

- Students will describe hopes they have for their future participation in missio Dei.

Unpacking

Closing Reflection (8–10 minutes)

Direct students to spend some time journaling in response to **JE 104 A Time of Reflection**. Then give them time to go back and read their entries in **JE 1 Reflection on Missio Dei**. Compare and contrast the two entries in a class discussion.

The Trees and Life Between Them (10–15 minutes)

Use the suggestions in the "Teacher's Preparation" section as a guide to lead students through a reflection on the concept of journeying with God on His mission in our time "between the trees." Ask the students to share specific new understandings they have gleaned from this course and how they might apply these insights in the future.

Racing to the Future (8–10 minutes)

Read "The Parable of the Race" from chapter 3 to your students. Lead them through a reflective time and discussion as outlined in the "Teacher's Preparation" section.

Journal Entry Activities (10–15 minutes or longer)

Direct students to **JE 105 Created in Christ Jesus to Do Good Works** and **JE 106 Next Steps** and give students time to complete these reflective activities.

If Time Activity

Watch the video *Nooma: Trees 003*, in which author and Mars Hill pastor Rob Bell (2005) presents his thoughts on the concept of life "between the trees."

Formal Assessment

- Unit 4 exam
- Getting to Know a People Group: An Ethnographic Study (the project presented between TE lessons 46 and 47)
- Missio Dei: The Journey (the culminating course portfolio)

What's Next

We have intentionally created some final reflection pages (**JE 107 My Journey with God … a Year Later** and some blank pages) so that students can return to the journal and reflect on their journey a year later or beyond. Encourage your students to take some time to read through their journal a year from now to reflect on where their journey with God has taken them. Perhaps this journal will become a tool God will use to clarify issues that are unresolved in their minds at this point or to act as a springboard for God's direction for future plans and opportunities.

Enjoy the journey of missio Dei!

References

Anderson, Neil T. 2001. *Who I am in Christ*. Ventura, CA: Regal.

Beaver, R. Pierce. 1999. The history of mission strategy. In Winter and Hawthorne 1999a, 241–52.

Bell, Rob. 2005. *Nooma: Trees 003*. DVD. Grand Rapids, MI: Zondervan.

Bird, Brad. 2004. *The Incredibles*. DVD. Directed by Brad Bird. Burbank, CA: Walt Disney Home Entertainment.

Blackaby, Henry T., and Claude V. King. 1994. *Experiencing God: How to live the full adventure of knowing and doing the will of God*. Nashville, TN: Broadman & Holman.

Blue, Ken. 1987. *Authority to heal*. Downers Grove, IL: InterVarsity Press. Quoted in Winter and Hawthorne 1999a, 72.

Bonhoeffer, Dietrich. 1954. *Life together*. Trans. John W. Doberstein. New York: HarperSanFrancisco. Orig. pub. as *Gemeinsames Leben* (Germany).

Bosch, David J. 1991. *Transforming mission: Paradigm shifts in theology of mission*. American Society of Missiology Series, no. 16. Maryknoll, NY: Orbis Books.

Bria, Ion. 1980. *Martyria/mission: The witness of the Orthodox churches today*. Geneva: World Council of Churches, 8–10. Quoted in Bosch 1991, 207–8.

Bubeck, Mark I. 1975. *The adversary: The Christian versus demon activity*. Chicago, IL: Moody Press.

Cornish, Rick. 2005. *5 minute church historian: Maximum truth in minimum time*. Colorado Springs, CO: NavPress.

Daniel, Orville E. 1996. *A harmony of the four Gospels: The new international version*. 2nd ed. Grand Rapids, MI: Baker Books.

Davis, Charles. 2008. The glory of God in the calling of the church. Sermon presented at the thirtieth anniversary celebration for Grace Church, October 12, in Tuscaloosa, AL.

Durback, Robert, ed. 1997. *Seeds of hope: A Henri Nouwen reader*. 2nd ed. New York: Image Books.

Egeler, Daniel. 2000. Honor your mother and father. Case study presented at the ACSI Pre-Field Orientation, June, Colorado Christian University, in Denver, CO.

Elmer, Duane. 2002. *Cross-cultural connections: Stepping out and fitting in around the world*. Downers Grove, IL: InterVarsity Press.

———. 2006. *Cross-cultural servanthood: Serving the world in Christlike humility*. Downers Grove, IL: InterVarsity Press.

Ewing, Bill, and Bart Gavigan. 2006. *End of the spear*. DVD. Directed by Jim Hanon. Century City, CA: 20th Century Fox.

Fab, Joe. 2003. *Paper clips: Changing the world ... one classroom at a time*. Documentary film. Directed by Elliot Berlin and Joe Fab. McLean, VA: Johnson Group.

Frost, Michael. 2006. *Exiles: Living missionally in a post-Christian culture.* Peabody, MA: Hendrickson.

Guder, Darrell L., ed. 1998. *Missional church: A vision for the sending of the church in North America.* The Gospel and Our Culture Series. Grand Rapids, MI: Wm. B. Eerdmans.

Hamilton, David Joel. 2008. The New Testament basis for the discipling of nations. In *His kingdom come*, ed. Jim Stier, Richlyn Poor, and Lisa Orvis, 47–76. Seattle, WA: YWAM Publishing.

Hawthorne, Steven C. 1999. The story of his glory. In Winter and Hawthorne 1999a, 34–48.

Hiebert, Paul G. 1999. Cultural differences and the communication of the gospel. In Winter and Hawthorne 1999a, 373–83.

Hiebert, Paul G., and Frances R. Hiebert. 1987. *Case studies in missions.* Grand Rapids, MI: Baker Book House.

Hill, Susan D. 2008. *Closer than your skin: Unwrapping the mystery of intimacy with God.* Colorado Springs, CO: WaterBrook Press.

Hirsch, Alan. 2006. *The forgotten ways: Reactivating the missional church.* Grand Rapids, MI: Brazos Press.

Hughes, John. 1985. *The breakfast club.* VHS. Directed by John Hughes. Hollywood, CA: A&M Films.

Irvin, Dale T., and Scott W. Sunquist. 2001. *History of the world Christian movement.* Vol. 1, *Earliest Christianity to 1453.* Maryknoll, NY: Orbis Books.

Jenkins, Philip. 2002. *The next Christendom: The coming of global Christianity.* New York: Oxford University Press.

Knight, Steven. 2007. *Amazing grace.* DVD. Directed by Michael Apted. Century City, CA: 20th Century Fox.

Koenig-Bricker, Woodeene. 1996. *Prayers of the saints: An inspired collection of holy wisdom.* New York: HarperOne.

Kraft, Charles H. 1996. *Anthropology for Christian witness.* Maryknoll, NY: Orbis Books.

———. 1998. Culture, worldview and contextualization. In Winter and Hawthorne 1999a, 384–91.

———. 2000. Two kingdoms in conflict. In *Behind enemy lines: An advanced guide to spiritual warfare*, ed. Charles H. Kraft with Mark White, 17–30. Eugene, OR: Wipf and Stock.

Ladd, George Eldon. 1959. *The gospel of the kingdom: Scriptural studies in the kingdom of God.* London, England: Paternoster Press. http://www.gospelpedlar.com/articles/Last%20Things/GK/gospel_of_the_kingdom.html.

Lewis, Jonathan, ed. 1994. *World mission: An analysis of the world Christian movement*, part 1. 2nd ed. Pasadena, CA: William Carey Library. Quoted in Winter and Hawthorne 1999a, 60–61.

Linton, Ralph. 1936. *The study of man.* New York: D. Appleton-Century.

Malinowski, Bronislaw. 1948. *Magic, science, and religion.* Glencoe, IL: Free Press.

Manning, Brennan. 2005. *The importance of being foolish: How to think like Jesus.* New York: HarperCollins.

McKinley, Rick. 2006. *This beautiful mess: Practicing the presence of the kingdom of God.* Sisters, OR: Multnomah.

McLaren, Brian D., and Tony Campolo. 2003. *Adventures in missing the point: How the culture-controlled church neutered the gospel.* Grand Rapids, MI: Zondervan.

McManus, Erwin Raphael. 2006. *Soul cravings: An exploration of the human spirit.* Nashville, TN: Thomas Nelson.

Miner, Horace. 1956. Body ritual among the Nacirema. *American Anthropologist* 58, no. 3:503–8. http://www.aaanet.org/publications/anthrosource/.

Moffett, Samuel H. 1987. Early Asian Christian approaches to non-Christian cultures. *Missiology* 15:484. Quoted in Bosch 1991, 204.

Murphy, Ed. 1992. *The handbook for spiritual warfare.* Nashville, TN: Thomas Nelson.

Neill, Stephen. 1986. *A history of Christian missions.* 2nd ed. Rev. by Owen Chadwick. New York: Penguin Books.

Newbigin, Lesslie. 2005. *A walk through the Bible.* Vancouver, BC: Regent College Publishing.

Nouwen, Henri J. M. 1994. *Here and now: Living in the Spirit.* New York: Crossroad. Quoted in Durback 1997, 47, 90.

Nussbaum, Stan. 2005. *A reader's guide to "Transforming mission."* American Society of Missiology Series, no. 37. Maryknoll, NY: Orbis Books.

Omartian, Stormie. 2002. *The power of a praying parent.* Calendar. May 27 entry. Siloam Springs, AR: Garborg's.

Ortberg, John. 2005. *God is closer than you think.* Grand Rapids, MI: Zondervan.

Ortberg, Nancy. 2008. *Looking for God: An unexpected journey through tattoos, tofu, and pronouns.* Carol Stream, IL: Tyndale House.

Paulson, Elliot. 2003. Between a rock and a hard place. *Mission Frontiers* (U.S. Center for World Mission) September–October:14–16.

Pierson, Paul. 1999. A history of transformation. In Winter and Hawthorne 1999a, 262–68.

Rasmus, Rudy. 2007. *Touch: Pressing against the wounds of a broken world.* Nashville, TN: Thomas Nelson.

Redemption in the day-to-day. 2006. *Discipleship Journal*, no. 156:52–61.

Robert, Dana L. 1996. *American women in mission: A social history of their thought and practice.* Macon, GA: Mercer University Press.

Robison, Gerald. 2007. Perspectives course. Lecture presented at Grace Church, February 13, in Tuscaloosa, AL.

Saint Benedict. 1993. *Saint Benedict's prayer book for beginners.* York, England: Ampleforth Abbey Press.

Sandras, Eric. 2004. *Buck-naked faith: A brutally honest look at Christianity.* Colorado Springs, CO: NavPress.

Shenk, Wilbert R. 1999. *Changing frontiers of mission*. American Society of Missiology Series, no. 28. Maryknoll, NY: Orbis Books.

Sjogren, Bob. 2000. *Notes for "Cat and dog theology" on DVD*, version 1.04. Mechanicsville, VA: UnveilinGlory.

Sjogren, Bob, and Gerald Robison. 2003. *Cat and dog theology*. Waynesboro, GA: Authentic Lifestyle.

Stanley, Charles. 1985. *How to listen to God*. Nashville, TN: Thomas Nelson.

Stewart, Meiji. 1995. *Keep coming back*. Center City, MN: Hazelden.

Sweet, Leonard I. 2007. *The gospel according to Starbucks: Living with a grande passion*. Colorado Springs, CO: WaterBrook Press.

Thiessen, Henry C. 1979. *Lectures in systematic theology*. Rev. by Vernon D. Doerksen. Grand Rapids, MI: Wm. B. Eerdmans. (Orig. pub. 1949.)

Thomas, Norman E., ed. 1995. *Classic texts in mission and world Christianity*. American Society of Missiology Series, no. 20. Maryknoll, NY: Orbis Books.

Tucker, Ruth A. 2004. *From Jerusalem to Irian Jaya: A biographical history of Christian missions*. 2nd ed. Grand Rapids, MI: Zondervan.

Wachowski, Andy, and Larry Wachowski. 1999. *The matrix*. DVD. Directed by Andy Wachowski and Larry Wachowski. Burbank, CA: Warner Home Video.

Walls, Andrew F. 1996. *The missionary movement in Christian history: Studies in the transmission of faith*. Maryknoll, NY: Orbis Books.

Winter, Ralph D. 1999a. Four men, three eras, two transitions: Modern missions. In Winter and Hawthorne 1999a, 253–61.

———. 1999b. The kingdom strikes back: Ten epochs of redemptive history. In Winter and Hawthorne 1999a, 195–213.

Winter, Ralph D., and Steven C. Hawthorne, eds. 1999a. *Perspectives on the world Christian movement: A reader*. 3rd ed. Pasadena, CA: William Carey Library.

Winter, Ralph D., and Steven C. Hawthorne, eds. 1999b. *Perspectives on the world Christian movement: The notebook*. Pasadena, CA: William Carey Library.

Wright, Christopher J. H. 2006. *The mission of God: Unlocking the Bible's grand narrative*. Downers Grove, IL: InterVarsity Press.

Wright, N. T. 2008. *Surprised by hope: Rethinking heaven, the resurrection, and the mission of the church*. New York: HarperOne.

Credits